Research Methods
for the Social Sciences

Research Methods for the Social Sciences

Practice and Applications

Robert J. Mutchnick

Indiana University of Pennsylvania

Bruce L. Berg

Indiana University of Pennsylvania

ALLYN AND BACON

Boston   London   Toronto   Sydney   Tokyo   Singapore

Executive Editor: Karen Hanson
Vice-President, Publisher: Susan Badger
Editorial Assistant: Sarah L. Dunbar
Executive Marketing Manager: Joyce Nilsen
Production Administrator: Annette Joseph
Editorial-Production Service: Karen Mason
Copyeditor: Susan Freese
Manufacturing Buyer: Megan Cochran
Cover Administrator: Suzanne Harbison
Cover Designer: Susan Paradise

Library of Congress Cataloging-in-Publication Data

Mutchnick, Robert J.
    Research methods for the social sciences : practice and
applications / by Robert J. Mutchnick and Bruce L. Berg.
        p.   cm.
    Includes bibliographical references.
    ISBN 0-02-385451-0
    1.   Social sciences—Methodology.   I. Berg, Bruce Lawrence
. II. Title.
    H61.M87   1995
    300'. 72—dc20   95-11824
                                                                CIP

Printed in the United States of America

10   9   8   7   6   5   4   3   2   1   00   99   98   97   96   95

To my family—Jill, Cate, and Alex
B. L. B.

To my mother, Bea, father, Herb, and daughters, Kathryn and Sarah
R. J. M.

To our students, from whom we continually learn
R. J. M. and B. L. B.

Contents

CHAPTER 3 Sampling and Design 73

CHAPTER 4 Technologies of Observation 115

CHAPTER 5   Data Organization and Analysis   181

Preface

We were having coffee one afternoon while attending a meeting of the American Society of Criminology, and our talk turned to work. We had both been teaching research methods for a number of years and had begun to grow weary of the usual lecturing style and traditional textbooks. In the course of our conversation, a great idea was born: What if we were to combine traditional research textbook material with exercises that allowed students to experience research in a controlled environment?

We acted on our idea and wrote this book, a companion methods text/manual for use with most traditional social scientific research textbooks. Our intention was to create a book that offers readers basic information about various methodological concerns; a series of brief readings (or *abstracted reprints,* as we call them), taken from published research articles; and a variety of practice exercises related to the readings.

We have condensed lengthy research articles to produce brief abstractions, which are largely methodological. The results are shorter, edited versions of the original articles. We have maintained the integrity of the articles, however. We have not added any new or additional material, and we have remained true to the presentation of information used in the abstracted reprints.

We believe that our book can be used as a supplement to more comprehensive methods textbooks or as a brief guide to methods and application practices during shorter summer semesters. We also believe our book might be used to introduce inexperienced researchers to basic research concepts and practices.

PLAN OF THE TEXT

The plan of this text is simple. Each chapter begins with a discussion of the elements relevant to a basic understanding of research methods. This material is intentionally brief because we are primarily interested in emphasizing the application of ideas expressed in each chapter. Numerous lengthy texts are available that will describe aspects of research methods more comprehensively. Although these other texts are informative, they do not provide students with the opportunity to actually experience research. A unique feature of our book is that students actually *do research.*

Following the informational section of each chapter are several abstracted reprints. These readings contain the basic introductions of published articles, along with their methodological descriptions and findings. The articles were selected because they illustrate certain kinds of methodological strategies or techniques.

Each reading is followed by an Application Exercise, which relates to the methodological procedure described in the abstracted reprint. All the exercises were designed to be completed by college students, bearing in mind that some of these students will be inexperienced in research methods. Completing these exercises will allow students to "get their hands dirty with data."

Reading the text and abstracted reprints and completing the exercises in this book will help fledgling researchers become more proficient in research methods. More importantly, we hope this book will show inexperienced researchers that there is nothing mystical or scary about designing or conducting research.

We would like to thank the following individuals, who reviewed this text for Allyn and Bacon and provided useful suggestions to us: Michael B. Blankenship, East Tennessee State University; Frank E. Hagan, Mercyhurst College; Jeffrey M. Jacques, Florida Agricultural and Mechanical University; Shirley R. Salem, Louisiana State University; and Susette M. Talarico, The University of Georgia.

R. J. M.

B. L. B.

Research Methods
for the Social Sciences

CHAPTER 1

Introduction

OBJECTIVES

This text/manual was written to provide both students and instructors of research methods with various options to learn and practice many frequently used basic techniques. Most traditional research methods texts provide students with a plethora of information about a wide range of topics by adding a few questions at the end of each chapter. The practice/study questions are rarely integrated throughout the text. Recently, approaches to education have begun incorporating interactive "learning-through-doing" techniques, which have been developed in the past few decades. The authors believe it is time to provide students and instructors of research methods with an option that incorporates a more hands-on, interactive approach to the subject.

This text/manual is designed to work with many of the popular social science research methods texts currently available. Instructors can use this text/manual in a variety of ways: (1) as a supplement to a standard methodology text; (2) as a stand-alone text supplemented with class lectures and some outside reading; or (3) as a self-paced text for students studying research methods on an individual or independent basis.

The material in this text/manual is provided to assist inexperienced students in better understanding and completing the practice assignments. Students can use the material to augment information provided in their core texts.

The main focus of this text/manual is on creating an environment where students learn various methodological techniques through a process that can include imitation, replication, and/or experimentation. Using the standard textbook approach, this book provides a brief presentation of a methodological topic or technique, followed by a number of current research examples culled from the social science journal literature. The research examples represent applications of specific methodological techniques. Each journal article has been abstracted to present a brief but informative demonstration of the methodological topic or technique while maintaining the integrity of the article. In some instances, more than one research article has been abstracted for a given methodological technique to provide instructors with options for instruction and application, depending on the discipline or perspective from which they wish to teach.

Immediately following each abstracted journal article is an application exercise, which is designed to provide students with an opportunity to practice and apply the technique being demonstrated. Some of the application exercises present readers with a set of questions that allow students to demonstrate their understanding of the methodological technique. Other exercises give students the opportunity to actually use the technique, either through replicating or adapting it using the data provided or collected.

The authors believe that the approach of abstracting journal articles and providing application exercises allows students to engage interactively in learning the research process. As indicated earlier, in a number of instances, more than one abstracted article and exercise is provided for a technique. While we do not expect that students will be required to demonstrate their knowledge of a technique using more than one of the abstracted articles and exercises, the additional materials could be used to reinforce a particular methodological procedure, when necessary. In some cases, the additional abstracted articles and exercises allow instructors and students some choice in selecting how to study and learn a particular methodological technique. And in other cases, depending on the academic discipline and the class at hand, one abstracted article and exercise might be more germane and interesting than another. We have provided articles from a broad range of refereed social science journals to allow the text/manual to be used by a host of social science disciplines, such as sociology, political science, anthropology, criminology, criminal justice, psychology, labor relations, and economics.

This text/manual is also designed to be used as a workbook, similar to those most of us used when we were students in elementary school and first learning to read or do math. Spaces are provided for students to respond directly to exercises, and the pages are perforated to facilitate removal, should instructors want to be able to review exercises for grading. The manual also can be used for self-paced, individualized instruction by allowing students to work on their own, completing and turning in exercises when they feel they have mastered particular methodological techniques. As a supplemental text, this manual can be used to highlight specific topics through the exercises or to allow students to demonstrate proficiency in specific methodological techniques. The pages of the exercises can be removed from the text and incorporated in a loose-leaf, three-ring binder; students can then add notes on specific methodologies.

This text/manual is designed to work with approaches that incorporate qualitative as well as quantitative methodologies. Exercises are provided that address the main aspects of each of these methodologies.

We assume that you are motivated, intelligent individuals who have had little or no exposure to the subject of research methods. With a little effort on your behalf and the guidance of your instructor, you should have no difficulty mastering the content of this text.

TABLE READING

A wealth of information often can be obtained from tables if only readers know what and how to look for it. The following material on table reading is designed primarily for readers with no regular table-reading experience. Those of you with some experience will also benefit from this section because of the systematic presentation of material on the subject. This section serves as a guide to the general components of a table. It should be noted that not all tables contain all the information presented, and the specific location of material might vary from table to table. Even so, the general principles remain the same and are important to know. Knowing how to read a table can save you valuable time in reading and understanding research.

It has been suggested that if you read the tables contained in a manuscript, you could cull from them the information necessary for understanding the whole research project. While this claim is not entirely true, it points to the value of reading and understanding tables.

Title

First, students should read the title of the table. Often, people dive directly into the body of the table, bypassing the title. This can be a mistake. Among the things the title of a table can inform us about are:

1. the content of the table
2. the names and types of variables included
3. the time frame for the data presented
4. the form in which the data are presented

By reading the title of Table 1.1, we learn that the table is about the results of the Graduate Record Examination (GRE), and the data are reported in the form of test scores. The title also tells us that the dependent variable in the table (i.e., the variable that is changed) is the score on the GRE, and the independent variable (i.e., the variable that caused the change) is the student's intended major. In addition, we can learn from this title that the data represent the scores of individuals who took the examination between 1987 and 1990.

The title of Table 1.1 has provided us with five pieces of important information before we have looked at the actual data. Knowing this information helps guide us in reading the content of the table and how to form statements about the content. For instance, we know before looking further that we will probably discover information about the relationship (if any) between GRE scores and intended majors.

TABLE 1.1 Graduate Record Examination General Test Scores by Intended Graduate Major Field, 1987–1990

Note: GRE General Test scores range from 200 to 800. These data include both foreign and domestic examinees.

	VERBAL		QUANTITATIVE		ANALYTICAL		N
	Mean	SD	Mean	SD	Mean	SD	
All Examinees	486	124	560	142	532	128	954,995
Seniors and Nonenrolled College Graduates[a]	500	117	572	135	562	124	424,612
Social Sciences[b]	508	110	535	123	555	120	71,621
Social Sciences, Other[c]	486	118	510	130	528	129	5,967
Criminal Justice/ Criminology	421	97	443	115	477	123	1,546

[a] Limited to college seniors and nonenrolled college graduates who earned their bachelor's degrees within two years of testing.

[b] Includes anthropology and archaeology, economics, political science, psychology, sociology, other.

[c] Includes American studies, area studies, criminal justice/criminology, geography, public administration, urban studies, social science, other.

Source: Educational Testing Service (1991) *GRE 1991–92: Guide to the Use of the Graduate Record Examinations Program.* Princeton, NJ: Educational Testing Service, Tables 1A, 1B, 4, and Appendix Table 4. Table constructed by *Journal of Criminal Justice Education,* Vol. 3 No. 1, Spring 1992. © 1992 Academy of Criminal Justice Sciences.

Headnotes

Some tables present the reader with headnotes, which are designed to provide information that helps clarify the data or variables in the table. In the case of our sample table (see Table 1.1), the headnote tells us about the range of the GRE scores, specifically, that they can range from 200 to 800. This information will be very useful when we try to interpret the data. Knowing the lowest and highest scores possible will allow us to assess the range of scores on the individual tests as well as what the possible range may be for the overall test. The headnote for Table 1.1 also tells us that the GRE was taken by both foreign and domestic individuals.

Source

What is the source of the data for the table? What do we know about the reliability of the data? Is the source reputable? In the case of our example (Table 1.1), the table was taken from a recognized, scholarly, refereed journal. Although the table was compiled by members of the editorial staff of the journal, the source of the specific data was the Educational Testing Service (ETS). ETS has an excellent reputation for accuracy and reliability. However, since the table was compiled by the editorial staff of the journal (i.e., the data did not exist in this form in the materials published by ETS), it is possible that an error could have been made: Were the data correctly reproduced? Were the numbers for the columns or rows transposed? Even if the editorial staff who compiled the data and constructed the table were entirely accurate, could a mistake have been made by the typesetter? How do you know that what is being presented is accurate?

In most instances, these types of errors are unlikely to get by the individuals responsible for proofreading the materials, but sometimes errors are missed. For example, as you read this text, you may discover a few typographical errors. They are inevitable, given the process that writing goes through before ending up as a publication. This is also true for tables. Regardless of the number of proofreadings, it is possible that an error will be made and go undetected and that some of the data in a table will be incorrect.

Therefore, before you can take the data in the table at face value, you need to assess the quality of the source. Usually, the more reputable the source, the more reliable, with regard to the presentation of data. Evaluating the credibility of a source is similar to seeking a doctor to treat an ailment. You would be more likely to use the services of someone who came highly recommended by people you trust. You would also be more likely to use the services of someone who had a list of established, verifiable credentials. You would be less likely to put your faith in someone who recently arrived in town, had no references, and had credentials that could not be verified. The same is true with sources of data. The reliability of the information tends to increase with the credibility of the source. Therefore, knowing the source of the data is helpful in assessing the accuracy of the information.

It is not always possible to determine the data source from the information provided in the table. Sometimes, you need to read the text of the research to ascertain the source. If the source is an original collection of data, you should consider who collected the data and under what conditions. If the answer is three high school students who were hired because they live in the researcher's neighborhood, not because of any data-collection experience, this should be reason to pause and raise questions about the credibility of the data. If, however, the source is three college students who were specifically trained and supervised by a researcher with extensive data-collection experience, the confidence in the data should certainly increase.

Knowing the source helps readers have faith in data and interpret them with greater confidence.

Footnotes

Footnotes clarify the uses of terms, categories, and abnormal aspects of a table. Sometimes, a footnote will be used to explain a whole column or row of data. In Table 1.1, there are three footnotes—"a," "b," and "c"—which explain what the categories represent. The second footnote, "b," defines the term *Social Sciences*. In this case, the category "Social Sciences" includes those examinees who intend to major in anthropology and archaeology, economics, political science, psychology, sociology, and "other." Footnote "c" indicates the other social sciences.

The authors of the table decided to separate the social sciences into two categories. Some would argue that this distinction between what are often referred to as the traditional social sciences and the new social sciences is appropriate. Obviously, the authors of the table believed that the information they wanted to communicate was best served by creating these separate categories. Given that the table was published in a criminal justice journal, it would seem that the editors of that journal are most interested in reaching their readership, which is most likely made up of criminal justice students, academics, and practitioners. We would have no knowledge of what is represented by the two categories without the footnotes. Therefore, it is often best to read the footnotes before examining the content of the table.

Column Heads and Table Body

Specific to Table 1.1, it would be helpful to review the rest of the table to see how much information is actually contained within it. The table column heads show that the exam is divided into three parts: "Verbal," "Quantitative," and "Analytical" sections. Each section has a maximum possible score of 800 (determined from the information in the headnote). The column heads also show that the table provides the mean as well as standard deviation (SD) scores for each of the three sections. The table does not provide the total mean score for each group taking the exam, but it would be easy to calculate by adding the mean scores for the "Verbal," "Quantitative," and "Analytical" sections.

Within the body of the table, we find from the first entry that 954,995 people took the Graduate Record Examination in the three-year time period (under column head "N," for "number"). Just under half this total of almost 1 million examinees were in the category "Seniors and Nonenrolled College Graduates." The mean scores for the individuals in this category were the highest of any group on two of the three sections of the GRE. The lowest mean scores were received by those examinees who intended to major in criminal justice/criminology.

Comparing examinees in the social sciences to the others provides some interesting information. For the overall group of examinees, as well as for the "Seniors and Nonenrolled College Graduates," the highest mean score on the GRE was on the "Quantitative" section. For those intending to major in the social sciences, the highest mean score was on the "Analytical" section. These findings could cause the reader to consider two issues:

1. Do people who intend to major in one of the social sciences tend to have greater analytical skills than examinees in general?
2. Are examinees whose analytical skills are stronger than their verbal or quantitative skills drawn to major in one of the social sciences?

Given the limited information in this table, it is not possible to answer these questions. Instead, the information in the table would help us formulate the questions.

THE RESEARCH PROCESS/ SCIENTIFIC METHOD

Knowing how to read tables is one method that assists readers in evaluating research, but it is not the only helpful tool available. In addition to table reading, a working knowledge of the typical steps involved in the research process is beneficial. A working knowledge of the research process not only allows you to evaluate existing research but also introduces you, as a potential researcher, to the skills necessary to develop a research project of your own.

Regardless of how individual writers diagram the research process, the basic elements are usu-

ally the same. Very simply, a problem or question is identified, and a methodology is selected or developed to attempt to answer the question. The goal of using the scientific method to engage in the research process is to establish a set of standards by which the research can be judged and interpreted.

The Research Wheel

Some writers have presented the research process as a wheel or circle, with no specific beginning or end (see Figure 1.1). The elements of the research process are parts of the circumference of the wheel, and even though they appear in a particular order, you can begin almost anywhere on the wheel with the research process. Typically, the research process begins with the selection of a problem and the development of research questions or hypotheses (Bailey, 1982, p. 10; Hagan, 1993, p. 1). It is possible that the results of previous research may generate new research questions and hypotheses for the consumer of the research. This suggests that research is cyclical, a vibrant and continuous process. When the researcher answers one question, the result is often the generation of additional or new questions, which plunges the researcher right back into the process of answering questions.

Identifying Research Questions/Problems: The Idea Stage

The first step in the research process is usually the identification of a problem or question that the researcher is interested in studying. Research questions can arise from a wide variety of sources:

1. They can be generated by the findings of an existing study.
2. They can be questions that a government or private agency needs to have answered.
3. They can be the result of intellectual curiosity.

Often, when an existing research study has been completed, more new research questions have been raised than answered.

FIGURE 1.1   The Research Wheel

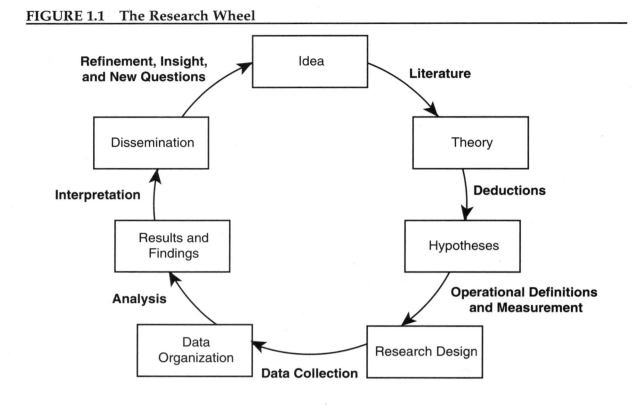

Assessing the Literature: The Theory Stage

Once the researcher has identified a particular problem or question, the next step in the research process is to assess the current state of the literature related to the problem or question. The researcher will often engage in a considerable amount of library work to ascertain what the existing literature, if any is available, has to say about the subject. Has the subject already been studied to the point that the questions in which the researcher is interested have been sufficiently answered? If so, can the researcher approach the subject from a previously untested or unexamined perspective? Sometimes, research questions have been previously explored but not brought to closure. If this is the case, it may be appropriate to examine the question again. It even may be appropriate to replicate a previous study to assess whether the findings reported were "not an accident or mere coincidence" (Bailey, 1982, p. 11) and that the findings are applicable today.

Formulating Hypotheses: The Hypothesis Stage

After the researcher has determined that the research problem or question is appropriate for

study, the next issue is directly related to the formulation of hypotheses. Is the subject under research consideration one that is "limited to bounds amenable to treatment or test" (Miller, 1991, p. 15)? One of the most difficult problems faced by the researcher, especially one new to the research endeavor, is identifying a manageable research question. Often, the focus of research questions has to be narrowed so that they can be studied before hypotheses can be formulated. Also, after brainstorming, research questions can contain many questions that would be legitimate for study. The researcher needs to decide which questions to study first. A review of the existing literature on the subject can often shed light in this area. Once this has been accomplished, hypotheses can be formulated for study.

In addition to formulating hypotheses, this phase of the research process requires the researcher to define terms and concepts. The definitions of terms and concepts must allow the researcher to operationalize them for study. In this sense, the term *operationalize* means to define the term or concept so that it can be tested or measured. If a term or concept is defined in a manner that does not allow its operationalization, it cannot be proved or disproved.

Criticism regarding operationalization has been leveled at various theories in the social sciences. For instance, Edwin H. Sutherland's (1947) work on differential association has been criticized because Sutherland did not fully define or explain some of his concepts. In one of the nine propositions of his theory of criminal behavior, Sutherland talks about an individual needing an excess of definitions favorable to the commission of a crime. At no time does he specifically indicate what he means by *excess,* and therefore, he has caused researchers considerable consternation when they have tried to test his theory.

Developing the Research Plan: The Design Stage

After the research questions have been identified and supported with existing literature, the hypotheses created, and the key concepts and terms defined, it is appropriate to move to the next component of the research process: development of the research design. In this phase, two specific questions need to be answered:

1. How are the variables of the study to be measured?
2. What group or population is to be studied?

The variables for a research study usually include independent, dependent, and control variables. The *dependent variable* is defined as the variable "we wish to explain" (Bailey, 1982, p. 47) or "predict" (Hagan, 1993, p. 15). For instance, we may be interested in understanding crime in a particular community, why people choose nursing as a career, or why people vote certain ways in elections. The *independent variable* is the variable that "causes, determines, or precedes in time the dependent variable" (Hagan, 1993, p. 15). Typical examples of independent variables are gender and race. A *control variable* is a "third variable that is controlled for or held constant in order to see whether it affects the relationship between two variables" (Bailey, 1982, p. 488).

At the same time the variables are identified and operationalized, the specific technique or methodology for answering the questions is determined. The methodological technique selected should be driven by the type of research question asked. Certain types of questions are best answered by using *quantitative* strategies, such as a survey of a large number of individuals. Other research questions are best answered by employing *qualitative* methods, for example, a case study of a single individual or participation of a researcher in some activity under study. In some instances, a combination of quantitative and qualitative techniques is appropriate. (Methodologies are discussed in detail in Chapters 2 and 3.) The method of *triangulation* means that "the correct data are gathered by comparison of the results of two or more methods" (Bailey, 1982, p. 273). (See Chapter 3 for additional information on triangulation.) The best method for answering the research questions should drive the selection of a methodological technique.

The second component of the development of the research design is selecting a population to be studied. How many people should be included, and what specific characteristics or minimum qualifying characteristics should they have? A variety of methods are available for selecting the group, or *sample*. Two general methods are *random* and *purposive*. (These two general methods are discussed at length in Chapter 2.)

Collecting and Organizing Data: The Data-Organization Stage

The next phase is the collection of the data. If a survey instrument is being used, it would be field-tested with a pilot group to assess the reliability and validity of the instrument. Once the survey instrument has been assessed to be reliable and valid, it can be used to gather data from the population under study.

Analyzing Data: The Results and Findings Stage

After the data have been collected, the next phase of the research process requires coding and analyzing them. At this point, various and appropriate statistical techniques are applied. (See Chapter 2 for more detail.)

Reporting and Interpreting Results: The Dissemination Stage

Reporting and interpreting the results is the final phase of the research process. At this stage, the results are reported and an assessment is made regarding the support or lack of support for the hypotheses tested. It is also at this stage that the researcher can posit additional research questions that may now need to be answered as a result of the research process. Should that be the case, the research process can begin again.

VALUE-FREE RESEARCH

One of the interests of the research process is that it be as void of personal biases or values as possible. Since every individual has preconceived notions about what causes behavior and events to take place, it is necessary that the research process neutralizes, as much as possible, the personal biases or values of the researcher.

In the natural, or "hard," sciences, the researcher often studies inanimate, or nonhuman, subjects. In the social sciences, the subjects are often human, whether individuals or groups. At times, the researcher may be a member of the group under study. At other times, though, the researcher will not be a member of the group; instead, he or she will interact with the group. This is especially true if the researcher is using a *participant observation* method, which involves the active participation of the researcher. The researcher who is collecting data through administering a survey may not be actively involved, but he or she can still have some involvement.

What influence can these contacts or memberships have on collecting and interpreting data and reporting results/conclusions? One problem is the effect of personal biases. One way to reduce the impact of personal biases and values is to identify them up front. When researchers acknowledge their biases and values, they are more likely to attempt to prevent them from influencing the results of their research. This acknowledgment also benefits consumers of research, who are allowed to place the results in an appropriate context when they are told of researchers' biases and values.

The scientific method, borrowed from the natural, or "hard," sciences, provides the social scientist with a vehicle relatively free of personal biases and values. According to Bierstedt (1957), the physical sciences offer a model for the social sciences that incorporates elements of ethical neutrality and objectivity. Specifically, Bierstedt states:

> Objectivity means that the conclusions arrived at as a result of inquiry and investigation are independent of the race, color, creed, occupation, nationality, religion, moral preferences, and political predispositions of the investigator. If his research is truly objective, it is independent of any subjective elements, any personal desires, that he may have. This kind of objectivity is difficult to achieve, because factors of many varieties distort the process of inquiry. (1957, p. 17)

With regard to ethical neutrality:

> The scientist, in his professional capacity, does not take sides on issues of moral or ethical significance. . . . The scientist, as such, has no ethical, religious, political, literary, philosophical, moral, or marital preferences. That he has these preferences as a citizen makes it all the more important that he dispense with them as a scientist. As a scientist he is interested not in what is right or wrong or good or evil, but only in what is true or false. (1957, p. 10)

In summary, what Bierstedt is telling us is what Joe Friday, from the old television show *Dragnet,* is famous for saying: "Just the facts, ma'am." The researcher is to report the facts, no matter how they turn out.

In addition to the elements of objectivity and ethical neutrality, relativism, skepticism, and parsimony are important to the scientific method. "*Relativism* refers to the fact that scientists not consider their conclusions as permanent. . . . Instead, they assume their conclusions are tentative and limited" (Fitzgerald & Cox, 1987, p. 22). With regard to *skepticism,* Fitzgerald and Cox refer to the researcher's willingness to question almost everything, "especially common sense and common knowledge, accepting little at face value and looking beneath the surface in an attempt to determine for themselves the validity of an argument or conclusion" (1987, p. 22).

The last element of the scientific method we need to discuss is that of *parsimony*.

> Parsimony . . . holds that the numerous alternative explanations of a particular phenomenon should be reduced to the smallest number possible. As scientific knowledge grows, competing explanations of the same phenomenon are incorporated into a more general theory or rejected as incorrect. (Fitzgerald & Cox, 1987, p. 23)

Together, these elements of the scientific method help the researcher avoid value-laden and biased explanations. We should note that some individuals consider it impossible to be value free. While this may be true, the scientific method at least points social scientists in the right direction.

INDUCTIVE AND DEDUCTIVE REASONING

One issue in the social sciences relates to where we start in the research process. This issue concerns the methods of induction and deduction. When the researcher begins with "an a priori assumption (before-the-fact reasoning), wherein a theoretical idea precedes any attempt to collect facts" (Hagan, 1993, p. 16), he or she is using a *deductive* reasoning technique. In this case, the research is based on a theory or hypothesis and the data are then collected and the results generalized to a larger population. When the reasoning begins with an "a posteriori assumption (after-the-fact reasoning)" (Hagan, 1993, p. 16), the researcher is engaging in *inductive* reasoning. In this latter case, the facts are used to develop a theoretical explanation. Said another way, "inductive logic moves from a number of particular and separate observations to a generalization" while "deductive logic . . . moves from the general to the particular" (Fitzgerald & Cox, 1987, p. 9).

When a researcher who is engaged in the research process begins with a theory about behavior, formulates a research strategy, and then collects the data to test the theory, he or she is using deduction. When the researcher starts with a set of findings or results from a study and

attempts to generate a theoretical explanation from the results, he or she is engaging in induction. Both approaches are useful to the research process and can provide beneficial results.

RESPONSIBILITIES TO SUBJECTS, COLLEAGUES, AND THE COMMUNITY

When a social scientist undertakes a research project, questions are raised about the responsibility of the scientist to the subjects of the study, the scientist's colleagues, and the community at large as opposed to the subject of science itself. There have been significant changes in the laws governing the activity of research, especially as it relates to the use of live subjects, both human and nonhuman.

To maintain academic and research integrity, many professional organizations have established codes of ethics for researchers to provide them with sets of guidelines that include integrity in reporting results of research. Such guidelines are especially important for the colleagues of researchers who rely on the academic integrity of others for purposes of their own research. The responsibilities of the researcher have been broadened even further to include the community at large, who often take the findings of research at face value. (Most of these issues are identified and discussed in Chapter 5.)

REFERENCES

Bailey, Kenneth D. (1982). *Methods of social research* (2nd ed.). New York: Free Press.

Bierstedt, Robert (1957). *The social order.* New York: McGraw-Hill.

Fitzgerald, Jack D., and Cox, Steven M. (1987). *Research methods in criminal justice.* Chicago: Nelson-Hall.

Hagan, Frank E. (1993). *Research methods in criminal justice and criminology* (3rd ed.). New York: Macmillan.

Miller, Delbert C. (1991). *Handbook of research design and social measurement* (5th ed.). Newbury Park, CA: Sage.

Sutherland, E. H. (1947). *Principles of criminology* (4th ed.). Philadelphia: Lippincott.

Inequality and Metropolitan Rape Rates: A Routine Activity Approach

David J. Maume, Jr.
Justice Quarterly
Vol. 6, No. 4, pp. 513–525, December 1989

Introduction

The relationship between inequality and patterns of violent crime has been a long-standing concern of sociologists and criminologists. On the basis of accumulated research findings, many social scientists would agree that (1) material deprivation produces in some individuals feelings of frustration, rage, and alienation (Blau and Blau, 1982; Braithwaite, 1979) and (2) criminal activity is one way in which people express their rage against a system that distributes resources unequally (Coser, 1968).

Theory

The routine activity perspective, which emerged in the late 1970s, argues that a crime occurs when three factors converge in time and space: (1) a motivated offender, (2) a suitable target, and (3) an absence of capable guardians. Following Hawley (1950), Cohen and Felson (1979) argue that the volume of crime is related to the nature of normal, everyday patterns of interaction. They state, "Daily activity may determine the location of property and persons in visible and accessible places at particular times" (1979:591). Over time, they contend, people's routine activities have taken place increasingly outside the home (e.g., women's increased labor-force participation, increased college attendance). Thus the potential for interaction between offenders and targets has increased, as has the number of unguarded homes. These increases explain the rising crime trends since the end of World War II.

Like Cohen and Felson (1979), others also argue that lifestyle differences associated with routine activities explain group differences in falling victim to a crime (Hindelang, Gottfredson, and Garofalo, 1978). For example, the young spend less time at home, and their chances of falling victim to a crime exceed those of the aged. Similarly, the victimization rates for the employed or for those in school are lower than for the unemployed because the first two groups spend less time on the street and more time in the company of guardians. Yet the employed and students have higher victimization rates than retired persons or homemakers because the latter groups spend more time at home (Miethe, Stafford, and Long, 1987).

Routine Activity Theory and Aggregate Rape Rates

I contend that income differences could affect rape activity because income constrains lifestyles. I assert that areas with an unequal distribution of income will have unemployment and poor housing. Belknap (forthcoming) found that women looking for work were the most likely and homemakers the least likely to fall victim to a rape. For men, high unemployment may increase the pool of motivated offenders. Regarding housing, one measure of poor housing is overcrowding. Gove and Hughes (1979) found that people who live in overcrowded housing spend more time on the street than those who do not. Other things being equal, spending time on the street increases the likelihood that potential offenders and victims will cross paths and that a crime will occur as a result.

Inequality also may influence the number of potential guardians against rape. Economically deprived areas exhibit higher rates of family disruption; Sampson's [1986] work ties family structure to the number of potential guardians against crime. One also could argue that separated or divorced women spend more of their time alone (going to work, shopping, going to restaurants) than do married women, and thus are at greater risk of being raped.

Housing status also has been shown to affect the chances of falling victim to rape. Belknap (forthcoming) found that renters were more likely than homeowners to experience rape. One could interpret this finding in terms of Sampson's discussion of the level of guardianship in a community: cities with high rates of rentership have higher rates of population turnover (Shannon, 1983). As a result, the residents of those areas would be more accustomed to seeing strangers and less vigilant in protecting their neighbors. I expect that as income disparities in an area increase, so does the rate of rentership, and consequently that rape rates are higher.

The Sample

The 318 standard metropolitan statistical areas (SMSAs) defined in 1980 constituted the sample for this study; because 34 SMSAs lacked data on the dependent variable, the final sample size was 284.

The choice of the unit of analysis is debatable. States may be a poor choice because, as Messner (1983:999) argues, they do not represent ecological areas in which offenders and victims come into contact with one another. Cities may be more meaningful ecological fields, but Gibbs and Erickson (1976) contend that when city boundaries form only a portion of the SMSA, suburbanites may visit the city and may fall victim to a crime. Counting these people in the number of crimes occurring within the city but not in the city's population base inflates the city's crime rate. If, in addition, these cities have a higher percentage of poverty and their suburbs wealth, the size of the city compared with the rest of the

SMSA may bias the inequality-rape relationship. Choosing the metropolitan area as the unit of analysis solves these measurement problems most effectively.

The Dependent Variables

The FBI's *Uniform Crime Reports* (UCR; Federal Bureau of Investigation, 1980–1982) provided the data for the dependent variable. I calculated a three-year average over the years 1980 through 1982 in order to minimize year-to-year variation in an area's rape rate. The FBI calculates the rape rate by dividing the total number of rapes by total population and multiplying the quotient by 100,000. Although no published study has taken this approach, one could argue that it would be more appropriate to divide the number of rapes by the number of women in constructing the rape rate. I decided against this method, however, so that my findings could be compared to those of prior studies. Finally, to correct for skewness, I calculated the base 10 logarithm of the average rape rate.

Independent Variables

The Census Bureau's Summary Tapes Files (U.S. Bureau of the Census, 1983) provide information necessary for operationalizing the independent variables. All of these variables were measured at the census date in 1980.

Results

Table 1 presents ordinary least squares regression results of the determinants of areal rape rates. Equation 1 in Table 1 presents results with the opportunity indexes omitted from the model; the second equation adds these variables into the model.

When the criminal opportunity indexes are omitted from the model, population size is shown to be the strongest determinant of geographic variation in rape rate (beta = .31); the Gini index of income inequality is the second strongest predictor. The racial inequality measure is related

TABLE 1   Determinants of (Log 10) Rape Rates, 1980–1982 (Standardized Coefficients in Parentheses)

PREDICTORS	EQUATION 1	EQUATION 2
Percent Black	.0044**	.0026
	(.1775)	(.1031)
Population Size (log 10)	.1748**	.1062**
	(.3105)	(.1886)
Percent Aged 15–34	.0078**	.0041
	(.1421)	(.0751)
South (= 1)	.0087	–.0620
	(.0171)	(–.1220)
Gini Index	2.2882**	.9678
	(.2351)	(.0978)
Racial Inequality	–.0022*	–.0009
	(–.1064)	(–.0432)
General Opportunity Lifestyles	—	.0394**
		(.4014)
Racial Differences in Lifestyle	—	.0170**
		(.2142)
Constant	–.6666	.3780
R^2	.3262	.4413

** Coefficient significant at the .05 level.
* Coefficient significant at the .10 level.

only weakly to the level of rape in an SMSA. As expected, the age and racial structure of an area predicts the rape rate strongly; yet the region dummy [variable] does not influence the dependent variables significantly.

The results in Equation 2 show that the general opportunity index is the most important predictor of geographic variation in rape (beta = .40); the index of racial differences in lifestyles is the second strongest predictor (beta =.21). Moreover, the addition of the index variables increases explained variation in areal rape rates by nearly 12 percent.

In addition, controlling for the index variables in Equation 2 causes a considerable weakening of the effects of the inequality measures on rape. This finding suggests that areas with a high degree of income inequality are structured to promote opportunities for the occurrence of rape. As income differences widen and racial disparities increase, male employment decreases and the community's rates of divorce, overcrowding, and renting increase. These community-level factors measure the number of motivated offenders, the number of suitable targets, and the degree of lack of guardians. As these three factors converge in space and time, the rape rate will increase. The results support my contention that inequality affects the violent crime rate indirectly via the organization of routine activities or lifestyles that are determined by economic conditions.

My results suggest that rape rates rise with racial composition because blacks live lifestyles that increase their exposure to criminal activity. Minorities make up a large share of unemployed, are more likely to suffer marital disruption, and live in poor housing. Thus they make up a disproportionate share of persons motivated to rape and of the pool of suitable targets. Blacks also live in areas where "guardianship" against crime is reduced because those areas are transient or are plagued with unstable family structure. Like the results for the Gini index, the index of racial differences in lifestyle mediates the effect of racial composition on rape.

References

Belknap, Joanne (forthcoming) "Routine Activity Theory and the Risk of Rape: Analyzing Ten Years of National Crime Survey Data." *Criminal Justice Policy Review*.

Blau, Judith R. and Peter M. Blau (1982) "The Cost of Inequality: Metropolitan Structure and Violent Crime." *American Sociological Review* 47 (February):114–29.

Braithwaite, John (1979) *Inequality, Crime, and Public Policy*. London: Routledge and Kegan Paul.

Cohen, Lawrence E. and Marcus Felson (1979) "Social Change and Crime Rate Trends: A Routine Activities Approach." *American Sociological Review* 44 (August):588–607.

Coser, Lewis A. (1968) "Conflict: Social Aspects." In David L. Sills (ed.), *International Encyclopedia of the Social Sciences*, Volume 3. New York: Macmillan, pp. 232–36.

Federal Bureau of Investigation (1980–1982) *Crime in America: Uniform Crime Reports*. Washington, DC: Government Printing Office.

Gibbs, Jack P. and Maynard L. Erickson (1976) "Crime Rates of Cities in Ecological Context." *American Journal of Sociology* 82 (November):605–20.

Gove, Walter R. and Michael Hughes (1979) "Overcrowding in the Home: An Empirical Investigation of Its Possible Pathological Consequences." *American Sociological Review* 44 (February):59–80.

Hawley, Amos (1950) *Human Ecology: A Theory of Community Structure*. New York: Ronald.

Hindelang, Michael J., Michael Gottfredson, and James Garofalo (1978) *Victims of Personal Crime*. Cambridge, MA: Ballinger.

Messner, Steven F. (1983) "Regional and Racial Effects on the Urban Homicide Rate: The Subculture of Violence Revisited." *American Journal of Sociology,* 88 (March):997–1007.

Miethe, Terance D., Mark C. Stafford, and J. Scott Long (1987) "Social Differentiation in Criminal Victimization: A Test of Routine Activities/Lifestyle Theories." *American Sociological Review* 52 (April):184–94.

Sampson, Robert J. (1986) "Neighborhood Family Structure and the Risk of Personal Victimization." In J.M. Byrne and R.J. Sampson (eds.), *The Social Ecology of Crime*. New York: Springer-Verlag, pp. 25–46.

Shannon, Thomas R. (1983) *Urban Problems in Sociological Perspective*. New York: Random House.

U.S. Bureau of the Census (1983) *1980 Census of the Population*. Washington DC: Government Printing Office.

Name of Student _____

Student ID # _____

Course Section # _____

Date _____

1. What are the possible limitations from using FBI data on rape?

_____

_____

_____

_____

_____

_____

_____

_____

2. According to the author, there is a relationship where *income* as an independent variable causes *rape*. Does this relationship have *practical validity?* Does this relationship have *theoretical validity?*

_____

_____

_____

_____

_____

_____

_____

_____

3. Given the size of the correlation coefficients, how *reliable* are the findings? Are the findings *valid?*

_____

_____

_____

_____

_____

_____

_____

_____

4. Again, considering the size of the correlation coefficients, how *significant* are the author's findings as an explanation for what causes rape?

_____

_____

_____

_____

_____

_____

_____

_____

Measuring Jail Use: A Comparative Analysis of Local Corrections

John Klofas
Journal of Research in Crime and Delinquency
Vol. 27, No. 3, pp. 295–317, August 1990

Introduction

In the past 10 years, interest in the measurement of the use of incarceration and other methods of correctional intervention has grown. Researchers have used measures of incarceration to examine numerous issues including sentencing practices, changes in corrections practice over time, prison crowding, and racial disparity within the criminal justice system. Measures of incarceration have also been central to investigations of deterrence and incapacitation and other important policy goals in criminal justice. The studies make it clear that adequate measures of incarceration are central to both research and policy in criminal justice.

Most research involving the measurement of incarceration has focused on the use of imprisonment. It is in this area, also, that most attention has been paid to the methodology of measurement. In recent publications of the National Institute of Justice, for example, Garofalo (1987) details several different measures of prison use. Along with rates of incarceration, he discusses the use of fraction in prison, as well as chance, prevalence, and duration of imprisonment as alternative indices of the use of prison resources.

The measures Garofalo (1987) discusses all relate to imprisonment, but they may not be useful when assessing other forms of incarceration. Jails, for example, serve significantly different functions than prisons. The local jail serves as a port of entry into the judicial system. It holds some people while they navigate that system, and it continues to hold some whose navigation has been unsuccessful and who are, therefore, being punished for criminal or even some civil violations. This complex role differs significantly enough from that of the prison to raise the ques-

tion as to whether a single approach to measurement is equally useful in both areas. This article will consider the problem of measurement of the use of local jails.

Measurement of Jail Use

Among researchers, jails are no longer the neglected institutions they once were. Until recently there was only a handful of original studies of local corrections (e.g., Mattick, 1974; Goldfarb, 1975). Although the research is still not abundant, these seminal works have been joined by a number of more narrowly focused studies of jails. Irwin (1985) has provided a provocative study of the jail's role in the community. Gibbs (1982) has produced insightful and useful analysis of inmate adjustment in jail. Other significant studies have been done on judicial intervention (Schafer, 1986; Champagne, 1983), subcultures (Garofalo and Clark, 1985), jail suicides (Hayes, 1983; Winfree, 1987), and jail management (Pogrebin, 1982; Kalinich and Postill, 1981). With the increasing size of the jail population, many useful studies have also been done on the causes and remedies for jail crowding (see Bolduc, 1985).

While jails perform similar tasks, there seems to be great variability across jails in their application of these tasks. In a study of Illinois jails (Klofas, 1987), average daily population rates across the 95 jails ranged from 1 to over 16 per 10,000 county residents, while annual booking rates per 10,000 ranged from 45 to 450. This variability suggests differences in the way communities deploy their resources for social control.

In the Illinois study, the measures of these processing and holding functions of the jails were only modestly correlated. Thus, assessment of jail use by either measure alone is inadequate for describing variation in the ways county jails facilitate social control. A more complete description of the jail use could be obtained by simultaneously considering both the booking and holding functions of the jail. To accomplish this, a typology was formed based on the possible combination of the ways the jail tasks could be performed. Some jails were described as "high-use" jails in that they booked and held county residents at a high rate. "Low-use" jails booked and held residents at a low rate. "Holding jails" had a high average daily population rate but a low rate of booking, and "processing jails" booked county residents at a high rate while maintaining a low average daily population rate. In the broad theoretical perspective, these types are assumed to represent differences in communities' approaches to social control.

Data

The data for this study were collected as part of the 1986 *Annual Survey of Jails* sponsored by the Bureau of Justice Statistics (1987) and were made available through the Criminal Justice Archive of the Inter-University Consortium for Political and Social Research.

   The survey used a stratified national sample of all jurisdictions containing jails but did not include police lockups. Federal, state, and privately administered facilities as well as the combined jail-prison systems of Connecticut, Delaware, Hawaii, Rhode Island, and Vermont were excluded. Data were collected on each jail and aggregated across the local jurisdiction if it contained more than one jail. In the large jurisdictions with multiple facilities, it is common for the institutions to serve different jail functions. Thus, some jurisdictions may use a "house of corrections" or "workhouse" for sentenced offenders only, while some have established specialized facilities for reception and short-term detention. Because our concern is with the totality of local incarceration in any jurisdiction, the analysis combined data from all facilities in a given jurisdiction.

Jail Use Typology

The findings suggest that the combination of similarities and differences in local jails may indeed be an elegant combination worthy of additional attention. The first step in focusing that attention is to examine the extent to which the jail use typology developed in the Illinois study can be applied to the national data.

   There are, however, consequences to invoking this typology. The most important of these is the reduction in sensitivity of the measures. The typology requires the conversion of continuous data to categorical data. This places limitations on the statistical measures appropriate in the analysis, but—more importantly—it implies reduced refinement in the ability to distinguish between the jails. Whether this loss is tolerable will depend on judgments about the value of the social control perspective in guiding measurement and about the usefulness of the results of the analysis. It can be argued that the precision of these continuous variables, absent some theoretical justification, is of little use and simply contributes to increased variance that is beyond explanation under the current crude theoretical models. As Mills (1959:72) has noted, "Precision is not the sole criterion for choice of method."

   Juxtaposing the jail population rate and booking rate so that they can be considered simultaneously also requires a decision about the cutting points that will convert the rates to categories. In this analysis, the distribution of each of the variables was biased at the median. Different cutting points or the creation of additional categories could have been used. Division at the median was selected in this research for two reasons. First, given the moderately strong correlation between variables, we can expect jurisdictions to be distributed unevenly among types. Division at the median allows us to determine if all four types are needed to describe jail use by seeing whether the smallest categories will contain enough jurisdictions to facilitate analysis or whether they are best seen as hypothetical types that do not exist in the data. Second, this division avoids producing types composed solely of juris-

TABLE 3   Typology of Jail Use Patterns

		BOOKING RATE	
		Low	High
Jail Population Rate	Low	Low-Use Jails	Processing Jails
		N = 130	N = 43
	High	Holding Jails	High-Use Jails
		N = 42	N = 130

dictions that are extreme along two dimensions. It is thus the least likely to reveal differences across the jurisdictions and, therefore, the most appropriate division for testing the typology's usefulness.

Table 3 presents the typology of jail use using the data from the large jail jurisdictions. [Tables 1 and 2 have been omitted in this abstract representation.] As expected from the positive correlation, the two most common patterns are for jurisdictions to be low or high on both of the dimensions. The low- and high-use categories each contain 130 jurisdictions. Less common are the split types, which are high on one dimension but low on the other. Forty-two of the jurisdictions can be described as containing holding jails in that their population rate is high but the rate of bookings is low. Forty-three jurisdictions display the opposite pattern, with high booking rates but low jail population rates. This array of jurisdictions indicates that none of the types can be eliminated from the analysis as nonexistent or as occurring so infrequently as to add little comparative analyses.

Discussion

Because of the variety of ways in which the local jail contributes to the social control function of communities, measuring its use is a different and arguably more complex problem than assessing imprisonment. Any approach to measurement should serve to facilitate comparative analyses that can identify the antecedents and consequences of differences in jail use. The approach taken here is useful from both a conceptual and an empirical point of view.

The efforts to predict the patterns of use suggest that comparative studies can move beyond the limitations inherent in viewing jail use as idiosyncratic. The analysis indicates that there are some similarities between variables that have been related to prison use and those related to jail use. Unexpectedly, however, the population of the jurisdiction contributed little to explaining the patterns. This suggests that the impact of large urban areas on jails may not be as important as is frequently believed. The impact of crime on jail use needs further analysis, but this research suggests that the impact is significant when daily population and booking rates are considered together.

References

Bolduc, A. 1985. "Jail Crowding." *Annals of the American Academy of Political and Social Science* 478:47–57.

Bureau of Justice Statistics. 1982. *State Court Organization 1980.* Washington, DC: Bureau of Justice Statistics.

—. 1987. *Jail Inmates 1986.* Washington, DC: Bureau of Justice Statistics.

Champagne, A. 1983. "The Theory of Limited Judicial Impact: Reforming the Dallas Jail as a Case Study." Pp. 87–9 in *The Politics of Criminal Justice,* edited by S. Nagel, E. Fairchild, and A. Champagne. Springfield, Illinois: Charles C Thomas.

Garofalo, J. 1987. *Measuring the Use of Imprisonment.* Washington, DC: National Institute of Justice.

Garofalo, J. and R. Clark. 1985. "The Inmate Subculture in Jails." *Criminal Justice and Behavior* 12:415–34.

Gibbs, J. 1982. "The First Cut Is the Deepest: Psychological Breakdown and Survival in the Detention Setting." Pp. 97–114 in *The Pains of Imprisonment,* edited by R. Johnson and H. Toch. Beverly Hills, CA: Sage.

Goldfarb, R. 1975. Jails: *The Ultimate Ghetto of the Criminal Justice System.* Garden City, NY: Anchor.

Hayes, L. M. 1983. "And Darkness Closes in . . . a National Study of Jail Suicides." *Criminal Justice and Behavior* 4:461–84.

Irwin, J. 1985. *The Jail: Managing the Underclass in American Society.* Berkeley: University of California Press.

Kalinich, D. and F. Postill. 1981. *Principles of County Jail Administration and Management.* Springfield, IL: Charles C Thomas.

Klofas, J. 1987. "Patterns of Jail Use." *Journal of Criminal Justice* 15:403–12.

Mattick, H. 1974. "The Contemporary Jails of the United States: An Unknown and Neglected Area of Justice." Pp. 777–849 in *Handbook of Criminology,* edited by D. Glaser. Chicago: Rand McNally.

Mills, C .W. 1959. *The Sociological Imagination.* New York: Oxford University Press.

Pogrebin, M. 1982. "Scarce Resources and Jail Management." *International Journal of Offender Therapy and Comparative Criminology* 26:263–74.

Schafer, N. E. 1986. "Jails and Judicial Review: Special Problems for Local Facilities." Pp. 127–45 in *Sneaking Inmates Down the Alley: Problems and Prospects in Jail Management,* edited by D. Kalinich and J. Klofas. Springfield, IL: Charles C Thomas.

Winfree, L. T. 1987. "Toward Understanding State-Level Jail Mortality: Correlates of Death by Suicide and Natural Causes, 1977 and 1982." *Justice Quarterly* 4:51–72.

Name of Student _____

Student ID # _____

Course Section # _____

Date _____

1. Create a typology using the data on "jail admissions and release" in *Sourcebook* for the years 1988–1992. Your typology should inform the reader about current trends for males, females, adults, and juveniles.

   _____

   _____

   _____

   _____

   _____

   _____

   _____

   _____

   _____

   _____

   _____

   _____

   _____

   _____

   _____

   _____

   _____

   _____

   _____

   _____

   _____

2. What are some of the implications of the current trends in population represented by admissions data?

   _____

   _____

   _____

   _____

   _____

_____

_____

_____

_____

_____

_____

_____

_____

_____

_____

_____

_____

3. Given the data on jail admissions and releases, if we assume that management of jail resources is an important policy consideration, what can be said about the effectiveness of jails in the United States?

_____

_____

_____

_____

_____

_____

_____

_____

_____

_____

_____

_____

_____

_____

_____

_____

_____

Gender and Varieties of White-Collar Crime

Kathleen Daly
Criminology
Vol. 27, No. 4, pp. 769–794, 1989

Introduction

Studies of gender and crime draw primarily on official arrest statistics. From such studies we learn a good deal about the frequency, but almost nothing of the nature, of men's and women's illegalities. These gaps are especially acute for white-collar crime.

Scholars typically use the Uniform Crime Reports (UCR) or Offender-Based Transaction Statistics (OBTS) arrest data on embezzlement, fraud, and forgery when assessing gender- or race-based rates of white-collar crime (e.g., Hirschi and Gottfredson, 1987; Manson, 1986; Simon, 1975), but their analyses are based on questionable assumptions. Simon (1975) argues, for example, that the increasing female share of embezzlement, forgery, and fraud arrests during the 1960s and early 1970s may be explained by increases in women's labor participation rate. She assumes that all three offenses are occupationally related.

It is imperative that we understand the characteristics of acts falling in the presumptive "white-collar" statutory domain, how they are organized both within and outside workplace settings, and their class-, gender-, and race-specific nature. The aim of this paper is to begin that process. The focus of the analysis is 1,342 defendants (14% female) who were convicted of white-collar offenses in U.S. federal district courts during the late 1970s. This is a select group of white-collar offenders, those who were prosecuted and convicted.

The issue of gender differences in "workplace opportunities" to commit white-collar crime has sparked debate over interpreting UCR arrest data. Simon (1975:106) argues that as women move into "those types of jobs that will provide them opportunities to commit offenses that are important enough to report," the female share of arrests for forgery, fraud, and embezzlement will increase. Critics take Simon to task on several grounds. Chapman (1980) and Messerschmidt (1986) say that the increasing female share of UCR white-collar arrests reflect women's economic and occupational marginality, not mobility; and Steffensmeier (1978) suggests that women's frauds and forgeries may not be occupationally related at all.

Plainly, the literature on gender and white-collar crime is long on speculation and short on evidence. Hence, five hypotheses that consolidate some of the major themes reviewed are explored in this paper:

H1: The female share of corporate (or organizational) crime is very low.
H2: The female share of occupational crime is low.
H3: Women are less likely to work in crime groups than men.
H4: Women's economic gains from crime are less than men's.
H5: Men's and women's motives for criminal involvement differ.

The Data

The Wheeler et al. (1982, 1988) data set used in this analysis was gathered in the following way. At seven federal district courts a sample of cases was drawn for defendants convicted during 1976–1978 of bank embezzlement, income tax fraud, postal fraud, credit fraud, false claims and statements, and bribery. In addition, all antitrust and securities fraud convictions in these and other federal districts were selected. The presentence investigation (PSI) report was obtained for each defendant, and a coding scheme was developed to quantify information in the PSI narrative. In selecting cases, Wheeler et al. (1982:642) took an offense-based approach and defined white-collar crime as "economic offenses committed through the use of some combination of fraud, deception, or collusion." Thus, the sample is not restricted by any offender-based criteria.

Results

The proportion of female defendants in each offense category varies dramatically: women were 45% of convicted bank embezzlers, but their numbers were negligible for antitrust violations, bribery, and securities fraud (n's of 1, 4, and 5, respectively). Offense categories in which there was a moderate share of women were postal fraud (18%), cash fraud (15%), and false claims and statements (15%). Generally, the higher the percentage of women in each offense, the higher the fraction of non-whites (predominantly Black) and those not completing four years of college. In fact, the results for the education variable are startling. If completing college is an indicator of status or occupational power, then most of the defendants, including those convicted of securities fraud and antitrust violations, do not fit the high-status profile.

Four findings are noteworthy. First, a high percentage of women (30 to 40%) and about one-fourth of the men convicted of postal fraud, credit fraud, and false claims and statements had no labor force ties. Second, 40 to 85% of the male offenders were professional or managerial workers, but only a majority of the very small number of women convicted for tax fraud, bribery, securities fraud, and antitrust violations were professionals or managers. Third, there is offense- and gender-specific variability in whether an offender used an occupational role to carry out the offense. As one would expect, bank embezzlement, securities fraud, and antitrust violations were occupationally related. Postal fraud and false claims, however, were more likely to be occupationally related for men than for women, and credit fraud was somewhat more likely to be occupationally related for women than for men.

Finally, a higher percentage of men's (14%) than women's (1%) cases involved indictments against corporations or businesses. The corporate nature of defendants' illegalities is moderate to low for men and almost negligible for women. Of the 194 women, only two cases had corporate indictments: the one woman convicted of antitrust violations and one of the five convicted of securities fraud. For the 162 men's cases involving corporate indictments, most were concentrated, not surprisingly, among the antitrust violators, and to a lesser degree, securities fraud offenders.

Summary and Implications

In this group of white-collar offenders, some men are "big fish," but most are "little fish" and do not comport with images of highly placed or powerful white-collar criminals. Men's white-collar crimes were both petty and major, but almost all the women's were petty. Although half or more of the employed men were managerial or professional workers, most employed women were clerical workers. Higher proportions of women were Black and had no ties to the paid labor force; fewer women had a four-year college degree.

References

Chapman, Jane Roberts
    1980   Economic Realities and the Female Offender. Lexington, Mass.: Lexington Books.

Hirschi, Travis and Michael Gottfredson
    1987   Causes of White-Collar Crime. Criminology 25:949–974.

Manson, Donald A
    1986   Tracking offenders: White-collar crime. Bureau of Justice Statistics, Special Report, NCJ-102867. Washington, D.C.: U.S. Department of Justice.

Messerschmidt, James W. 1986
    Capitalism, Patriarchy, and Crime: Toward a Socialist Feminist Criminology. Totowa, N.J.: Rowman and Littlefield.

Simon, Rita J. 1975
    Women and Crime. Lexington, Mass.: Lexington Books.

Steffensmeier, Darrell J. 1978
    Crime and the Contemporary Woman: An Analysis of Changing Levels of Female Property

Crimes, 1960–75. Social Forces 57:566–584.

Wheeler, Stanton and Mitchell L. Rothman
1982   The Organization as Weapon in White-Collar Crime. University of Michigan Law Review 80:1403–1426.

Wheeler, Stanton, David Weisburd, Nancy Bode, and Elin Waring
1988   White Collar Crime and Criminals. American Criminal Law Review 25:331–357.

Name of Student _____
Student ID # _____
Course Section # _____
Date _____

1. What is the difference between a *null* and an *alternative* hypothesis?

    _____
    _____
    _____
    _____
    _____
    _____
    _____
    _____
    _____
    _____
    _____
    _____
    _____

2. Create two null hypotheses appropriate for a study of white-collar crime.
    H1: _____

    _____
    _____

    H2: _____

    _____
    _____

3. Create two alternative hypotheses for a study of white-collar crime.
    Alt. 1: _____

    _____
    _____

    Alt. 2: _____

    _____
    _____

4. How would you operationalize concepts in each of your hypotheses? In other words, what variables might be used to measure each concept represented in each hypothesis?

_____

_____

_____

_____

_____

_____

_____

_____

CHAPTER 2

Issues of Measurement

In this chapter, we will consider abstracts of articles that deal with measurement. *Measurement* is defined as the process by which concepts are transformed through operationalization into variables. We will illustrate various types of measuring strategies and provide opportunities to practice many of these techniques. First, however, we need to introduce a number of terms and concepts and explain the importance of measurement.

A research study usually begins with a fairly simple idea. A researcher poses a question to himself or herself: for example, "Does marijuana use affect students' academic performance?" Next, the researcher may start thinking about hypotheses or may ask other tentative questions about the topic. At the same time, the researcher begins reading literature on the subject. At this point, he or she has a kind of informal theory about the topic, a personal theory. As the researcher continues to read about the subject matter, he or she will refine propositions and eventually develop a formal theory.

Theories are composed of sets of logically linked concepts. But since theories are neither directly observable nor testable, these concepts must be transformed into variables. In many ways, measurement is the process by which this transformation takes place.

The task of transforming elements of theory into measurable indices—*variables*—is one of the toughest challenges facing social scientists. Some of the concepts that arise during a given research project are relatively easy to measure because there is broad consensus on how to evaluate their underlying properties. For example, an individual's "age," "educational level," and "income" are concepts that are relatively easy to measure; these concepts have properties that are clear, objective, concrete, and easy to assess. However, many concepts have more elusive properties. For example, "friendship," "involvement," "socialization," "social status," "value," and "social class" are among the many thousands of concepts that are regularly measured but have vague properties.

Consider, for example, "religiosity"—an important concept in many social scientific studies but quite a difficult concept to measure. One way to consider the *variable* "religiosity" is to think about various ways in which people indicate being religious. Initially, we think about various practice issues, organizational memberships, identifiable beliefs, perhaps rituals and foods, or even verbal declarations of religious identification. Each of these, then, represents a kind of subcategory of religiosity, and each can be transformed into a measurable index.

Measurement provides researchers with means by which to make evaluations, assessments, and comparisons of various kinds. These analytic activities, in turn, are the stuff that give meaning to our everyday reality. For example, we might want to know if the crime rate in a given community has gone up or down, if individuals' religious attitudes have anything to do with becoming involved in certain kinds of crime, if alcohol use impacts the commission of predatory crime, and so forth. To answer any of these questions, the researcher must measure something.

As several of the abstracts reprinted in this book demonstrate, measurement in the research context is not always clear cut or strictly numerical. When someone asks "How dangerous is it to walk through this neighborhood?" a response such as "very dangerous" or "a little dangerous" is not immediately quantifiable. Thus, research on the subject "fear of crime" requires the researcher to consider what measures can be identified and used to represent various degrees of perceived danger.

WHY DO SOCIAL SCIENTISTS MEASURE VARIABLES?

Sometimes, a numerical representation of frequency of occurrence or the magnitude of some event or phenomena is sufficient measurement for a study. In other cases, more specific measures may be required.

Social scientists also often devise measures to describe properties associated with various social ideas and phenomenon. The ideas "social class" and "social status," for example, conjure images in our minds, yet those images may be slightly different for each of us. For some, "social class" may bring to mind images of income levels, relative levels of education, certain patterns of consumer buying, and various kinds of lifestyles or economic strata in our society. "Social status," for some people, may prompt identical images. But for others, "social status" may evoke images of certain careers, access to restricted social organizations, specific categories of occupations, or even rankings of certain occupations in a given society.

Many of the ideas and events we value are conceived of in terms of an essentially arbitrary system of measurement. In order for more than a single individual to appreciate the meanings of these concepts, some form of systematic measurement must be declared by the researcher. The process of formally defining how a concept will be measured is called *operationalization*.

Operationalization is perhaps the most difficult task a researcher must undertake. The reason for this difficulty is that operationalization involves moving from the abstract, namely, a concept, to the concrete, a variable. Throughout most of our socialization in American educational settings, we have been trained to take concrete items and make them abstract. If asked to write about a topic such as a tree on Arbor Day or if asked to describe how a bicycle works, most of us would have little trouble moving from the concrete to the abstract. But if asked to take an abstract concept such as "social class," many of us would find it difficult to derive concrete measures of this term. We might decide that "social class" is made up of several elements for which we can identify concrete measures. Certain levels of income and edu-

cation, for example, may be thought to represent different social class strata. By identifying people who fit into different income and educational groups, we could establish a hierarchy intended to represent the social class rankings of a given population. Doing so would bring us to an operationalized definition of "social class": Social class is an individual's placement in one of the hierarchy of categories representing income and class.

RELATIONSHIPS BETWEEN VARIABLES

Measurement also permits examination of and comparisons between various variables. Analysis of such comparisons permits researchers to make predictions and assessments about variable relationships. Does a student's Graduate Record Examination (GRE) score accurately represent his or her potential to succeed in graduate school? A well-designed operationalized variable representing the concept "success" could be used to assess this question. Does a baccalaureate degree increase the likelihood that an individual will get a job in his or her area of choice? Do members of minorities with baccalaureate degrees have the same likelihood of obtaining jobs of choice as similarly educated Whites do? By carefully operationalizing "areas of choice," "minorities," and categories of "jobs," we could potentially assess these questions.

Now that we have established what measurement is and suggested how it works in social science research, we must consider various kinds of measurement. Typically, measurement is classified into four groups or levels of data, namely, nominal, ordinal, interval, and ratio. These categories are conceived in terms of their increasing and cumulative mathematical properties.

MEASURES OF CENTRAL TENDENCY

To offer a general description of a mass of data, we might consider several things. For example, we could summarize the distribution of certain variables and indicate what is typical for the mass of data, or we could identify what was average for the data. Finally, we could examine how most of the data are distributed. In the language of quantitative methodologists, these three approaches provide insight to measures of central tendency.

The *mode,* the *mean,* and the *median* are the labels used to describe central tendencies. In effect, each indicates a single score or value that represents the center of a frequency distribution. Yet each measure is slightly different.

The *mode* represents the variable or value observed most frequently in a mass of data. For instance, if a class comprises 25 females and 20 males, the modal category would be "female." Determining the mode requires no calculation. We simply examine the distribution of categories or variables and identify which occurs most frequently. It is possible for more than one value or variable to be the mode. If two variables in a mass of data appear with equal frequency (and are the most frequent), then they would both be the mode and the data would be *bimodal.* For example, consider the following data regarding the ages of students in a class:

AGE	FREQUENCY
19	5
20	11
21	10
22	11
23	5
	42

Given these data, the ages 20 and 22 are the modes, since both occur 11 times.

The *mean* is the arithmetic average of a set of data. It describes the distribution of variables as if they were distributed equally. In other words, the mean is the sum of scores divided by the number of scores. Using the data on students' ages, we multiply each category of age times its frequency of occurrence. For instance, for the age 19, there are 5 individuals, which yields a score of 95 (19 × 5 = 95). If we multiply each age category by its frequency and then total these scores, the results are as follows:

AGE	FREQUENCY	(AGE × FREQUENCY)	=	PRODUCT
19	5	19 × 5	=	95
20	11	20 × 11	=	220
21	10	21 × 10	=	210
22	11	22 × 11	=	242
23	5	23 × 5	=	115
	42			882

The next step in calculating the mean is to sum the frequency and product categories. Next, we divide the sum of the product by the sum of the frequency. In our example above, doing so results in a mean of 21 (882/42 = 21). Therefore, the mean age category for the given sample of students is 21.

The *median* identifies the score (with a real or hypothetical case) that separates all occurrences of a given variable or value into two equal-sized groups. The median can be described as the score of the middle value or case and is therefore *positional* in character. If the distribution contains an odd number of cases or variables, the median is the middle case ($[N + 1]/2$, where N is the number of cases or variables). If the distribution contains an even number of cases or variables, the median is the *hypothetical score* between the two equal-sized groups. Before calculating the median, we must make sure the cases are arranged from lowest score to highest score. For instance, in our student example, the cases are already arranged ordinally from 19 through 23 for the 42 cases (students). The median is 21.5 ($[42 + 1]/2 = 21.5$). Therefore, in our sample, the median case for age of the students falls halfway between the 21st and 22nd scores, which is 21.5.

What if we have an odd number of cases? Suppose we have 35 students (cases) with IQ scores as follows:

IQ SCORE	FREQUENCY
95	2
100	5
115	10
120	10
125	5
130	3
	35

For these data, the median score is 18 ([N + 1]/2 = 36/2 = 18). The median is the IQ value associated with the 18th case, which is 120.

Once we understand the mode, the median, and the mean, we can calculate the *mean deviation,* which is the average distance from the mean. In doing so, we are not concerned with whether the deviation is plus or minus from the mean but only with the distance. We can use the student age data to demonstrate how to calculate the mean deviation.

The *absolute value* represents the distance from the mean without regard to direction. Therefore, in our example, the age 19 has an absolute value of 2.0 while 21 has an absolute value of 0.0. Once we have determined the absolute value for each score, we multiply the absolute value for each score by its frequency. In the data that follow, for the age 19, we multiply the frequency of 5 by the absolute value of 2.0, resulting in 10.0 deviation points. Once we have done this for each score, we sum the deviation points to determine the total deviation points. We then divide the total deviation points by the total frequencies to determine the mean deviation. The size of the mean deviation tells us how spread out the scores are. The higher the mean deviation, the greater the dispersion of the scores and therefore the greater the heterogeneity.

One way to avoid working with absolute values, as we do in calculating the mean deviation, is to square the deviations. The *variance* is the mean of the squared deviations. Again, using the student age example, we create a table as follows:

AGE	FREQUENCY	DEVIATION $(X - \overline{X})$	ABSOLUTE VALUE	DEVIATION POINTS
19	5	21.0 – 19.0 = +2.0	2.0	5 x 2.0 = 10.0
20	11	21.0 – 20.0 = +1.0	1.0	11 x 1.0 = 11.0
21	10	21.0 – 21.0 = 0.0	0.0	10 x 0.0 = 0.0
22	11	21.0 – 22.0 = –1.	1.0	11 x 1.0 = 11.0
23	5	21.0 – 23.0 = –2.0	2.0	5 x 2.0 = 10.0
$N = 42$				Total Deviation Points 42.0

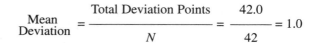

$$\text{Mean Deviation} = \frac{\text{Total Deviation Points}}{N} = \frac{42.0}{42} = 1.0$$

Although the method of ignoring positive or negative signs and using absolute values was once popular, it is no longer used. Today, the method used to eliminate negative signs is to square each number. When we square any number, the result is always positive. In this method, we usually square each mean deviation and then find the average of these squared values. This measure of dispersion is called the *variance.* Using the same example, we create a table as follows:

AGE	FREQUENCY	MEAN DEVIATION	SQUARED DEVIATION
19	1	+2.0	4.0
20	1	+1.0	1.0
21	1	0.0	0.0
22	1	–1.0	1.0
23	1	–2.0	4.0
	5		10.0

Given these data, the population variance is 2.0 (10/5 = 2.0).

The population variance has one drawback: Because it is based on the squares of the deviations from the mean, it is difficult to create a mental picture of the distribution. If we calculate the *population standard deviation,* it simplifies the visualization of the dispersion. The population standard deviation is calculated by taking the square root of the sum of squares of the deviations from the mean and dividing it by N, the number of cases. This is represented by the following formula:

σ = population standard deviation
Σx^2 = sum of mean deviation squares
N = number of cases

$$\sigma = \sqrt{\frac{\Sigma x^2}{N}}$$

The last point to be made regarding the standard deviation is that the formula is for a population, not a sample. If we would use the same formula for a sample, we would get a biased estimate of the population variance because we would systematically underestimate the population variance.

We can correct this bias by decreasing the N in the formula by 1, thereby creating the following formula:

s = standard deviation for a sample
$\sum x^2$ = sum of mean deviation squares
$N-1$ = number of cases minus 1 for bias correction

$$s = \sqrt{s^2} = \sqrt{\frac{\sum x^2}{N-1}}$$

This discussion of measures of central tendency is intended to be preliminary or introductory. You should consult one of the numerous statistical texts available for an in-depth explanation of the measures of central tendency, especially as they relate to grouped data.

LEVELS OF MEASUREMENT

Nominal Level

The nominal level of measurement involves sorting elements to be measured into discrete categories. For example, we could measure people's hair color by categorizing them as "brown," "blond," "red," and "black." In terms of the mathematical properties associated with nominal-level data, we can use only operations related to relationships that are equal or not equal. Stated simply, nominal-level data involve assigning names or numbers to categories. These names and numbers have no literal mathematical meanings.

Many of the variables that social scientists find interesting are of the nominal type. Gender, race, marital status, political preference, and religious preference are typical examples. Gender is usually depicted as involving two categories—"male" and "female"—but no underlying mathematical meaning is imputed to these categories. We cannot order them nor can we add them in the same way we can add a quarter and a nickel and derive the sum 30 cents. Even if we assign numbers to these categories ("male" = 1, "female" = 2), adding the numbers makes no sense. Certainly, "male" + "female" does not equal 3.

The categories in any nominal set must meet two criteria:

1. They must be *mutually exclusive,* so that each case is counted in only one category.
2. They must be *logically exhaustive,* so that every case belongs in one category.

The fact that nominal-level measures have no mathematical properties does not mean that mathematical operations are inappropriate in every case. We may not be able to order or average the categories, but mathematical functions can be performed and used to compare between and across categories. The mathematical operations most frequently used on nominal-level measures are the calculations of frequencies (e.g., number of males = 15; number of females = 10), simple proportions (males = 15/25; females = 10/25), and percentages (males = 32%, females = 68%).

Ordinal Level

Unlike nominal-level measures, ordinal-level measures do possess basic mathematical properties. Ordinal-level data are ordered or ranked, usually involving a rising order of inequality between categories from lowest rank to highest. We could, for example, take the midterm examinations from a class and order the students from lowest to highest scores. This would provide us with a means for ranking each student in the class. However, this simple ranking would not tell us how far apart the students are in academic performance.

We can consider another example from the world of horse racing. When a horse "places" in a race, we immediately know it has come in second. But we do not know whether this second-place horse has edged out the "show" horse (the third-place horse) or has beaten it by several lengths, nor do we know whether the "place" horse has followed the winning horse (the first-place horse) by inches or meters. We do know, however, the first-, second-, and third-place rankings of the horses.

All ordinal-level measures incorporate this mathematical property of order or rank. Here are several other examples of ordinal measures.

VOLUME	MILITARY RANK	SIZING
5 gallon	5 captain	5 extra large
4½ gallon	4 lieutenant	4 large
3 quart	3 sergeant	3 medium
2 pint	2 corporal	2 small
1½ pint	1 private	1 petite

For such measures, rank is assigned (1) according to the number of categories and (2) in ordered sequence (from less to more of a property).

Interval Level

The third level of data is interval measure. In addition to possessing the mathematical property of order, interval-level scales assume an equal distance between points representing order. In an interval scale, the distance between the points on a measuring instrument is known, and this value is equal throughout the scale. For example, the difference between 40 and 50 correct answers on an aptitude test is the same as the difference between 70 and 80. Thus, the ratio of measured intervals is meaningful. In other words, any given interval is exactly equal to every other interval in the scale, regardless of its position in the series of units.

However, we would not be accurate in saying that an individual with a score of 80 is twice as smart as someone with a score of 40 on the same aptitude test. The reason for this is that in interval measures, we operate with an arbitrary zero point. The placement of zero on this scale is arbitrary, since the best we can do is operationally define the absence of the property being measured. For instance, if an individual received a score of zero on an aptitude test, this would not mean that he or she had absolutely no aptitude.

Mathematically, interval measures possess several basic properties. Operations of addition, subtraction, multiplication, and division normally can be performed on interval scales. When measuring various cognitive, perceptual, and behavioral phenomena, social scientists frequently employ the use of an arbitrary zero.

If we were to measure student perspectives about the death penalty, for example, we could assume that the difference between scores of 2 and 3 is the same as that between scores of 6 and 7. However, accounting for individuals who have no feelings about the death penalty (neutrality) still requires an arbitrary placement of zero.

Ratio Level

Ratio measures incorporate both the mathematical properties already mentioned (order and equal intervals) and one additional property: the presence of a natural or absolute zero. The ratio level of measurement is based on an ordered series of equal intervals, beginning with an absolute or natural zero. In situations where the zero on a ratio scale is absolute, it represents a condition where the absence of a property is measured: "none of something."

For example, if you withdraw all your savings from a bank account, you reach the natural origin of zero. If you replace $25, you increase the balance to a positive $25. If you add a second deposit of $50, your balance increases to $75 (assuming no other deposits or withdrawals have occurred). At this point, the balance is three times as large as it was following your first deposit. This example demonstrates that when we work with a natural zero, the numbers on the scale represent the actual amount of a property following the first deposit. Because the actual amount of a property is scaled, mathematical operations are possible with ratios. The ratio of $75 to $25 is 75/25, or 3/1. In other words, we can legitimately claim that $75 is three times as much as $25.

Another commonly employed example of a ratio-level measure is age, where the moment of birth (in most Western cultures) represents a natural zero. Accepting this natural zero point allows the social scientist to suggest that a person who has lived 50 years has lived twice as long as someone who is 25.

Overview of Levels of Measurement

For most concepts, there is no single correct measure. In fact, most concepts can be transformed into variables in many different ways. It is also possible to have different measures of a given concept represented at different levels. Which measure the researcher chooses for a given concept will depend on what measures are selected, what measures previously have been used in similar research, and which measures previously have been proven effective. At least two major techniques are used in the social sciences for constructing measures: single-measure indicators and scales.

Single-Measure Indicators

A single-measure indicator can be constructed in just two steps: The researcher decides (1) what observations to use as measures of a concept and (2) what procedure to use for combining these observations operationally. For instance, we might decide to use the number of law violations reported to the police as an approximate indicator of the annual crime rate. Although operationally possible, such an indicator would be limited, since as many as half of the violations against persons are not reported officially to the police and an indeterminable number of violations (e.g., tax and insurance fraud) may never be discovered let alone reported.

Social scientists, then, must make decisions about how fruitful a selected indicator will be toward measuring a given concept. The researcher also must decide whether a single limited indicator will be sufficient or several indicators might yield more satisfactory results. One way to use several indicators of a concept and to measure these together operationally is through scaling.

Scales as Measures

The term *scale* refers to a special type of measurement in which numbers are assigned to positions, indicating varying degrees of the property under consideration. When a concept is measured using a scale, the result is usually a single score for an individual, representing the degree to which that individual possesses the property being measured. Many different types of scales are used in social science research. We will discuss only two major types, namely, rating scales and questionnaire-based scales.

Rating Scales

Speaking generally, rating scales all have one feature in common: The person or object being rated is placed in one category within an ordered set, in which numerical values are assigned to categories. Rating scales can be used to secure individuals' ratings of themselves or others. If we want to transpose this type of categorical scaling strategy to a more qualitative mode, this, too, is possible. By assessing either self-perceptions or perceptions of others, we could create various types of categorical or typological schemes. Three of the most commonly used rating scales are the graphic rating scale, the itemized rating scale, and the comparative rating scale.

An alternative scaling technique uses a measured line, usually 10 centimeters in length. At one end, the researcher places a 0 or a term such as "Low," "Disagree," or "Never." At the other end, the researcher places a 10 or a term such as "High," "Agree," or "Always." In response to a question or statement, the subject places a mark on the line in relation to how he or she rates something—for instance, high or low. Since the questionnaires are identical (i.e., each line is exactly 10 centimeters long), each subject's rating can be determined and scaled.

Graphic Rating Scales

Graphic rating scales are those constructed with (1) a designated number of ordered scale points and (2) a written description for every other scale point. It may help to think of a graphic rating scale as analogous to a ruler. Unlike the 10 centimeter line, which shows starting and ending points, graphic rating scales show points positioned at equal intervals, and written descriptions are supplied for most or all points. The subject is told to select the one written description (and hence the corresponding scale point) that most closely approximates his or her position. For example, [look at the table at the top of the next page].

Itemized Rating Scales

Itemized rating scales are composed of series of ordered statements to which point values have been assigned. In some scales, subjects are instructed to read the statements and to select *all* those statements with which they agree. In other cases, subjects may be asked to read all the state-

CONFIDENCE IN PERSONAL SECURITY AND PROTECTION OF PROPERTY

1	2	3	4	5	6

High confidence in personal security. Free movement night and day, for both sexes. High sense of security of property. Locking homes is optional.	Moderate confidence in personal security. Confidence of men is high in personal security, but women are warned to take precautions. Movements of women are restricted to daytime. Simple property precautions are essential.	Low confidence in both personal security and protection of property. Men and women restrict all movements at night to predetermined precautions. Many property precautions are obligatory. Extensive use of locks, dogs, and guards.

ments and select *only one* statement that best describes their view. Usually, the statements vary in terms of intensity, with the middle statement expressing a relatively neutral position. Statements also may vary in length, from a single sentence to several sentences or illustrations. The clearer the distinction between statements, the more vivid the scale positions and the more reliable the scale. For example, consider the following statements in the order presented:

1. The Bible is God's word, and all it says is true.
2. The Bible was written by men inspired by God, but it contains some human errors.
3. The Bible is a good book because it was written by wise men; God had nothing to do with it.
4. The Bible was written by men who lived so long ago that it is worth very little today.

Comparative Rating Scales

Comparative rating scales ask subjects to position themselves or others on scales where the positions are judged relative to other individuals or groups. This type of scale differs from an itemized scale, since it does not require that subjects rate some objects or people in reference to others. In effect, subjects are asked to rate on the basis of their knowledge about something or someone. For example, when a professor is asked to evaluate a student seeking entrance into a graduate, law, or medical program, he or she is frequently asked to rate the student's performance in comparison with the performances of other students. A typical question might look like the following:

Of the students you have known, is this student in the top:

1. 5%
2. 10%
3. 25%
4. 50%

To make this evaluation, the professor must have a clear picture of this student in relation to other students with whom he or she has worked.

Questionnaire-Based Scales

Questionnaire-based scales are scales in which series of statements are tallied in order to create single composite scores or indexes. The use of the phrase *questionnaire based* is not meant to imply that *rating scales* are not included on these questionnaires. This phrase is only meant to suggest that questionnaire-based scales are formatted much like questionnaires, since they contain series of questions or statements.

The usual format for a questionnaire-based scale asks the subject to respond to every statement. Several questionnaire-based scales have received general acceptance in social science research, including the Thurstone, Likert, and Guttman scales.

Thurstone Scales

The Thurstone scaling technique, named after its originator, L. L. Thurstone, is generally held to be the most elaborate version of a questionnaire-based scale. Thurstone scales are one means of measuring attitudes. In the traditional Thurstone scale, a set of statements are arranged along a continuum, on which the scale points vary from 1 to 11, ranging from the least favorable responses to the most favorable ones; the midpoint, the 6 position, represents a neutral response. The locations of the statements along the continuum are decided by a panel of judges who are knowledgeable about the topic area. The judges respond to each statement in terms of its meaning, not in terms of their personal views. A final Thurstone scale typically consists of about 24 statements, allowing approximately 2 statements for each scale point. These reflect the positions on the scale to which all the judges have agreed.

Stated in general terms, the steps for creating a Thurstone scale are as follows:

1. A concept is selected for measurement. For example, we might be interested in measuring attitudes toward homosexuality, the death penalty, or victimization issues.
2. Next, the concept is transformed into measurable variables.
3. To measure the concept, the researcher collects or constructs a wide variety of statements about it. These statements may be collected from newspapers, magazines, books, individuals, broadcasters, or oneself and should represent a wide variety of opinions about the concept, since the end result is to identify statements that can be positioned at 11 different positions on the scale. For example, if we were interested in attitudes about victimization, some of the statements might be:
   - People who walk in poorly lit places are looking for trouble.
   - It is dangerous to go into certain neighborhoods at night.
   - Most muggings are entirely avoidable.
   - Locked doors are important for safety in the home.

   The researcher assembles about 100 different statements, recording them on file cards for convenience, a single statement per card.
4. In the next phase of development, the researcher identifies a panel of 200 to 300 judges, each knowledgeable on the subject "victimization," in our example. Each judge is asked to sort the statement cards into 11 piles, labeled "A" through "K," with "A" representing the most negative statements, "K" the most positive, and "F" neutral. In order for this procedure to work, the researcher must accept the assumption that the statements placed in each pile are equal distance from statements placed in every other successive pile, as assigned by the judges. In other words, those statements placed in pile A are assumed to be equal distance from those statements placed in pile B, which are assumed to be equal distance from those in pile C, and so on.
5. If the sortings of several judges are drastically different from those of the other judges, those few judges' piles are eliminated and the assumption is made that they were careless in paneling statements. Once this cross-checking has been completed, scale values for each statement are calculated by computing the median scale values of each pile. The spread of judgments about the median is also computed. Some researchers prefer to use the mean and the spread of scores about the mean. The general rule is to use both measures when the size of the panel of judges is large. In this case, the two measures should give approximately equivalent results. When the panel of judges is small, the median measure is usually considered the most appropriate. Calculation of either the mean or the median assumes conversion of the scale to a number continuum, where $A = 1$, $B = 2$, $C = 3$, and so on.
6. Final selection for the scale is made from those statements that have been calculated as having the smallest spread and that are equally spaced along the scale. Each of the numbered intervals is assigned 2 statements, so that the final scale contains 22 statements. When each pile contains many statements to choose from, the general rule is to select those statements that are the most clearly and concisely worded.

The scale is administered by having respondents check only those statements with which they agree, and each respondent's score is the mean scale value for all the statements he or she has endorsed.

Likert Scales

Shortly after development of the Thurstone scale, Renis Likert (1932) offered a less time consuming and complicated alternative. Like Thurstone, Likert began by compiling a large number of questions, usually 30 or more, all of which focused on the interest area (e.g., "victimization"). In practice, however, Likert scales frequently are employed using far fewer statements than 30.

We begin construction of a Likert scale with the assumption that each individual statement involves at least an ordinal level of measurement. This represents a major difference between Thurstone and Likert scales. With Thurstone scales, no scale weights are given with the statements, and respondents are asked to check only those statements with which they agree. With Likert scales, respondents are asked to indicate the degree of agreement or disagreement for each statement on the instrument using a five-point scale. In other words, five response categories are provided for each statement: "Strongly Agree," "Agree," "Neutral," "Disagree," and "Strongly Disagree."

Next, a numerical value is assigned to each response category for scoring: for instance, "Strongly Agree" (SA) = 5, "Agree" (A) = 4, and so on. The statements used may be either favorable or unfavorable, provided the researcher is consistent in his or her weighting:

	SA	A	N	D	SD
Favorable Statements	1	2	3	4	5
Unfavorable Statements	5	4	3	2	1

The respondent will be assigned a total score, which is the sum of the numerical values of his or her responses to all questions.

It is a good idea to have both positively and negatively worded statements. Sometimes, when all the statements are worded in only one direction, a *response set* develops (sometimes called an *acquiescent response set*), which represents a tendency to answer all statements the same. If all the statements were positively worded, for example, a respondent might mark "Agree" for each statement without reading any of the statements carefully.

A second difference between Likert and Thurstone scales is in the scoring. Whereas Thurstone scales are scored by computing the mean (or median) value of those statements endorsed, Likert scales are scored by simply summing the weights for all statements. With a 20-statement Likert scale, for example, we would expect a minimum score of 20 and a maximum score of 100. (Both these values assume that all 20 statements were answered.)

Guttman Scales

A third prominent measurement technique, developed by Louis Guttman and his associates and introduced in the 1940s, is Guttman scaling. This technique, sometimes referred to as *cumulative scaling,* is a scoring technique that assumes that indicators of a concept can be arranged along a unidimensional continuum and that each indicator differs from the others in intensity. In other words, knowledge of a total score allows us to predict a subject's responses to individual statements. The statements assume an a priori order, such that agreement with any particular statement assumes agreement with the statements preceding it.

Reiss (1967), for example, used the concept "premarital sex" to develop a Guttman scale. In this scale, indicators ranged from "kissing" to "sexual intercourse." Reiss reasoned that anyone who approved of heavy petting also would approve of light petting and kissing. Conversely, anyone who disapproved of light petting also would disapprove of heavy petting, oral contact, and full sexual intercourse. This type of question series might be expressed as follows:

1. Do you approve of kissing someone you are dating?
2. Do you approve of light petting with someone you are dating?
3. Do you approve of oral/genital contact with someone you are dating?

4. Do you approve of heavy petting with someone you are dating?
5. Do you believe in having sexual intercourse with someone you are dating?

If these five statements were given to a subject, treated as having ordinal properties, and 1 point was scored for each statement the subject approved of, we could predict the subject's degree of premarital sexual permissiveness. For example, if the subject scored 5, we would know that he or she approved of having intercourse with someone he or she was dating. If the subject scored 4, we would know that he or she approved of a number of sexual activities while dating but not intercourse. If the subject scored 0, we would know that the subject did not approve of any of the sexual activities indicated in the statements. The ability to predict accurately, of course, lies in the assumption that the statements represent a cumulative character along the same continuum (in this case, along the continuum of attitudes about premarital sexual behavior).

REFERENCES

Guttman, L. (1947). The Cornell technique for scale and intensity analysis. *Educational and Psychological Measurement, 7,* 247–279.

Likert, Renis. (1932). A technique for the measurement of attitudes. *Archives of Psychology, 140,* 5–55.

Reiss, I. L. (1967). *The social context of premarital sexual permissiveness.* New York: Holt, Rinehart & Winston.

What Is the Perceived Seriousness of Crimes?

Mark Warr
Criminology: An Interdisciplinary Journal
Vol. 27, No. 4, pp. 795–821, November 1989

Introduction

Social judgments concerning the seriousness of criminal offenses have been a subject of continuous study in criminology since the publication of the landmark work *The Measurement of Delinquency* (Sellin and Wolfgang, 1964). Research on the subject has grown to include cross-cultural comparisons of seriousness ratings as well as a substantial literature on social consensus among Americans on the perceived seriousness of crimes (e.g., Normandeau, 1966; Rossi et al., 1974). The recent publication of the National Survey of Crime Severity, a sample survey in which 60,000 Americans rated the seriousness of crimes, attests to a continuing interest in this issue (Wolfgang et al., 1985).

The heart of the issue lies in the fact that the notion of seriousness can have more than one meaning. Consider, for example, the following offense: shoplifting $4 worth of goods from a large retail store. There are two central ways in which the seriousness of this act might be judged. First, one might consider the moral gravity of committing the act, that is, the moral culpability or blameworthiness that would accrue to an individual committing the act. Such a judgment is clearly a normative evaluation of the act and, hence, this dimension will be referred to here as the perceived *wrongfulness* of criminal offenses. On the other hand, the action might be judged on the basis of the harm or damage that the action brings upon the victim. Here, the judgment is not a normative evaluation of the act at all, but rather a factual assessment of the consequences of the offense for the victim. Since the judgment in this instance is based on an assessment of consequences, we will refer to this type of judgment as the perceived *harmfulness* of offenses.

The distinction between harmfulness and wrongfulness has been overlooked in the seriousness literature, but it appears in fields as varied as jurisprudence, developmental psychology, ethics, and social psychology. In the *Moral Judgement of the Child,* for example, Piaget (1932) reports that, as they grow older, children come to distinguish between the harmfulness of an act (or its "material consequences") and its moral wrongness ("naughtiness"). That is, an action (e.g., lying) may be morally wrong, even when it causes no harm, and an action that results in substantial harm (e.g., injury to a sibling) may be morally blameless, when, for example, it occurs by accident or is committed under duress or in self-defense. Similar reasoning is found throughout Western criminal law in such doctrines or concepts as *mens rea,* strict liability, negligence, and defenses to crime. In sociology, Durkheim (1949) was among the first to point out that acts (e.g., violating food taboos, burning the flag, working on the Sabbath) may be deviant even when they are devoid of objective harm (see also Gibbs, 1966).

This study examines how seriousness judgments are formed, concentrating on the contributions of harmfulness and wrongfulness to seriousness judgments. The analysis will show that there is considerably more structure and complexity to seriousness judgments than commonly supposed and that individuals differ in how they determine seriousness.

Data and Methods

The data for this study were obtained through a mail survey of Dallas residents. A Texas city was chosen so as to benefit from the reputation of the University of Texas in the state, and Dallas appears to be the Standard Metropolitan Statistical Area (SMSA) in Texas that most closely resembles SMSAs in the United States as a whole. The composition of the Dallas SMSA with regard to education, marital status, sex, age, and ethnicity is close to that of all SMSAs (Bureau of the Census, 1986). The median income for Dallas residents is somewhat higher than the national figure, but that is unlikely to have any bearing on the results.

The survey was designed in accordance with Dillman's (1978) methods for mail surveys. Respondents were chosen randomly from the Dallas telephone directory. One week after the initial mailing, all respondents received a reminder postcard. A letter and replacement questionnaire were mailed to nonrespondents three weeks after the initial mailing. Dillman recommends yet a third follow-up to nonrespondents after seven weeks, but it was omitted because it was thought to be intrusive and because the marginal returns would be small.

To determine the sources of seriousness judgments, respondents were first asked to rate the seriousness of a set of offenses ranging from petty crimes (e.g., trespassing and petty vandalism) to multiple homicide. In subsequent questions respondents were asked to rate the same offenses according to (1) how morally wrong they are and (2) the degree to which they harm or damage the victim.

The seriousness question, which used wording similar to that of Rossi et al. (1974), follows:

> There are many different kinds of crimes. Some are considered to be very serious, others not so serious. Below is a list of different types of crime. We are interested in your opinion about how serious each type of crime is. If you think it is among the least serious, then circle the number 0 beside the crime. If you think it is among the most serious, then circle the number 10 beside the crime. If you think the crime falls somewhere between the least serious and the most serious, then circle the number between 0 and 10 that best indicates how serious you think the crime is. Remember that the seriousness of a crime is only a matter of opinion, and it is your opinion that we want.

The question was followed by a list of 31 offenses with an 11-point (0–10) scale printed beside each offense. The words "least serious" were printed above the number 0 and "most serious" appeared above the number 10.

Following the seriousness question were two questions measuring wrongfulness and harmfulness. . . .

Findings

An initial inspection of the response structure to the three questions revealed that respondents fell into two clearly discernible groups based on responses to the wrongfulness question. Unlike either the seriousness question or the harmfulness question, a substantial minority (26%) of respondents rated all or nearly all of the offenses as equal when it came to moral gravity, usually assigning the number 10 to all offenses.

Discussion and Conclusion

The findings of this study support several conclusions. Among those who discern differences in the moral gravity of offenses, wrongfulness and harmfulness are distinct dimensions and conventional classes of crime (property, personal, public order) systematically differ on the two dimensions. The seriousness scores assigned to crimes by this group appear to reflect the dominant or primary feature of all crimes, either their wrongfulness or their harmfulness.

Among those who do not perceive differences in the moral gravity of crimes, wrongfulness, being a constant, is unrelated to judgments of either harmfulness or seriousness, and harmfulness alone is used in assessing the seriousness of crimes. Although the seriousness judgments of this group display enormous relative agreement with those of discriminators, nondiscriminators perceive crimes to be slightly more serious and more harmful than do their counterparts.

References

Bureau of the Census
1986   Statistical Abstract of the United States. Washington, D.C.: Government Printing Office.

Dillman, Don A.
1978   Mail and Telephone Surveys. New York: John Wiley & Sons.

Durkheim, Emile
1949   The Division of Labor in Society (trans. George Simpson). Glencoe, N.Y.: Free Press.

Gibbs, Jack P.
1966   Conceptions of deviant behavior: The old and new. Pacific Sociological Review 9:9–14.

Normandeau, Andre
1966   The measurement of delinquency in Montreal. Journal of Criminal Law, Criminology and Police Science 57:172–177.

Piaget, Jean
1932   The Moral Judgement of the Child. New York: Harcourt Brace.

Rossi, Peter H., Emily Waite, Christine E. Bose, and Richard E. Berk
1974   The seriousness of crimes: Normative structure and individual differences. American Sociological Review 39:224–247.

Sellin, Thorsten and Marvin E. Wolfgang
1964   The Measurement of Delinquency. New York: John Wiley & Sons.

Wolfgang, Marvin E., Robert M. Figlio, Paul E. Tracy, and Simon I. Singer
1985   The National Survey of Crime Severity. Washington, D.C.: Government Printing Office.

Name of Student _____

Student ID # _____

Course Section # _____

Date _____

1. Each of the following three pages contains a list of 10 crimes and a scale. The first scale is a "Seriousness Scale"; it lists 10 crimes and is designed to assess the degree of seriousness you associate with each crime. Please mark an "X" at the point on the continuum that best represents how serious you believe each crime is. A mark on the 7 indicates that you believe the crime is among the most serious. A mark on the 1 indicates that you believe the crime is among the least serious. A mark placed somewhere between the 1 and the 7 represents a middle degree of seriousness, from low to high. Please place an "X" on each scale to indicate the degree of seriousness you believe the crime represents.

    The second scale is a "Moral Wrongfulness Scale." Again, place an "X" at the appropriate place on each scale to represent the degree of moral wrongfulness each crime represents. An "X" on the 1 represents your belief that the crime is among the least morally wrongful, and an "X" over the 7 represents your belief that the crime is among the most morally wrongful.

    The third scale, a "Harmfulness Scale," is designed to assess the degree of harm or damage you believe each crime has done to the victim. As with the other two scales, an "X" over the 1 indicates the least severity, and an "X" over the 7 indicates the most severity.

Seriousness Scale

Directions: Place an "X" at the place on each scale that best indicates your belief about the seriousness of the crime.

1. A parent sexually abusing a child

```
|_____|_____|_____|_____|_____|_____|
1        2        3        4        5        6        7
```
Least serious   *Most serious*

2. Leaving a restaurant without paying the bill

```
|_____|_____|_____|_____|_____|_____|
1        2        3        4        5        6        7
```
Least serious   *Most serious*

3. Selling drugs to junior high school students

```
|_____|_____|_____|_____|_____|_____|
1        2        3        4        5        6        7
```
Least serious   *Most serious*

4. Pouring toxic waste into a river that serves as a source of drinking water

```
|_____|_____|_____|_____|_____|_____|
1        2        3        4        5        6        7
```
Least serious   *Most serious*

5. Cheating on your federal income tax

```
|_____|_____|_____|_____|_____|_____|
1        2        3        4        5        6        7
```
Least serious   *Most serious*

6. Robbing a local store and killing the cashier

```
|_____|_____|_____|_____|_____|_____|
1        2        3        4        5        6        7
```
Least serious   *Most serious*

7. Breaking a window of an empty house

```
|_____|_____|_____|_____|_____|_____|
1        2        3        4        5        6        7
```
Least serious   *Most serious*

8. A store overcharging for repairs

```
|_____|_____|_____|_____|_____|_____|
1        2        3        4        5        6        7
```
Least serious   *Most serious*

9. Stealing a car

```
|_____|_____|_____|_____|_____|_____|
1        2        3        4        5        6        7
```
Least serious   *Most serious*

10. Taking a telephone from your place of employment to use in your home

```
|_____|_____|_____|_____|_____|_____|
1        2        3        4        5        6        7
```
Least serious   *Most serious*

Wrongfulness Scale

Directions: Place an "X" at the place on each scale that best indicates your belief about the moral wrongfulness of the crime.

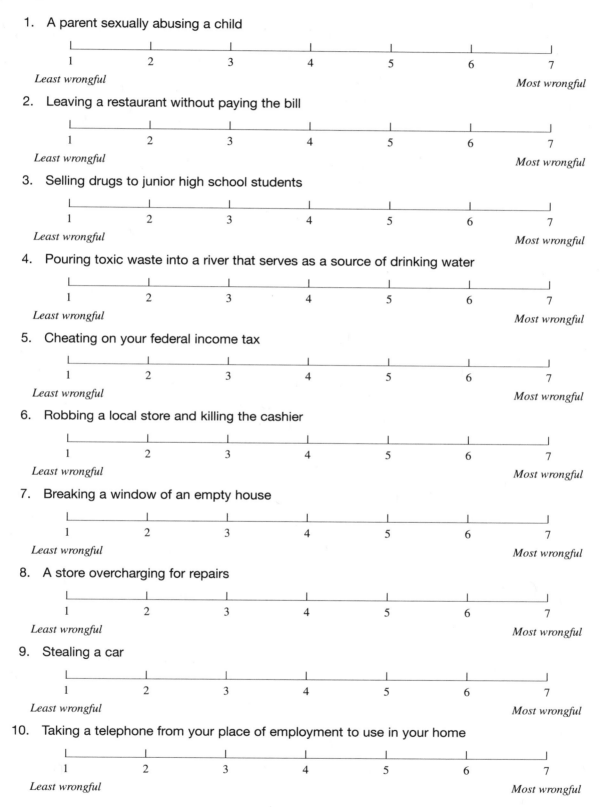

1. A parent sexually abusing a child

| 1 | 2 | 3 | 4 | 5 | 6 | 7 |

Least wrongful   *Most wrongful*

2. Leaving a restaurant without paying the bill

| 1 | 2 | 3 | 4 | 5 | 6 | 7 |

Least wrongful   *Most wrongful*

3. Selling drugs to junior high school students

| 1 | 2 | 3 | 4 | 5 | 6 | 7 |

Least wrongful   *Most wrongful*

4. Pouring toxic waste into a river that serves as a source of drinking water

| 1 | 2 | 3 | 4 | 5 | 6 | 7 |

Least wrongful   *Most wrongful*

5. Cheating on your federal income tax

| 1 | 2 | 3 | 4 | 5 | 6 | 7 |

Least wrongful   *Most wrongful*

6. Robbing a local store and killing the cashier

| 1 | 2 | 3 | 4 | 5 | 6 | 7 |

Least wrongful   *Most wrongful*

7. Breaking a window of an empty house

| 1 | 2 | 3 | 4 | 5 | 6 | 7 |

Least wrongful   *Most wrongful*

8. A store overcharging for repairs

| 1 | 2 | 3 | 4 | 5 | 6 | 7 |

Least wrongful   *Most wrongful*

9. Stealing a car

| 1 | 2 | 3 | 4 | 5 | 6 | 7 |

Least wrongful   *Most wrongful*

10. Taking a telephone from your place of employment to use in your home

| 1 | 2 | 3 | 4 | 5 | 6 | 7 |

Least wrongful   *Most wrongful*

Harmfulness Scale

Directions: Place an "X" at the place on each scale that best indicates your belief about the harmfulness of the crime.

1. A parent sexually abusing a child

1	2	3	4	5	6	7

    Least harmful   *Most harmful*

2. Leaving a restaurant without paying the bill

1	2	3	4	5	6	7

    Least harmful   *Most harmful*

3. Selling drugs to junior high school students

1	2	3	4	5	6	7

    Least harmful   *Most harmful*

4. Pouring toxic waste into a river that serves as a source of drinking water

1	2	3	4	5	6	7

    Least harmful   *Most harmful*

5. Cheating on your federal income tax

1	2	3	4	5	6	7

    Least harmful   *Most harmful*

6. Robbing a local store and killing the cashier

1	2	3	4	5	6	7

    Least harmful   *Most harmful*

7. Breaking a window of an empty house

1	2	3	4	5	6	7

    Least harmful   *Most harmful*

8. A store overcharging for repairs

1	2	3	4	5	6	7

    Least harmful   *Most harmful*

9. Stealing a car

1	2	3	4	5	6	7

    Least harmful   *Most harmful*

10. Taking a telephone from your place of employment to use in your home

1	2	3	4	5	6	7

    Least harmful   *Most harmful*

2. Now that you have completed the three scales, determine the mean and median scores for each of the 10 crimes.

> 1. Child sexual abuse   *Show your calculations here*
>   Mean Score   _____
>
>
>   Median Score   _____
>
>
> 2. Leaving restaurant without paying bill   *Show your calculations here*
>   Mean Score   _____
>
>
>   Median Score   _____
>
>
> 3. Selling drugs to junior high school students   *Show your calculations here*
>   Mean Score   _____
>
>
>   Median Score   _____
>
>
> 4. Pouring toxic waste into river   *Show your calculations here*
>   Mean Score   _____
>
>
>   Median Score   _____

5. Cheating on federal income tax   *Show your calculations here*

    Mean Score   _____

    Median Score   _____

6. Robbing store and killing cashier   *Show your calculations here*

    Mean Score   _____

    Median Score   _____

7. Breaking window of empty house   *Show your calculations here*

    Mean Score   _____

    Median Score   _____

8. Store overcharging for repairs   *Show your calculations here*

    Mean Score   _____

    Median Score   _____

9. Stealing car

   Mean Score   _____

   Show your calculations here

   Median Score   _____

10. Taking telephone from place of employment

    Mean Score   _____

    Show your calculations here

    Median Score   _____

Love, Sex, and Self-Esteem

Anthony Walsh and Grace J. Balazs
Free Inquiry in Creative Sociology
Vol. 18, No. 1, pp. 37–41, May 1990

Introduction

There is broad agreement among social and behavioral scientists that, to a large extent, human destiny is determined by the esteem in which we hold ourselves. In Allport's (1961:155–156) multiple drive theory, self-esteem "takes precedence over all other drives," and Kaplan (1975:1) has contended that "the self-esteem motive is universally and characteristically . . . a dominant motive in the individual's motivational system." Moderate to large correlations are consistently found between self-esteem and many psychological and somatic indices of illness and well-being: depression (Rosenberg, 1965), satisfaction with life (Crandall, 1973), various somatic symptoms (Bachman, 1970), and coping with multiple sclerosis (Walsh and Walsh, 1987). In short, self-esteem is the image we have of ourselves in an evaluative sense (a person of great or little worth, and all judgments in between). If the image is positive, we have a firm foundation for coping with life's problems and for gathering its bounties. If the image is negative, we cope less well and achieve very little.

While there is a body of literature comparing the male and female experience of love, it is unfortunately almost exclusively limited to romantic love. Romantic love is certainly an important form of love, but by no means does it exhaust the many meanings attached to it. We are concerned here with love as a broad form of human relatedness that encompasses caring, trust, respect, appreciation, friendship, concern, as well as filial and romantic love. We do observe in the affiliation literature that females are far more likely than males to be with other people rather than to be alone in a variety of social situations (Latane and Bidwell, 1977).

In addition to love, other independent variables determined by prior research to be significantly related to self-esteem are included in this study as control variables: occupational status and age (Rosenberg, 1979) and marital status (MacDonald et al., 1987).

The following hypotheses are proposed: (1) Males will be shown to have higher self-esteem than females. (2) Love will be the most powerful predictor of self-esteem among both men and women. (3) Love will have a more powerful impact on self-esteem among women than among men.

Methods

Subjects

Subjects are a non-probability sample of 253 adults in the Boise, Idaho, area who responded to mailed questionnaires. There are 155 females and 98 males in the sample, 107 subjects were married at the time of the sampling, and 146 were either never married, divorced, separated, or widowed. These 146 were grouped together as "unmarried." Ages of the subjects ranged from 24 to 80 (mean = 40.9). Breaking down the sample by occupational status, we find that 28 listed themselves as unskilled, 66 as skilled, 34 as lower white-collar, 33 as being in managerial or technical positions, and 6 as executives or professionals. Eighty-six of these subjects either did not reply to this question or listed themselves as students and/or housewives. Occupational status scores were based on Van Dussen and Zill

(1975). Years of education ranged between 10 and 20 years (mean = 13.99).

Self-Esteem

Self-esteem was measured using Rosenberg's Self-Esteem Scale (1965). We computed a reliability coefficient of .87 for this scale. Self-esteem scores ranged between 18 and 50 (mean = 37.8, s = 6.7).

Love

Love is measured in two different ways. The first measure is Miller's (1971) Positive Affect Scale. This six-item scale asks the subject to check the number of people with whom he or she has "fairly regular and frequent contact" who (1) show appreciation of you, (2) make you feel that they admire you very much, (3) show understanding and acceptance of you, (4) act in ways that show they sincerely like you, (5) seem to really care about you, and (6) seem to really love you. The reliability coefficient computed for this scale from our data is .91. Positive affect scores ranged between 12 and 24 (mean = 20, s = 3.3).

Social Isolation

The second measure of love is Neal and Groat's (1974) Social Isolation Scale. This is an indirect measure of love based on the assumption that social isolation indices that the individual has few opportunities to experience the love and affection of others or to extend the same to others. The coefficient of reliability computed from our data is .78.

These two (direct and indirect) measures of love are mirror images of one another: those who are socially isolated are less likely to be in frequent contact with sources of positive affect. The "mirror" image nature of the two measures can be ascertained by the correlations between them and self-esteem. The Pearson correlation between positive affect and self-esteem is .44 and between social isolation and self-esteem it is −.43. Consequently, it was decided to combine the two indices (positive affect minus social isolation) to create a more parsimonious love variable. The computed reliability coefficient for this created composite scale is .88.

Discussion

All three research hypotheses were supported by our data. As expected from prior research, males had higher self-esteem than females. The significant zero-order effect of sex on self-esteem was enhanced when the effects of the other independents were included in a multiple regression model. Contrary to the findings of MacDonald et al. (1987), marital status was not significantly related to self-esteem at the zero-order level; it was able to uniquely account for a statistically significant, albeit small percentage of variance in self-esteem when the effects of other variables in the model were adjusted for. In contrast to MacDonald et al. (1987), it was the unmarrieds who had the higher level of self-esteem. Different models, of course, produce different results. MacDonald and her colleagues controlled for masculinity and femininity scores in their model, and were only able to account for 5 percent in self-esteem variance.

Love was overwhelmingly the most powerful variable in the model. Aside from marital status, only age was significantly (negatively) related to self-esteem. The effect of age on self-esteem was primarily due to its influence on males.

Of greatest interest is the sex-differentiated effect of love on self-esteem. . . . [L]ove was found to be about 2.8 times more important in accounting for variance in self-esteem for women than for men, although love was most important in explaining male self-esteem also. The respective adjusted R squared values indicate that accounting for self-esteem among males is a more complicated business than accounting for it among females. The model accounts for almost half of the variance in self-esteem among females, but the same variables only account for about one-fifth of the variance among males.

Whether women are innately more oriented to and embedded in emotional relationships than men is an intriguing question. If women do have such an innate foundation for this capacity to respond more strongly than males to emotional cues, culture certainly builds upon and reinforces that foundation (Rossi, 1984). Certainly, the data presented here clearly shows that love is much more important to how women evaluate themselves than it is to men. Women who are secure in the knowledge that they are loved, and who have the opportunity to love in return, feel worthwhile. Love proved to be such an important variable in explaining self-esteem among both sexes that we have little hesitation in recommending that behavioral scientists pay greater attention to it in future research.

References

Allport G 1961 *Pattern and Growth in Personality*. NY: Holt, Rinehart and Winston

Bachman J 1970 *Youth in Transition, Volume II: The Impact of Family Background and Intelligence on Tenth-Grade Boys*. Ann Arbor MI: U Michigan Survey Research Center

Crandall R 1973 The measurement of self-esteem and related constructs. in J Robinson, P Shaver eds *Measures of Social Psychological Attitudes* Ann Arbor, MI: U Michigan Survey Research Center

Kaplan H 1975 *Self-Attitudes and Deviant Behavior* Pacific Palisades, CA: Goodyear

Latane B, and L Bidwell 1977 Sex and affiliation in college cafeterias *Personality Soc Psychol Bull* 3 571–574

MacDonald N, P Ebert, S Mason 1987 Marital status and age as related to masculine and feminine personality dimensions and self-esteem *J Soc Psychol* 127 289–298

Miller R 1971 Positive affect: an empirical study of social relationships. Unpublished MA thesis, U Toledo

Neal A, H Groat 1974 Social class correlates of stability and change in levels of alienation: a longitudinal study *Sociol Qrtly* 15 548–558

Rosenberg M 1965 *Society and the Adolescent Self-Image* Princeton: Princeton U Press

— 1979 *Conceiving the Self* NY: Basic Books

Rossi A 1984 Gender and parenthood: American Sociological Association 1983 Presidential Address *Amer Sociol Rev* 49 1–19

Van Dussen R, N Zill 1975 *Basic Background Items for U.S. Household Surveys* Washington, DC: Social Science Research Foundation

Walsh P, A Walsh 1987 Self-esteem and disease adaptation among multiple sclerosis patients *J Soc Psychol* 127 669–671.

Name of Student _____
Student ID # _____
Course Section # _____
Date _____

1. Complete this Love Measurement Scale. For each of the following items, indicate the number of people with whom you have *fairly regular and frequent contact* who:

    1. Show appreciation of you   _____

    2. Make you feel that they admire you very much   _____

    3. Show understanding and acceptance of you   _____

    4. Act in ways that show they sincerely like you   _____

    5. Seem to really care about you   _____

    6. Seem to really love you   _____

    2. Using the scales completed by your class as a group, code all responses into a systematic answer key.

    Item 1 _____

    _____

    _____

    _____

    _____

    _____

    _____

    _____

    _____

    Item 2 _____

    _____

    _____

    _____

    _____

    _____

    _____

    _____

Item 3

Item 4

Item 5

Item 6

3. Next, calculate the mean and standard deviation for each item using the class data.

Item 1   *Show your calculations here*

Mean Score   _____

Standard Deviation   _____

Item 2   *Show your calculations here*

Mean Score   _____

Standard Deviation   _____

Item 3   *Show your calculations here*

Mean Score   _____

Standard Deviation   _____

Item 4   *Show your calculations here*

Mean Score   _____

Standard Deviation   _____

Item 5   *Show your calculations here*

Mean Score   _____

Standard Deviation   _____

Item 6   *Show your calculations here*

Mean Score   _____

Standard Deviation   _____

4. Finally, compute a reliability coefficient for your data.

Neighborhood Differences in Attitudes toward Policing: Evidence for a Mixed-Strategy Model of Policing in a Multi-Ethnic Setting

Roger G. Dunham and Geoffrey P. Alpert
The Journal of Criminal Law and Criminology
Vol. 79, No. 2, pp. 504–523, 1988

Introduction

There are prevalent in society two general conceptions of the duties of the police officer. Middle class people feel that he should enforce the law without fear or favor. Cornerville people and many of the officers themselves believe that the policeman should have the confidence of the people in his area so that he can settle many difficulties in a personal manner without making arrests. These two conceptions are in a large measure contradictory. [Whyte 1943]

William Foote Whyte made these general observations more than forty years ago in *Street Corner Society.* The sharply contrasting social pressures that existed in different neighborhoods were important consequences of urban life. Whyte noted, more specifically, that the police must adapt to these different standards of acceptable conduct prevalent in different neighborhoods. His observations have been echoed by many, but tested by few. Other researchers have continued Whyte's theme that in the context of community policing, effective policing requires an understanding of the different citizens' expectations and values toward police practices.

The purpose of this article is to examine the differences in agreement and disagreement with various police practices among the residents of ethnically distinct neighborhoods in Miami, Florida. The findings provide needed empirical evidence for determining whether William F. Whyte was correct, and whether significant differences among neighborhoods really do exist. Further, these findings can guide police training to meet citizens' expectations for acceptable and effective policing. Research comparing ethnically distinct neighborhoods has not fully examined this aspect of neighborhood influences on policing.

This article will show that communities vary considerably in residents' expectations for police services. Residents of various culturally distinct neighborhoods may have different values dictating the appropriateness of police behavior and of the police styles used in specific situations. These preferences and dislikes may be interwoven into the fabric of the culture, the attitudes toward general authority, and more specifically toward police authority. In turn, police strategies and practices incongruent with the basic culture and values of a neighborhood would likely be ineffective and perhaps even counterproductive to maintaining order and controlling crime.

Methods and Procedures

The present article involves a sample of neighborhoods in Miami, Florida, and a sample of individuals within those neighborhoods. Each sample was chosen to allow for the most advantageous study of the issues central to our concerns: the relationships between the police and communities. The sample of neighborhoods allows for comparisons between areas with high versus low crime rates and distinct ethnic and social class compositions. Within each neighborhood, the survey data allows for study of how individual attitudes and values towards various policing practices form the aggregate patterns unique to each neighborhood.

Neighborhood Samples

Neighborhoods were selected because of their uniqueness, rather than to represent a balanced cross section of Miami or Dade County, Florida. Indeed, the overall population of Dade County is so segmented by ethnicity and social class that any overall characterization of the population would be difficult, if not impossible. With the assistance of police officials, officials from the Dade County Planning Department, and the 1980 census data, five neighborhoods, each representing a meaningful geographic unit to the police units operating in these areas, were chosen.

1. Rolling Oaks   Rolling Oaks is a relatively small community of about 150 recently built homes. Nearly all of the residents are upper-middle-class black professionals. Every third house was studied to complete a sample of fifty households.

2. James Scott Housing Project   The James Scott Housing Project is a government subsidized housing project populated almost exclusively by low-income blacks. There are a total of 858 units, most of which are occupied. Every sixteenth unit was surveyed to complete a sample of fifty units.

3. 1960 Cuban Entrants   The third neighborhood is a combination of middle-class and working-class homes that contain a very high percentage of Latin residents, most of whom are Cubans who immigrated during the first wave of Cuban immigration in the 1960s. There are nearly 700 homes in the neighborhood, and every fourteenth residence was surveyed to yield a sample of fifty residences.

4. 1980 Cuban Entrants   The procedure used to sample the fourth neighborhood represents an attempt to identify the attitudes of a new group of Cuban immigrants in the Miami area. Officials from the planning department identified a neighborhood of Cubans who arrived in this country during the 1980 boatlift. Interviewers screened prospective subjects and interviewed only those who immigrated from Cuba during the 1980 Mariel Boatlift.

5. Kendall Area   The fifth neighborhood is a well-established Anglo middle- and upper-middle-class area. There are about 900 houses in the particular Kendall neighborhood chosen, and every eighteenth home was surveyed to yield a total of fifty homes.

A sampling procedure was developed to select the member of the household to be interviewed to insure a representative sample of individuals living within households. Interviewers sampled only adults 18 years of age or older. Interviewers asked the number of adults and the number of men and women living in the house. The interviewer then used a table of random selections to decide which adult to interview. Provisions were made for the inability to contact the selected person after two visits. Substitutions of an under-represented group were allowed for, but such substitutions were made in less than 15% of the houses.

Measures

In order to determine the attitudes toward policing practices held by the residents of the neighborhoods selected, an exhaustive review of the literature was conducted. There are numerous studies on the interrelationship between the police and community, with numerous arrays of questions concerning attitudes toward policing. We selected scales and sets of questions that were relevant to our research that withstood the test of time with regard to reliability and validity of testing. This resulted in thirty questions coming from a variety of attitude scales. The thirty questions were scored on a one to five Likert-type scale. A "one" signified strong agreement. A "two" represented agreement, a "three" meant undecided, a "four" signified disagreement, and a "five" represented strong disagreement.

Factor Analysis

In the present study, these thirty items were administered to a sample of 451 high school students and a sample of 296 Dade County police officers, in addition to the study population of

250 Dade County residents. The data from the additional samples were used to provide a wide variety of respondents for scale construction.

The expectation was that certain, specific attitudinal domains would emerge from the combination of the 997 subjects. An effort was made to reduce the total number of items, eliminate those which were highly correlated, and identify the concepts which were believed to be the most important by the subjects. In other words, there was a search for attitude domains which can be identified by groups of questions which are answered in patterned ways.

The Five Scales

Demeanor   This scale consists of eight questions which measure the subject's perceptions of the general demeanor of police officers of his orientation toward citizens. Specific questions illicit responses concerning courteousness, friendliness, rudeness and concern or respect for citizens displayed by police officers. This scale includes the eight questions measuring specific behaviors represented by a comprehensive measure of police officer demeanor. The lower the score, the stronger the perception of a positive demeanor.

Responsibility   This scale consists of two questions concerning the role of the police and citizens in controlling crime: "only the police can control crime in Dade County/my neighborhood." The lower the score, the stronger the agreement with the statement that most of the responsibility for controlling crime rests with the police.

Discretion   Two questions are involved in this scale, which measures agreement with the need for variability in enforcing the law, and especially in stretching procedural safeguards in some neighborhoods or areas. The lower the score, the stronger the agreement with the need for variability in enforcement and applying procedural safeguards.

Ethnic   This scale consists of three questions concerning the justification for the suspicion that certain ethnic groups are more crime prone. The three questions are identical except

each makes reference to a different ethnic group: black, hispanic and anglo. The lower the score, the stronger the agreement with the idea that certain ethnic groups need to be watched more closely than others.

Patrol   Two questions comprise this scale, which measures the approval of active patrol strategies, such as stopping and questioning people walking down the street and stopping cars for random checks. The lower the score, the stronger the agreement that active patrol strategies are appropriate and necessary to control crime.

Discussion and Conclusions

It is very clear that there is more variation on attitudes toward police practices among neighborhoods than within neighborhoods. In fact, a surprising degree of consensus was found within neighborhoods. In all the scales, with the exception of the demeanor scale, there is enough variation among neighborhoods to suggest a need for differences in police practices, in at least one of the neighborhoods.

Variation on the responsibility scale indicated that it is believed by residents of the Cuban neighborhoods that crime control is mainly a police matter and that there is very little that citizens can do to help. In contrast, Kendall residents had the strongest disagreement with this notion. Residents of the middle-class Kendall area are heavily involved in Citizen's Crime Watch and similar programs that actively involve citizens in crime control. Obviously, the police need to approach crime control in each of these areas in a different manner. They will receive much more help and support in the Kendall area, but should begin to change the attitudes of the Cuban residents by educating them on how they can help the police control crime more efficiently. The fact that the Cubans had higher levels of disagreement over this idea than any of the other groups leads to the belief that a significant change in attitudes could take place. . . .

[V]ariation of the scores on the ethnic scale indicate a different grouping of neighborhoods than was found on the other scales. The residents of the James Scott Housing project and the 1980 Cubans, to a lesser degree, are the only groups that did not show significant disagreement with the appropriateness of ethnic suspicion. It is ironic that they are not strongly opposed to it, because residents of these two neighborhoods are the most likely to be victims of ethnic suspicion in Miami. Apparently, the majority of the residents in these neighborhoods are law-abiding citizens living in high crime areas. These residents call for more and tougher police protection. It may be that they view, first hand, the extent of the crime and violence in their neighborhoods and believe that there is some justification for ethnic suspicion.

Analysis of the responses to the scale on active patrol strategies indicates that there is more variation on this scale than on any of the others. The 1960 Cuban entrants report consid- erable agreement with active patrol strategies, as do, to a lesser degree, the 1980 Cubans. Middle- class blacks, such as those residing in Rolling Oaks, report the strongest disagreement with active patrol strategies. The active strategies gain more support and cooperation in the 1960 Cuban neighborhood and in the 1980 Cuban neighbor- hood than in the other neighborhoods. These same strategies, however, would cause some concern in the middle-class black neighborhood. The police may be more effective if they find some alternative strategy for this neighborhood.

References

W. Whyte, Street Corner Society, New York: Free Press, 136 (1943).

Name of Student _____
Student ID # _____
Course Section # _____
Date _____

1. Create Likert-type measures that could be used in four factors for each of the following concepts. Use the following scale: 1 signifies "Strong Agreement"; 2 represents "Agreement"; 3 means "Undecided"; 4 signifies "Disagreement"; and 5 represents "Strong Disagreement."

   1.   Good police protection

   2.   Home security

   3.   Neighborhood safety

   4.   Campus safety

For example:

Concept: Delinquent Act

Factor 1: Property Offenses

	Strong Agreement	Agreement	Undecided	Disagreement	Strong Disagreement
I have broken street lights.	1	2	3	4	5
I have broken windows.	1	2	3	4	5
I have painted or drawn on building walls.	1	2	3	4	5
I have overturned garbage cans.	1	2	3	4	5
I have overturned grave tombstones.	1	2	3	4	5

Factor 2: Theft Offenses

	Strong Agreement	Agreement	Undecided	Disagreement	Strong Disagreement
I have taken things worth $2 to $50.	1	2	3	4	5
I have taken things worth less than $2.	1	2	3	4	5
I have taken things from desks at school.	1	2	3	4	5
I have taken a car without permission.	1	2	3	4	5
I have taken things worth more that $50.	1	2	3	4	5

Factor 3: Incorrigibility

	Strong Agreement	Agreement	Undecided	Disagreement	Strong Disagreement
I usually disobey my parents.	1	2	3	4	5
I say mean things to get even with others.	1	2	3	4	5
I usually disobey my teachers.	1	2	3	4	5
I make harassing telephone calls.	1	2	3	4	5
I frequently stay out all night.	1	2	3	4	5

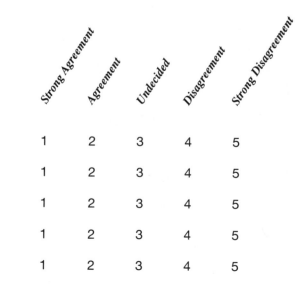

Factor 4: Drug Involvement

	Strong Agreement	Agreement	Undecided	Disagreement	Strong Disagreement
I smoke marijuana.	1	2	3	4	5
I have used cocaine more than twice.	1	2	3	4	5
I drink alcohol when my parents are away.	1	2	3	4	5
I keep alcohol in my school locker.	1	2	3	4	5
I use drugs at least once a week.	1	2	3	4	5
I use drugs more than three times weekly.	1	2	3	4	5

Gender and Adolescent Drinking Problems: The Effects of Occupational Structure

Kevin M. Thompson
Social Problems
Vol. 36, No. 1, pp. 30–47, February 1989

Introduction

Despite evidence that girls' prevalence rates of alcohol use now resemble rates for boys (Johnson et al., 1985; Rachal et al., 1980; Downs, 1985; Figueira-McDonough, 1985), drinking-related problems are still markedly more of a boys' than a girls' province (Radosevich et al., 1980; Wisniewski et al., 1985; Schuckit et al., 1977). In comparison with girls, boys' alcohol use is more likely to result in damage to social relations (Rachal et al., 1975; Wisniewski et al., 1985; Donovan et al., 1983), trouble with the law (Schuckit et al., 1977; Rachal et al., 1975), and accidents (Smart and Liban, 1981; Kane and Patterson, 1972). Boys also appear more likely than girls to continue a pattern of problem drinking over time (Donovan et al., 1983), thereby delaying or hampering the transition to responsible adult status.

Explaining Gender Differences in Problem Drinking

Efforts to explain gender differences in drinking problems among adults and adolescents have often attended to the structural influences of ethnicity and age. For example, the marianismo-machismo dichotomy has often been invoked to account for the marked gender drinking differential among Hispanics (Abad and Suarez, 1975; Johnson and Matre, 1978). Investigators have also coupled age with gender to understand how differential experiences in the life course tend to magnify gender differences in drinking problems over time (Donovan et al., 1983; Wilsnack and

Wilsnack, 1979; Smart and Liban, 1981; Jessor and Jessor, 1977).

What is missing from this literature is an accounting of whether boys' and girls' drinking problems are shaped by social position, and if so, whether the influences that deserve attention are unique to different groups. A few studies have examined whether socioeconomic status (SES) shapes gender differences in adult drinking behavior (Knupfer and Room, 1964; Johnson, 1982; Robins and Smith, 1980). These studies show that the consumption patterns of the sexes diverge as we descend the SES scale. Regrettably, these studies stop short of addressing why gender rates are more pronounced at the bottom of the SES scale or why SES suppresses gender differences as we ascend the socioeconomic scale. Even so, gradational measures of status do not foster theoretically meaningful accounts of deviant behavior (Colvin and Pauly, 1983).

An approach with more potential is to conceive of the relationship between gender and drinking as shaped by occupational structure. Occupational measures of class provide an indicator of how much control individuals have in the workplace (Marx, 1967). Structural arrangements in the workplace are also a source of values transmitted in the home (e.g., degree of supervision, alienation; Kohn and Schooler, 1969, 1973). In neo-Marxist schemes occupational structure is typically operationalized by attending to whether persons own, manage, sell, or fail to sell labor (Hagan et al., 1985; Singer and Levine, 1988). Occupational indicators of class are attractive for several reasons. First, they allow us to introduce and test for intervening variables that receive a theoretical grounding in the social position literature as well as research on gender differences in drinking practices. Second, they facilitate tests of Bonger's (1916) prediction regarding the role of social position in shaping the gender distribution of problem behavior.

Problem Drinking and Unemployment: A Neo-Marxist View

Based on the writings of Marx (1967), Suttles (1968), and Rubin (1976), I argue that the relationship between gender and drinking problems will be strongest among the segment of the population in which occupational control is the weakest, that is, households that are beset by periods of unemployment.

Methods

Survey Design

The data for this investigation comes from a 1974 national survey on adolescent drinking conducted by the Research Triangle Institute (RTI) for the National Institute on Alcohol Abuse and Alcoholism; a detailed description is given in Rachal et al. (1975). A two-stage stratified cluster sample included approximately 15,000 students in grades 7 to 12 from the contiguous 48 states. Selection of 50 primary sample units was stratified by census region, community size, and ethnic characteristics. Careful attention to economically disadvantaged communities facilitated adequate representation from the lowest stratum, allowing us to avoid the top-heavy class models that have plagued studies of deviance (Hirschi, 1969; Kornhauser, 1978).

Each student was asked to complete an anonymous self-administered questionnaire, which included items on drinking behavior, contexts and consequences of drinking, deviant behavior, and selected demographic, attitudinal, and personality characteristics. The overall response rate was 72.2 percent.

Measures

Drinking Problems Drinking problems among adolescents are much more difficult to operationalize than determining whether adolescents are drinkers or categorizing drinkers by consumption level (Schuckit et al., 1977). In the generic sense, drinking problems refer to all drinking that either is used as a way of escaping personal-internal discomfort or results in some kind of trouble for the individual (Zucker and Devoe, 1975). Others have conceptualized drinking problems in terms of symptoms indicative of alcoholism (Wilsnack and Wilsnack, 1979; Smart and Liban, 1981). This implies that drinking problems are really a multidimensional phenomena, requiring factor analytic techniques to examine the varying content of drinking problems in adolescence.

Occupational Structure Occupational categories were constructed on the basis of whether the respondent's father or mother owned, managed, sold, or did not sell their labor. In two separate questions, respondents were asked to specify their father's and mother's occupation. If respondents were living with both parents, father's occupation was used. If respondent was living apart from the father, mother's occupation was used.

Intervening Variables I have drawn four factors described in previous research that may mediate the larger predicted gender differential among the unemployed. Degree of parental controls was represented by items related to how often respondent's (1) lied to their parents, (2) stayed out all night without parents' permission, and (3) damaged something belonging to parents after having an argument with them. Rejection of educational institutions was represented by four items measuring how strongly respondents would like to (1) get at least a B average, (2) be considered a bright student by teachers, (3) come out near the top of the class on exams, and (4) go to college. Three items appear to be related to rejection of religious organizations. In a series of questions respondents were asked how important it was for them to (1) attend religious services, (2) join and participate in religious youth programs, and (3) be able to rely on religious counsel or teaching when they have a problem. The data set contained several items that seemed to reflect Bakan's (1966) concept of communion. These include how much respondents would like to be (1) a loving, affectionate person, (2) a sympathetic person, (3) a generous person, and (4) a reasonable, rational person.

Control Variables

Four variables are controlled in the regression analysis on the possibility that they could confound the relationship between gender and drinking problems. Race was dummy variable coded with whites (77.8 % of the sample), functioning as the reference category for Hispanics (12.9 %) and blacks (7.9 %). Community size was dichotomized with SMSAs (45.7 % of the sample) coded 0 and non-SMSAs coded 1 (54.3 %). The mean grade level of respondents in the study was just a little over ninth grade (Mean = 9.3, sd = 3.9). To eliminate the possibility that drinking problems are simply a function of respondents' purchasing power, I controlled for reported weekly spending money. In 1974 dollars this scale ranged from none (1) to more than $10 (6) (Mean = 4.1, sd = 1.2).

Results

The data . . . show that the gender ratio of adolescent drinking problems is largest among the unemployed, supporting our hypothesis and corroborating patterns that have surfaced in studies of adults. These patterns are clearly a function of larger variation in boys' drinking since the means for girls are roughly similar in each case. Gender differences are consistently smallest among children of owners. In fact, daughters of owners are as likely as sons of owners to use alcohol to cope with psychological discomfort. The gender convergence in the owner stratum appear to be attributed to boys' low scores on the index rather than elevated scores among girls. This suggests that sons of owners may adopt alternative ways to cope with distress than sons of managers, workers, or persons out of work.

Comparisons of full frequency distributions may mask differences in the persistence of drinking problems between boys and girls. . . . [G]ender ratios are more pronounced within the unemployed population. Among the unemployed boys, odds of encountering frequent drinking

problems are 1.6 to 4.4 times higher than they are for girls. Comparing gender ratios between the unemployed population and all other categories, we find that these ratios average 1.42, 1.63, and 1.59 for the symptoms, consequences, and distress scales, respectively. These odds ratios are an indicator of how much more boys can expect to encounter frequent drinking problems over and above that of girls when their father or mother is unemployed. It should be noted that gender ratios are quite similar for sons and daughters of owners. While the odds of encountering repeated negative consequences of drinking are 1.77 times higher for boys than girls among owners, this ratio is two-and-a-half times smaller than gender ratio registered among the unemployed. Hence, it is safe to suggest that occupational structure not only influences gender differences over the entire range of these scales, but that occupation also shapes boys' and girls' odds of drinking in ways that are likely to come to the attention of authorities.

Discussion

Despite the fact that class and gender have been united to account for a variety of problem behaviors, we know little about the distribution of boys' and girls' drinking problems as shaped by occupational structure. We know less yet about how occupation might shape gender differences in drinking problems. Consequently, efforts by the National Institute on Alcohol Abuse and Alcoholism to target services for special population groups may be imprecise if our matrix includes children from various occupational groups and gender (see U.S. Department of Health and Human Services, 1981).

This investigation assembles evidence that shows that gender ratios of adolescent drinking problems are shaped by occupational structure. The findings show that the gender gap in drinking problems is most pronounced among youths who reside in homes where parents are chronically or episodically unable to sell their labor. Among children of the unemployed, the gender differential in symptoms of alcohol dependence is partially accounted for by boys' rejection of communal values and weak parental controls. The gender coefficient for the negative consequences scale is entirely due to boys being more weakly supervised than girls. Since parental controls do not mitigate the gender differential among children of workers, managers, or owners, we might cautiously conclude that parental monitoring practices may be unique in explaining gender differences in certain forms of drinking in the unemployed population.

References

Abad, Vincente and J. Suarez
  1975   "Cross-cultural aspects of alcoholism among Puerto Ricans." Proceedings of the 4th Annual Alcoholism Conference of the National Institute on Alcohol Abuse and Alcoholism. Washington, DC: Department of Health, Education, and Welfare.

Bakan, David
  1966   The Duality of Human Existence. Chicago: Rand McNally.

Bonger, William
  1916   Crime and Economic Conditions, Book 2. Boston, MA: Little, Brown.

Colvin, Mark and John Pauly
  1983   "A critique of criminology: toward an integrated structural-Marxist theory of delinquency production." American Journal of Sociology 89:513–51.

Donovan, John E., Richard Jessor, and Lee Jessor
  1983   "Problem drinking in adolescence and young adulthood." Journal of Studies on Alcohol, 44:4, 109–37.

Downs, William R.
  1985   "Using panel data to examine sex differences in causal relationships among adolescent alcohol use, norms, and peer alcohol use." Journal of Youth and Adolescence 14:6, 469–86.

Figueira-McDonough, Josefina
  1985   "Are girls different? gender discrepancies between delinquent behavior and control." Child Welfare 64:3, 273–89.

Hagan, John, A.R. Gillis, and John Simpson
  1985   "The class structure of gender and delinquency: toward a power-control theory of common delinquent behavior." American Journal of Sociology 90:6, 1151–78.

Hirschi, Travis
  1969   Causes of Delinquency. Berkeley, CA: University of California Press.

Jessor, Richard and Shirley L. Jessor
  1977   Problem Behavior and Psychosocial Development: A Longitudinal Study of Youth. New York: Academic Press.

Johnson, Paula B.
  1982   "Sex differences, women's roles and alcohol use: preliminary national data." Journal of Social Issues 38:2, 93–116.

Johnson, L. V. and Marc Matre
  1978   "Anomie and alcohol use: drinking patterns in Mexican-American and Anglo neighborhoods." Journal of Studies on Alcohol 39:5, 894–902.

Johnston, Lloyd D., Jerald G. Bachman, and Patrick M. O'Malley
  1985   Drugs and American High School Students: 1975–1984. U.S. Department of Health and Human Services Publication. Washington, DC: U.S. Government Printing Office.

Kane, Robert L. and Elizabeth Patterson
  1972   "Drinking attitudes and behavior of high school students in Kentucky." Quarterly Journal of Studies on Alcohol 33:635–46.

Knupfer, Genevieve and Robin Room
  1964   "Age, sex, and social class as factors in amount of drinking in a metropolitan community." Social Problems 12:224–40.

Kohn, Melvin L. and Carmi Schooler
  1969   "Class, occupation, and orientation." American Sociological Review 34:659–78.
  1973   "Occupational experience and psychological functioning: an assessment of reciprocal effects." American Sociological Review 38:97–118.

Kornhauser, Ruth R.
  1978   Social Sources of Delinquency: An Appraisal of Analytic Models. Chicago: University of Chicago Press.

Marx, Karl
  1967   Capital, Vol. I. New York: International Publishers.

Rachal, J. Valley, L. Lynn Guess, Robert L. Hubbard, Stephen A. Maisto, Elizabeth R. Cavanaugh, Richard Waddell, and Charles H. Benrud
  1980   The Extent and Nature of Adolescent Alcohol and Drug Use: The 1974 and 1978 National Sample Studies. Report prepared for the National Institute on Alcohol Abuse and Alcoholism. Research Triangle Park, NC: Research Triangle Institute.

Rachal, J. Valley, Jay R. Williams, Mary L. Brehm, Betty Cavanaugh, R. Paul Moore, and William C. Eckerman
  1975   A National Study of Adolescent Drinking Behavior, Attitudes, and Correlates. Final report, Contract No. HSM-42-73-80, to the

National Institute on Alcohol Abuse and Alcoholism. Research Triangle Park, NC: Research Triangle Institute.

Radosevich, Marcia, Lonn Lanza-Kaduce, Ronald L. Akers, and Marvin D. Krohn
1980   "The sociology of adolescent drug and drinking behavior: a review of the state of the field: part II." Deviant Behavior 1:145–69.

Robins, Lee N. and Elizabeth M. Smith
1980   "Longitudinal studies of alcohol and drug problems: sex differences." Pp 203–32 in Oriana J. Kalant (ed.), Alcohol and Drug Problems in Women, Vol. 5 in Research Advances in Alcohol and Drug Problems. New York: Plenum.

Rubin, Lillian B.
1976   Worlds of Pain: Life in the Working Class. New York: Basic Books.

Schuckit, Marc A., Elizabeth R. Morrissey, Nancy J. Lewis, and William T. Buck
1977   "Adolescent problem drinkers." Currents in Alcoholism 2:325–55.

Singer, Simon I. and Murray Levine
1988   "Power-control theory, gender and delinquency: a partial replication with additional evidence on the effects of peers." Criminology 26:627–48.

Smart, Reginald G. and Carolyn B. Liban
1981   "Predictors of problem drinking among elderly, middle-aged and youthful

drinkers." Journal of Psychoactive Drugs 13:2, 153–63.

Suttles, Gerald
1968   The Social Order of the Slum. Chicago: University of Chicago Press.

U.S. Department of Health and Human Services
1981   Alcohol and Health. Fourth Special Report to the U.S. Congress. Washington, DC: U.S. Government Printing Office.

Wilsnack, Sharon C. and Richard W. Wilsnack
1979   "Sex roles and adolescent drinking." Pp. 183–224 in Howard T. Blane and Morris E. Chafetz (eds.), Youth, Alcohol and Social Policy. New York: Plenum.

Wisniewski, Nadine M., David S. Glenwick, and John R. Graham
1985   "McAndrew scale and sociodemographic correlates of adolescent alcohol and drug use." Addictive Behavior 10:55–67.

Zucker, Robert A. and C. I. Devoe
1975   "Life history characteristics associated with problem drinking and antisocial behavior in adolescent girls: a comparison with male findings." Pp. 109–34 in Robert D. Wirt, G. Winokur, and Merrill Roff (eds.), Life History Research in Psychopathology, Vol. 4. Minneapolis, MN: University of Minnesota Press.

Name of Student _____
Student ID # _____
Course Section # _____
Date _____

1. How might differential reporting among boys and girls affect the results in the study?

_____

_____

_____

_____

_____

2. What other factors might serve as mitigating or biasing factors regarding a study of gender differences in drinking problems?

_____

_____

_____

_____

_____

3. What validity checks might have been used to improve this study?

_____

_____

_____

_____

_____

4.   Complete the following index items:

Please indicate your gender: [1] Male   [2] Female

A. Symptoms of Alcohol Dependence

1.   Drunkenness—Number of times drunk in the past year?
[1]   None
[2]   Once during the past year
[3]   Two to four times during the past year
[4]   Five to eight times during the past year
[5]   Once a month during the past year
[6]   Twice a month during the past year
[7]   Three times a month during the past year
[8]   Once a week or more during the past year

2.   Forget—How often do you forget what you did while drinking?
[1]   Never
[2]   Rarely
[3]   Sometimes
[4]   Frequently

3.   Fun—How often do you need a drink to have fun?
[1]   Never
[2]   Rarely
[3]   Sometimes
[4]   Frequently

4.   Drinking and Driving—How often do you drink beer, wine, or liquor while driving around or sitting in a car?
[1]   Never
[2]   Rarely
[3]   Sometimes
[4]   Most of the time

B. Negative Consequences of Drinking

1.   School Authorities—In the past year, how often have you been in trouble with teachers or principals because of your drinking?
[1]   Never
[2]   Once
[3]   Two to four times
[4]   Five to seven times
[5]   Eight or nine times
[6]   Ten or more times

2. Dating Partners—In the past year, how often have you been criticized by someone you were dating because of your drinking?
   [1] Never
   [2] Once
   [3] Two to four times
   [4] Five to seven times
   [5] Eight or nine times
   [6] Ten or more times

3. Police—In the past year, how often have you been in trouble with the police because of your drinking?
   [1] Never
   [2] Once
   [3] Two to four times
   [4] Five to seven times
   [5] Eight or nine times
   [6] Ten or more times

C. Distress Drinking

1. Pressure—Positive functions of drinking: How often do you drink when there are too many pressures on you?
   [1] Never
   [2] Rarely
   [3] Sometimes
   [4] Frequently

2. Block—Positive functions of drinking: How often do you drink because it makes things such as doing well in school seem less important to you?
   [1] Never
   [2] Rarely
   [3] Sometimes
   [4] Frequently

3. Alone—How often do you drink alone?
   [1] Never
   [2] Rarely
   [3] Sometimes
   [4] Frequently

5. Using the responses from your class, calculate the mean and standard deviation.

    Mean   _____   *Show your calculations here*

    Standard Deviation   _____   *Show your calculations here*

6. Next, collect and copy sheets from each student. Separate the answer sheets into two groups, male and female. Calculate a ratio for each item of the three scales to indicate comparisons of male and female responses.

    Ratios for Males

    Scale 1   Scale 2   Scale 3   *Show your calculations here*

    _____   _____   _____

    Ratios for Females

    Scale 1   Scale 2   Scale 3   *Show your calculations here*

    _____   _____   _____

CHAPTER 3

Sampling and Design

One of the goals of any social scientific study is to describe or identify certain characteristics (variables) about some group or population in relation to those of another. When the population being studied is small, such as a group of 12 or 15 patients in an intensive care unit of some hospital, the research easily could be accomplished by interviewing or observing all these patients. However, if the group to be studied is large, such as all U.S. adolescents who use marijuana, it would be both impossible and highly inefficient to attempt interviewing, surveying, or observing *all* these individuals.

Happily, it is not necessary to systematically observe every member of a *working population* (the full group with the characteristics of interest to the researcher). Rather, we need only select a *sample* of this full population. If this sample is to represent the larger population accurately, it must be drawn carefully and according to certain rules of probability.

Typically, representative sampling strategies are used in survey research. However, the same basic strategies can be applied when identifying subjects for experimental studies, documents used in a textual content analysis, or people or places for observation (Berg, 1989).

The main objective of drawing a sample is to make inferences about the larger population from the smaller sample. Regardless of how carefully the sample is drawn, it is unlikely that it will be identical to the larger population from which it came. We can, however, reasonably expect that the sample will closely resemble the larger group. Since use of the smaller group allows the research to proceed, we must accept the possibility of slight discrepancies.

PROBABILITY SAMPLING

In a probability sampling strategy, the researcher specifies each segment of the population that will be represented in the sample. Basically, the sample is created by selecting units from the larger population. In a probability sample, the manner in which the sample units are selected is very important. The process usually entails drawing subjects from an identified population such that every unit in the larger population has precisely the same chance or probability of being selected as every other unit in that population. This process is known as *randomization*. In it, the researcher assumes that, since every unit in the larger population has precisely the same chance of being selected for the sample, characteristics possessed by the sample members resemble characteristics possessed by members of the larger population.

In order to accomplish this randomization, or *random sample,* the researcher can use several different strategies. Among the most commonly used procedures is the random numbers table. Usually, the researcher arbitrarily selects a number with which to begin and then moves up, down, forward, backward, or across the table to continue selecting numbers. By identifying two points—a number for the vertical column and another for the horizontal row—we can locate a starting point for selecting a sample from a population listing. Ten blocks of random numbers are arranged horizontally, and ten are arranged vertically. Random numbers tables are usually found as appendixes of most statistics textbooks (see, for example, Appendix B).

To illustrate use of a random numbers table, take a dollar bill from your pocket. Look at the first and last numbers of the serial number on the bill. These can be used as the vertical and horizontal guide numbers to enter a random numbers table. Let's say your numbers were 8 and 6. Go to the table and move to the eighth column of blocked numbers and the sixth row of blocked numbers. Now select any number between 1 and 5. Assume you select 3. Now move across the row three numerals and down three numerals. This identifies your random number; let's say number 3.

At this point, some researchers would go through their list of people in the full population and identify every third name as part of the sample until the sample was filled. Other researchers would repeat this random number selection and go through the list selecting the individual who corresponds to the randomly identified number from the table. This might mean selecting for a sample the third, eighth, twelfth, fifteenth, and so on. In the first case, the researcher would be conducting a *systematic sampling* strategy. You should be aware that systematic samples may be classified as probability or nonprobability samples, depending on how the starting point is selected and whether every possible element has an equal chance for inclusion. In the second case, the research would be using a *simple random sampling* protocol.

Other strategies for identifying a random sample may include placing all the names of potential subjects in a hat, shaking them up, and simply drawing out names for the sample. Some researchers prefer to computerize their population list and have the computer randomly select some proportion of the full population. In general, there is no absolutely right or wrong way to identify a sample. The single principle that must be maintained is that every unit of the full population must have an *equal chance* of being drawn into the sample.

Stratified Cluster Sampling (Multistage Sampling)

In *random* or *systematic probability* sampling, we sample the actual individuals or elements intended for inclusion in the study. In *stratified cluster* sampling, we begin by grouping elements that share certain characteristics. These groupings

or strata are then used as categories to divide the working population. Our sample involves elements from every stratum. Cluster sampling, then, involves dividing the population into several large groups, or clusters. The sampling actually occurs as we draw elements from each of these larger clusters.

In other words, stratified cluster sampling involves several stages. The first stage is to divide the working population into various strata, and the second stage is to draw the sample from these strata. This process can be repeated as many times as necessary to cluster the elements of the population into appropriate categories.

For example, we might use students attending U.S. colleges and universities as the working population to study collegiate drinking patterns. One method of sample selection could be to use stratified cluster sampling. The first step would be to create a list containing the names of all colleges and universities awarding four-year baccalaureate degrees. The second step would be to categorize these institutions according to some criteria; for instance, four regional categories could be used: "North," "South," "East," and "West." Now, we could sample equally from each category using a simple random selection process.

Alternately, we could determine the proportion of colleges and universities in each category and randomly draw a sample based on those proportions. For instance, suppose that the "North" category contained 650 colleges and universities, the "East" 250, the "South" 150, and the "West" 300. Calculating the proportion for each category and rounding appropriately, the four categories would represent the following proportions, respectively:

CATEGORY	NUMBER	PROPORTION
North	650	48.2%
East	250	18.5%
South	150	11.1%
West	300	22.2%
	1350	100.0%

Now assume that time and budget only allow us to have a sample of 100 schools. Using appropriate rounding techniques, we would produce a sample of 100 schools as follows:

CATEGORY	NUMBER
North	48 schools
East	19 schools
South	11 schools
West	22 schools
	100 schools in sample

Sampling Error

Whenever we use probability samples, it is possible that the elements we include in a particular sample may produce findings identical to those of another sample drawn from the same population. This phenomena, referred to as *sampling error,* arises because samples often vary slightly, even when two samples from the same population are drawn at the same time, under the same conditions.

For example, suppose we have a population of college students from which to select a random sample for a questionnaire about grades and majors. It is possible that the mean grade score for the working population may be 3.5 on a 4.0 scale. Yet even with repeated selection of different random samples, the mean of the sample may never equal exactly 3.5. The sample mean may be higher or lower than the population mean. However, if we select a number of different samples from the population and average the means of the samples, then the average mean should begin to approximate more closely the population's mean grade point average of 3.5.

It is also important to note that larger samples are more likely to offer mean scores that closely approximate the population means, since larger samples more closely represent the population.

Sample Size

Some researchers go by the general rule "More is better." Thus, the larger the sample, the better the results. However, in deciding how large a sample is sufficient, we cannot just say "The larger, the better." To do so would be similar to answering the question "What time is it?" by saying "Late."

Determining sample size depends on a number of different factors. First, size can be determined on the basis of how closely the sample approximates the population from which it is drawn. If the population is fairly homogeneous (e.g., all Cub Scouts in a given region), the sample can be smaller than if the population is heterogeneous (e.g., all children in social clubs in a given region). Considering this factor will ensure that the various characteristics in the heterogeneous population are represented in the sample.

A second useful guideline suggests that when statistics will be used, the sample should contain a minimum of 150 subjects. For greater statistical reliability, 250, 500, 1,000, or even 1,500 subjects should be used. As we increase the number of subjects, we also increase the degree to which the sample approximates the population and the accuracy of statistical procedures used in the analysis. Beyond 1,500 subjects, the amount of improved statistical accuracy is rather small.

The number of subjects actually included in a sample is often determined by factors of cost and time. The more subjects included, the greater the cost and the time required both to collect and analyze data. When time and money are not at issue, most researchers seek as large a sample as possible, frequently exceeding 1,500 subjects.

NONPROBABILITY SAMPLING

Nonprobability samples usually find their way into studies where probability samples would be extremely expensive or when precise representativeness of the sample is not crucial. There also are many occasions when a full population cannot be completely defined. For example, Glassner and Berg (1980) sought to examine drinking patterns among American Jews. Since no complete list of all Jews existed from which to draw a random sample, Glassner and Berg created a "master list" of Jews residing in one northeastern community. This list was quite comprehensive and was composed of a number of smaller lists obtained from various Jewish organizations and synagogues in the area. When complete, this list contained the names of over 3,500 Jewish families. Although Glassner and Berg used rigorous systematic sampling strategies, including use of a random numbers table to locate the *n*th name for each selection on this list, their overall sampling strategy was nonetheless a nonprobability strategy.

Nonprobability sampling strategies include a number of different protocols, including convenience or accidental samples, purpose samples, snowballing techniques, and quota sampling.

Convenience Samples

Convenience, or *accidental, samples* are typically comprised of subjects who are close at hand or easily accessible. For instance, it is fairly common for college and university professors to use students in their classes as subjects in survey research. This type of sample is attractive to some researchers because it tends to be inexpensive and easy to obtain. Hence, the researcher trades some degree of accuracy for increased efficiency.

Under certain circumstances, this strategy is an excellent means of obtaining preliminary information about some research question quickly and inexpensively. For example, if a researcher wanted to know about college drinking patterns, he or she could justify using a convenience sample of college students. If, however, the researcher was interested in knowing about drinking patterns among Iroquois Indians, he or she could not use the college student sample and ask them to pretend that they are Iroquois when answering the questions. In other words, convenience samples must still be evaluated for appropriateness of fit for a study.

Another variation of the convenience sample is the *haphazard sample,* in which inhabitants of an area of investigation are surveyed or interviewed by virtue of their presence. This type of sample is common in some field research studies.

Purpose Samples

Sometimes when a researcher identifies a sample, his or her intention is to assure that certain characteristics are represented. This is usually accomplished on the basis of a judgment or certain available information that the researcher possesses about some population or group. In some instances, *purpose samples* are selected after field investigation has ensured the location of people displaying attributes desirable for the study.

For example, if we were interested in studying car theft by adolescents involved in drug and alcohol use, it would be nearly impossible to select a random sample. After conducting a field study, however, we might be able to identify a cluster of youths who are involved in drugs and alcohol and who also steal or have stolen cars. Again, what the researcher may lose in generalizability, he or she will gain in accuracy of information by assuring that the appropriate subjects have been obtained for the study.

Snowballing Techniques

In some situations, the use of *snowballing* techniques may be the best way to locate subjects with certain attributes or characteristics necessary in a study. The basic strategy involves first identifying several persons with relevant characteristics and interviewing or administering the survey to them; these subjects are then asked for the names of other persons who possess the same attributes they do.

For example, suppose we are interested in examining drug use or theft by nurses. By using a probability sampling strategy, we might identify few or no subjects (i.e., nurses who use or steal drugs). But through the use of informants, field investigations, or other strategies, we might identify a small number of nurses with these characteristics. By asking these subjects for referrals of additional nurses, the sample eventually "snowballs" from few subjects to many subjects.

Quota Samples

A *quota sampling* strategy is similar, in some ways, to a *stratified random sample.* Stratified random samples rely on various strategies of chance to fill variable cells, or *stratum.* The quota sample uses a nonprobability method for filling stratum in a sample in approximately the same proportions as in the full population.

For instance, we might be interested in studying fear of crime among people in the United States, with a special interest in fear among people who are aged. Since census data would give us reasonable estimates of the aged, young adult, and child populations in the United States, we could determine the proportions of people in these age groups. Next, we could select a region of the country and sample people in these three categories, or *age cohorts,* in the same proportions as represented in the census data. Quota samples work best with highly objective variables, such as age or socioeconomic status, rather than subjective variables, such as viewpoints or perceptions.

TYPES OF RESEARCH DESIGNS

One of the major designs used both in the natural and social sciences is experimentation. The *experimental method* allows the researcher to assess the possibility of *cause and effect.* This means that, based upon the experiment, the researcher is able to determine whether variable A caused variable B to occur. Other methods tell about variables A and B, or whatever other variables are of interest to the researcher. However, only through the experimental method can the researcher determine whether the relationship between given variables is causal.

Experimental Design

There are actually several variations on the design of the traditional, or true, experiment used in the social sciences. We can identify these variants as three general categories of design: *pre-experimental*, *quasi-experimental,* and *classical.*

One of the main ways in which each of these variants is different is in the degree of control imposed on the variables under study. On an imaginary continuum, the pre-experimental design has the least control; the quasi-experiment, more control; and the classical experiment, the most control. The more control a researcher has over the variables in a study, the greater his or her ability to attribute cause.

In part, when we speak about the ability of the researcher to control variables, we also imply that the researcher has the ability to control the experimental environment. This implication addresses the degree of randomness by which each design type operates. Previously, we mentioned the con-

cept of *randomization* in reference to sampling; in that context, we referred to the equal opportunity by chance of every unit in a full population to be selected into the sample. Similarly, we can apply randomization to experimental design.

First, as in the general discussion on sampling, randomness applies to the selection of subjects to be used in the experiment. Second, in experimental design, subjects will be *randomly* assigned to different groups. In this case, the task is to make sure all the subjects in the sample have an equal chance of being placed into one group or another. Finally, once subjects have been assigned to their groups, the researcher assumes that each group is approximately equivalent and randomly selects which groups are to receive what experimental treatments.

Pre-Experimental Design

A pre-experimental design does not use random selection in identifying subjects from a working or full population, nor does this type of design employ any control groups or, for that matter, control over any possible intervening variables. For example, we might observe that whenever a friend has the hiccups, she hops on one foot and sings "The Star-Spangled Banner." We might also observe that each time she does this, she cures her hiccups.

Left alone, the hiccups would likely have stopped by themselves. Yet we might still reach the conclusion (weak as it is) that hopping on one foot and singing "The Star-Spangled Banner" will cure the hiccups. Unfortunately, there is little legitimate generalizability of this conclusion from this experiment. It is not clear what, if any, group our friend represents and no controlled comparison to show that the hopping and singing work better than other remedies or doing nothing at all.

Research textbooks sometimes refer to this type of study as a "one-shot study design." It follows the logical sequence of having a single group (haphazardly identified) being administered a treatment (in this case, the hopping and singing) and then making a post-test observation (in this case, the observation that the hiccups had stopped).

A problem with this type of experimentation is aptly demonstrated by an old joke. A young boy is standing in front of a barricade blocking a small side street in a Wisconsin suburb. The boy is holding a large menacing-looking rifle and has a pistol on each hip. A car pulls up, and the driver asks the boy what he is doing. The boy replies, "I'm guarding against stampeding elephants!" The driver of the car responds in shocked tones, "But son, there isn't a stampeding elephant within 30,000 miles of here." The boy smiles and answers, "See what a good job I'm doing."

There are several serious problems with the pre-experimental design type, the most obvious of which is its inability to accurately assess cause and effect. A pre-experimental design is useful, however, when the researcher is speculating about possible relationships between variables that occurred at one time and what potential effects they may have on later behavior.

Quasi-Experimental Design

As suggested above, it is highly desirable in experimental design to establish random protocols for selecting and assigning subjects. In some situations, the random selection of subjects may simply be impossible or impractical. For example, it would be difficult to randomly select as subjects a group of blind persons who use seeing-eye lead dogs. It would be similarly difficult to identify a random sample of Ph.D.'s in humanities with specialty interests in criminal justice.

While procedures can be established to identify appropriate samples or meet these characteristics, the design would not be strictly random. This sort of study design, then, represents a quasi-experiment. In other words, the design lacks full control over the randomness of the original sample selection, even though, once identified, the subjects may be randomly assigned to groups and the groups randomly identified for treatment.

The logical sequence in this type of design is as follows:

1. A sample of subjects is somehow identified.
2. Each subject is assigned to one group or another. (The groups are assumed to be roughly equivalent in their ability to represent the larger population from which they have been drawn.)
3. Each group is randomly assigned either to receive or not receive some experimental treatment.

4. The results are observed after the treatment has been administered to see whether there is any difference between the group receiving the treatment (the *experimental group*) and the group receiving no treatment (the *control group*).

In a quasi-experiment, the researcher has considerable control over the research environment and limited control over the degree of randomness used in the design. Although they are not perfect, conclusions from quasi-experiments are usually regarded as more or less accurate predictors of cause-and-effect relationships between variables.

Classical Design

The classical experimental design is the most rigorous of experimental types. It imposes all the random selection steps previously discussed and uses at least one control group for post-treatment comparisons. The basic underlying assumption in the classical experiment is that randomly selecting a sample and randomly assigning these subjects to groups produces equivalent groups for comparison. After a treatment has been applied to one group, it can safely be assumed that any change in the group, when compared with the post-test control group, can be attributed to the treatment.

Descriptive Studies

Traditionally, when a researcher undertakes a descriptive study design, he or she is not interested in drawing inferences or making generalizations about a population. Instead, the researcher is interested in describing what he or she can uncover about the group or population. Some textbooks talk about descriptive studies as attempts to "delineate the way things are" (Guy et al., 1987, p. 102). Others describe descriptive studies as obtaining "observations with insight" (Leedy, 1989, p. 140). Regardless of how descriptive studies are defined, it is agreed that a primary goal of this type of design is to accurately portray how things relate to some phenomenon, event, or characteristic.

Perhaps the most widely used example of a descriptive study is the U.S. Census, which is undertaken every 10 years to update information describing people residing in the United States. Data from the census indicate the numbers of males and females; how many are married, single, and divorced; what average level of education they have; what their average household income is; how many children most families have; and what racial and religious groups they belong to.

Descriptive studies are highly concerned with precision and completeness, rather than representativeness and randomization. They are often very useful endeavors that precede more exacting random or systematic studies.

Exploratory Design

Frequently, the terms *exploratory* and *descriptive* research are used interchangeably. In some instances, they are used simultaneously— *exploratory descriptive research.* In many ways, these uses illustrate accurate ways of thinking about exploratory and descriptive studies; they are, in fact, quite similar. They are not, however, entirely the same. Usually, when a researcher conducts exploratory research, he or she is entering the fabled "black box" of research. In other words, the researcher is working in an uncharted and underresearched (if not unresearched) area. The purpose of the exploration is to better understand some group, event, or phenomenon about which little or no previous research has been done.

Exploratory designs also may be used in areas in which data have been previously obtained but may reflect changing attitudes. For example, we might be interested in how resident advisors (RAs) in college dormitories see their role in enforcing university drinking regulations. By surveying or interviewing a number of RAs, we could learn what those regulations are and what RAs see as their responsibilities in enforcing them. While this survey may not produce an objectively accurate picture of how drinking rules are or ought to be enforced, it will produce an interesting picture of how RAs see themselves as rule enforcers.

The chief shortcoming of exploratory research is that it seldom produces highly generalizable answers to research questions. Nonetheless, this strategy can offer highly important insights into how things are or how people understand phenomena or events. Once again, the main reason that most exploratory studies offer definitive results is that they usually do not use representative samples.

CAUSALITY

In quantitative research, one of the ultimate goals is the identification of *cause.* In the so-called hard sciences, it is possible to control all the variables of an experiment and thus to prove causality with reasonable certainty. But in the social sciences, in the strictest sense, it is not possible to prove causality with certainty, given the complexities of social life and social reality. The social sciences typically use humans as subjects of study. Because human behavior is not absolutely predictable, it becomes impossible to predict accurately how, why, or when humans may act in certain ways. Also, because of ethical considerations, it is not appropriate to control or deceive subjects, to endanger or harm them, or to expose them to risks.

From a less strict perspective, causality cannot be established with certainty mathematically. For example, even though we may have thrown an apple into the air and watched it fall to the ground 99 times, we cannot be certain that the next time we toss the apple, it will fall to the ground. Perhaps a large bird might be lurking in the tree, watching hungrily as the apple goes up and down. The bird might swoop down and intercept the apple on the 100th toss. Or maybe the apple will be caught by an updraft, blown into the tree, and caught among the limbs, such that it will be unable to fall to the ground. Regardless of why the apple might not return to the ground, we cannot say for certain that it will.

Consider several more examples. If we flip a coin 99 times and get heads each time, there is no guarantee that the next time we flip the coin, it will come up heads. In fact, the laws of probability would suggest that it is more likely that the next toss will come up tails. Probability provides a predetermined degree of likelihood that something will happen; it does not provide certainty. At the racetrack, even if a horse has come in first during its last 15 races, we cannot be sure that in race number 16, the horse will win. On the other hand, if we know that a horse has won its last 15 races, we will be more likely to bet on that horse than on a horse who has lost its last 15 races.

So it is with causality and probability. If we observe that the occurrence of a particular variable, X, is regularly followed by the occurrence of another variable, Y, it may be reasonable to assume that X causes Y. However, three conditions must be met in order to accept a causal statement:

1. *Temporal requirement*—Variable X must precede variable Y in time.
2. *Covariance requirement*—For every change that occurs in variable X, a subsequent change must occur in variable Y. In other words, if variable X increases, then variable Y must either increase or decrease. Thus, Y is dependent upon X.
3. *Elimination of alternative explanation requirement (spuriousness)*—The possibility must be eliminated that other factors actually cause variable Y. (In the social sciences, this is probably the most difficult requirement to meet.)

When these three conditions have been met, we generally accept that a cause-and-effect relationship exists between the two variables. In such a relationship, the X variable is identified as the *independent* variable and the Y variable as the *dependent* variable.

In the social sciences, not all relationships can be positively identified as causal. Certain variables that seem to occur at approximately the same time are said to be *concomitant*. Concomitance provides for plural explanations because it suggests that variables occur at approximately the same time as opposed to one variable causing the other. For example, many people eat lunch at approximately noon. We can ask, however, whether hunger occurs at noon or whether lunchtime has become ritualized at that hour. If lunchtime has become ritualized, then does the upcoming noon hour possibly trigger pangs of hunger?

Therefore, in the social sciences, we traditionally talk about relationships and their strengths. In a causal relationship, we can statistically measure the strength of the relationship and the probability that it is significant.

VALIDITY AND RELIABILITY

Validity and *reliability* are two important considerations in research. Generally, it is believed that considerations of validity should precede considerations of reliability because validity examines the instrument of measurement while reliability addresses the consistency of responses. Validity asks the question: Does the measurement instrument accurately measure the concept it is intended to measure? Reliability, on the other hand, considers the regularity of particular responses given by subjects. Consequently, if an instrument is reliable, it will provide fairly uniform and stable measures of responses, even when the same questions are asked in repeated studies. (This assumes that the questions have already been assessed as being valid.)

Types of Validity

Researchers can assess a wide variety of types of validity. In this section, we will highlight a few of the most common types, including *face, content, construct,* and *predictive and practical* validity.

Face
Face validity addresses whether a specific question appears, on the surface (i.e., "on the face of it"), to measure what the researcher intended. For example, suppose an exam is given to students in an introductory anthropology class. For previous exams in this class, the result has been a normal distribution of grades over a standard scale. In other words, the majority of the students passed the exam with various levels of success. This time, however, a majority of the students fail the exam. As students discuss the exam with the instructor in class, they discover a heading on the test that indicates it was really intended for an upper-level anthropology class. Somehow, the exams were switched. Therefore, this exam lacked face validity for the introductory class because it was not designed for them.

Content
Content validity assesses whether each item of the measurement instrument accurately measures the

concept is was intended to measure. On a history test, for instance, suppose that a student answered questions 9 and 12 incorrectly and questions 14 and 17 correctly. When the exam is gone over in class, he discovers that everyone else in the class got the same two questions wrong and the same two questions right. He also notices that all four questions relate to a topic that the instructor did not discuss in class and that was not covered in the assigned reading material. Naturally, none of the students has any concern about questions 14 and 17, since everyone got them right. But the students are concerned about the two questions they got wrong, numbers 9 and 12. The class points out to the instructor that these questions are not appropriate since they measure content not covered by lecture or reading material. In fact, the two questions that everyone answered *correctly* also lack content validity because they relate to the same subject material.

Construct

Construct validity is one of the most difficult types of validity to assess because it is basically theoretical in nature. Construct validity is concerned with whether individual questions actually measure the specific concept under study. It is also concerned with whether a set of questions used to create a scale assesses the full range of behaviors or responses that are intended to be assessed.

For example, suppose we are interested in assessing degree of liberalism. In compiling a set of questions designed for this purpose, we would need to include questions pertaining to all degrees or levels of the characteristic. For instance, if we wanted to assess how the subject feels about minority groups, we could design a set of questions about how geographically close he or she would want minorities to reside. The first question could ask: "Would it be acceptable to have minorities live in the same country with you?" The second question could ask about having minorities live in the same state, the same city, and so on until the final question asks about having minorities live next door. To be sure of the construct validity of this set of questions, we could submit the set to a panel of experts to review inclusiveness and determine whether geographic proximity of minorities is a reasonable measure of liberalism.

Predictive and Practical

Predictive validity addresses the accuracy of an instrument of measurement using checks outside the instrument itself. For example, most graduate schools rely on Graduate Record Examination (GRE) scores for admission and financial aid distribution decisions, expecting that candidates with high GRE scores will be successful, as measured by completing the graduate program. Thus, someone with a score of 1,400 out of 1,600 on the GRE is presumed to have a greater likelihood of completion than someone with a 1,000 score. Yet GRE scores lack predictive validity to the extent that many students with scores in the 1,000 range complete their graduate studies while not all those in the 1,400 range do. Therefore, records of successful completion rates constitute the test of the predictive ability of the GRE.

Practical validity similarly checks validity outside the instrument. In this case, the researcher examines real-world situations being measured by the instrument and considers how well the results fit reality. For example, a research instrument may suggest that murderers tend to have red hair and wear size 14 shoes. If we were to examine the hair color and shoe size of a population of murderers, perhaps located in several different prisons, we could determine how much practical validity this suggestion has. If the population of murderers indeed has red hair and wears size 14 shoes, then the instrument has a high degree of practical validity. Conversely, if the population of murderers is generally blond and wears size 8 shoes, then the instrument has very low practical validity.

REFERENCES

Berg, B. (1989). *Qualitative research methods for the social sciences.* Boston: Allyn and Bacon.

Glassner, B., & Berg, B. (1980). How Jews avoid alcohol problems. *The American Sociological Review, 45(1),* 647–664.

Guy, R., Edgley, C., Arafat, I., and Allen, D. (1987). *Social research methods.* Boston: Allyn and Bacon.

Leedy, P. (1989). *Practical research.* New York: Macmillan.

Delinquency and Drug Use: Temporal and Developmental Patterns

David H. Huizinga, Scott Menard, and Delbert S. Elliott
Justice Quarterly
Vol. 6, No. 3, pp. 419–455, September 1989

Introduction

There is general consensus that drug use and delinquent behavior are related. This relationship has been demonstrated in a number of cross-sectional studies which indicate that levels of drug use vary with levels of general delinquent behavior. Although there is some disagreement about this relationship for alcohol use (see Blane and Hewitt 1977) and at least one dissenting study for amphetamine use (see Scott and Wilcox 1965), this cross-sectional relationship between drug use and delinquency is consistent across studies of detected drug users, studies of adjudicated delinquents, and studies employing samples of the general youth population.

In light of this general finding from cross-sectional studies, three postulated causal relationships are often suggested: (1) drug use leads to crime; (2) crime leads to drug use; and (3) both drug use and crime are manifestations of a general orientation towards deviance and delinquency (i.e., they are not causally related but are the result of other underlying variables or subcultural orientations). Empirical studies show considerable consensus about certain aspects of the three basic drug/crime hypotheses as applied to youth. Almost all studies report that involvement in both minor and serious delinquent behavior precedes use of illicit drugs (except for alcohol). Although the strongest evidence for this finding comes from longitudinal studies of general youth populations employing self-report measures of delinquency and drug use, studies employing arrest data and studies employing known drug-using groups commonly reach a similar conclusion. This evidence is inconsistent with the notion that in general, drug use results in or leads to the initiation or onset of delinquent behavior.

Although it is generally agreed that delinquency usually precedes drug use, many authors conclude that the "delinquency leads to drug use" hypothesis is in error. Instead they argue that the drug/delinquency relationship, at least for marijuana, is spurious and reflects adoption of a general deviant orientation, or involvement in a general deviant subculture (Goode 1970, 1972; Hindelang and Weis 1972; Jessor 1976; Jessor, Jessor, and Finney 1973; Johnson 1973; Johnston, O'Malley, and Eveland 1978; Kandel 1978; Polonsky, Davis, and Roberts 1967; Scott and Wilcox 1965). There is general consensus that underlying deviant orientations explain the observed marijuana/delinquency relationship, but available data on explanations of the relationship between delinquent behavior and other illicit drugs are limited and inconclusive.

In regard to the three hypotheses concerning the observed relationship between drug use and delinquency, the above discussion illustrates that current research provides few definitive generalized findings. Most commonly, delinquency precedes drug use of any kind, so that drug use cannot generally be said to initiate delinquent behavior. It would also appear that the relationship between marijuana and delinquency is based on the underlying deviance-proneness of the youth involved. Beyond these limited conclusions, however, lack of information or contradictory findings are the rule.

Research Questions

This report is in part a replication and in part an extension of results found in previous studies. We begin by asking to what extent self-reported delinquency and drug use are related to one

Source: David H. Huizinga, Scott Menard, and Delbert S. Elliott, *Justice Quarterly,* Vol. 6, No. 3, pp. 419–455, copyright © 1989. Reprinted with permission of the Academy of Criminal Justice Sciences.

another. Earlier reports (Elliott and Huizinga 1984; Huizinga and Elliott 1981; Johnson, Wish, and Huizinga 1986) confirmed the existence of a moderately strong cross-sectional relationship between drug use and delinquency by showing that more serious delinquents are more likely to use drugs and to use them more often than less serious delinquents, and by showing that more serious drug users (those who use more than marijuana or alcohol) are more likely to commit delinquent acts and to do so more frequently than less serious drug users. Our first research question is whether this cross-sectional relationship can be replicated longitudinally: do those who are ever involved in one of the two behaviors (delinquency or drug use) have a higher probability of ever being involved in the other?

After establishing the strength of the relationships among different measures of delinquency and drug use, we examine the question of temporal priority. That is, we attempt to determine whether the onset of delinquency is a plausible cause of the onset of drug use, or whether the onset of drug use is a plausible cause of the onset of delinquency. This process . . . involves replication of past research . . . in conjunction with the results from the first analysis, answers to the question of temporal order may allow us to eliminate some possible causal patterns and to ascertain whether certain types of behavior are in some sense prerequisite to others.

A third question deals with short-term temporal relationships between drug use and delinquency. Focusing on index offenses, we ask what proportion of these offenses is immediately preceded by alcohol use, drug use, or by both. . . . It is entirely possible, for example, that delinquency leads to drug use rather than vice versa, but that once drug use has been initiated, it increases the extent of delinquent behavior.

Our final research question focuses on repeated serious (index) delinquency and repeated serious (polydrug) substance use, and asks to what extent individuals move from one type of behavior to the other. In this report, "serious delinquency" refers to the commission of three or more index offenses in one year; "serious drug use" (hereafter "polydrug use") refers to the use of one or more substances (amphetamines,

barbiturates, cocaine, hallucinogens, or heroin) four or more times in one year.

Methods

Sample: The National Youth Survey

The National Youth Survey (NYS) is a prospective longitudinal study of delinquent behavior, alcohol and drug use, and other problem behavior in the American youth population. To date, seven waves of data have been collected on this national youth panel, covering the period from 1976 to 1986. The data reported in this paper are limited to the first six waves of data and cover the period from 1976 to 1983.

The National Youth Survey employed a probability sample of households in the continental United States based on a self-weighting, multistage cluster sampling design. The sample was drawn in late 1976 and contained 2,360 eligible youths aged 11 to 17 at the time of the initial interview. Of these, 1,725 (73 %) agreed to participate in the study, signed informed consents, and completed interviews in the initial (1977) survey. An age, sex, and race comparison between non-participating eligible youths and participating youths indicates that the loss rate from any particular age, sex, or racial group appears to be proportional to that group's representation in the population. Further, with respect to these characteristics, participating youths appear to be representative of the total 11- through 17-year-old population in the United States as established by the U.S. Census Bureau.

Annual involvement in delinquent behavior and drug use was self-reported by members of the youth panel in confidential, personal (face-to-face) interviews. In most instances these interviews occurred in the respondent's home. . . . Respondents were guaranteed that any information they provided in the interview was confidential and could not be released to any agency without their written consent.

Conclusion

The results of the present study are consistent with prior research on the relationship between

Correlations among Ever-Prevalence Measures

AGE IN 1976: 11–17/11–12	MINOR DELINQUENCY	INDEX OFFENDING	ALCOHOL USE	MARIJUANA USE	POLYDRUG USE
Minor delinquency	1.00/1.00	.32/.33	.15/.17	.30/.31	.25/.22
Index offending		1.00/1.00	.16/.20	.33/.29	.35/.32
Alcohol use			1.00/1.00	.33/.38	.19/.23
Marijuana use				1.00/1.00	.50/.53
Polydrug use					1.00/1.00

drug use and delinquency in finding a positive correlation among different types of delinquency and drug use. . . . In addition, by making a distinction between minor and index delinquency and among different types of substance use, we find that the strength of the relationship between delinquency and drug use is generally comparable to the strength of the relationship between different types of delinquency (minor and index) and among different types of substance use.

References

Blane, H.T. and L.E. Hewitt (1977) *Alcohol and Youth: An Analysis of the Literature.* Final Report to the National Institute on Alcohol Abuse and Alcoholism. Washington, DC: Department of Health, Education, and Welfare.

Elliott, D.S. and D. Huizinga (1984) "The Relationship between Delinquent Behavior and ADM Problems." Proceedings of the Alcohol, Drug Abuse, and Mental Health Administration/Office of Juvenile Justice and Delinquency Prevention Research Conference on Juvenile Offenders and Serious Drug, Alcohol, and Mental Health Problems. Washington, DC: U.S. Government Printing Office.

Goode, E. (1970) *The Marijuana Smokers.* New York: Basic.

——— (1972) "Excerpts from *Marijuana Use and Crime.*" In National Commission on Marijuana and Drug Abuse, *Marijuana: A Signal of Misunderstanding.* Appendix, Volume 1. Washington, DC: U.S. Government Printing Office, pp. 447–469.

Hindelang, M.J. and J.G. Weis (1972) "The BC-TRY Cluster and Factor Analysis System: Personality and Self-Reported Delinquency." *Criminology* 10:268-94.

Huizinga, D. and D.S. Elliott (1981) "A Longitudinal Study of Delinquency and Drug Use in a National Sample of Youth: An Assessment of Causal Order." National Youth Survey Report Number 16. Boulder: Behavioral Research Institute.

Jessor, R. (1976) "Predicting Time of Onset of Marijuana Use: A Developmental Study of High School Youth." *Journal of Consulting and Clinical Psychology* 44:125-34.

Jessor, R., S.L. Jessor, and J. Finney (1973) "A Social Psychology of Marijuana Use: Longitudinal Studies of High School and College Youth." *Journal of Personality and Social Psychology* 26:1-15.

Johnson, B.D. (1973) *Marijuana Users and Drug Subcultures.* New York: Wiley.

Johnson, B.D., E.D. Wish, and D. Huizinga (1986) "The Concentration of Delinquent Offending." In B.D. Johnson and E.D. Wish (eds.), "Crime Rates among Drug Abusing Offenders," Final Report to National Institute of Justice (80-IJ-CX-0049). New York: Interdisciplinary Research Center, Narcotic and Drug Research, Inc., pp. 106-43.

Johnston, L.D., P.M. O'Malley, and L.K. Eveland (1978) "Drugs and Delinquency: A Search for Causal Connections." In D.B. Kandel (ed.), *Longitudinal Research on Drug Use: Empirical Findings and Methodological Issues.* New York: Wiley, pp. 137-156.

Kandel, D.B. (1978) *Longitudinal Research on Drug Use: Empirical Findings and Methodological Issues.* New York: Wiley.

Polonsky, D., G.F. Davis, and C.F. Roberts, Jr. (1967) *A Follow-up Study of the Juvenile Drug Offender.* Sacramento: Institute for the Study of Crime and Delinquency.

Scott, P.D. and D.R. C. Wilcox (1965) "Delinquency and the Amphetamines." *British Journal of Psychiatry* 61:9-27.

Name of Student _____
Student ID # _____
Course Section # _____
Date _____

Answer the following questions, based on your reading of the Huizinga, Menard and Elliott article:

1. *Hypotheses:* What hypotheses do Huizinga, Menard, and Elliott indicate they are going to test?

   _____

   _____

   _____

   _____

2. *Variables:*

   a.   Identify the independent variable(s) in the study.

   _____

   _____

   _____

   _____

   b.   Identify the dependent variable(s) in the study.

   _____

   _____

   _____

   _____

3.   A review of the table at the end of the article points out that one of the relationships appears to be considerably stronger than the others. Which correlation is strongest, and what could possibly explain the strength of this relationship in comparison to the others?

   _____

   _____

   _____

   _____

   _____

   _____

   _____

   _____

_____

_____

_____

_____

_____

4. *Selection of a Simple Random Sample (SRS):* Using the most recent version of your campus telephone directory available and the random number table at the back of this text (see Appendix B), select a simple random sample of 25 students.

   a. Explain in detail the steps you took to select this sample.

   _____

   _____

   _____

   _____

   _____

   _____

   _____

   _____

   b. Did you select with replacement or without replacement?

   _____

   c. What is the difference between selecting with and without replacement?

   _____

   _____

   _____

   _____

   _____

   _____

   _____

Questionably Adult: Determinants and Effects of the Juvenile Waiver Decision

Carole Wolfe Barnes and Randal S. Franz
Justice Quarterly
Vol. 6, No. 1, pp. 116–135, March 1989

Introduction

Significant changes have occurred in the juvenile justice system over the past 20 years. At both the state and the federal level, court decisions and legislative acts have gradually redefined the philosophy and practice of the nation's juvenile courts, transforming a social agency with a treatment ideology and few due process protections into a legal institution with adversarial procedures and most of the due process protections accorded to adults in this society.

With increasing legalization of the procedures have come increased demands for accountability from young offenders. States created varying mechanisms in response to these demands; some lowered the age of adult court jurisdiction, while others defined or broadened the list of offenses dictating adjudication as an adult (Hamparian et al. 1982a). Many states have revised the statutes governing the procedure by which juveniles are transferred from juvenile to adult court. Described variously as "judicial waiver," "transfer," or "remand," the procedure has been facilitated and encouraged by the legislative restructuring which followed the U.S. Supreme Court decision in *Kent* vs. *the United States*.[1] That 1966 decision granted juveniles the right to a hearing, representation by counsel, access to relevant records, and appropriate justification when the waiver decision is made.

Like other states, California permits adjudication of serious youthful offenders in adult court. Persons 18 years of age and over are charged and tried originally as adults. Those under 16 cannot be tried as adults. Sixteen- and 17-year-olds, however, though charged originally as juveniles, may have jurisdiction waived to adult court if the alleged offense is serious and if the juvenile's record indicates a history of prior offense, failed rehabilitative efforts, and significant criminal sophistication. Introduced in 1909 and revised in 1949 and 1961, the waiver process was amended in 1977 by California Assembly Bill 3121 (AB 3121) to include two types of waiver motions (Hamparian et al. 1982b:CA-4).

The two motions, 707A and 707B, are distinguished by the nature of the alleged offense and by the burden of proof.

Although the present study offers a complete sample of all youth considered for waiver over a six-year period and considers a broad range of legal, demographic, and organizational variables, it shares some of the limitations [of previous studies]. The sample size (206) is barely adequate for multivariate analyses; selectivity on demographic variables at arrest or at intake is not controlled. Furthermore, because precise standards for waiver are lacking in most states (Fagan et al. 1987:275; Feld 1987), results from a state with well-articulated guidelines may be atypical.

---

[1] Kent vs. the United States, 1966, 383 U.S. 541, 16 L. Ed. 2d 84, 86 S. Ct. 1045. In addition, the decision's appendix prescribed the following criteria to be considered by the juvenile court judge in deciding the waiver issue: seriousness of the alleged offense, nature of the offense (personal vs. property), manner of commission (aggressive, premeditated, violent), quality of the evidence, jurisdiction in which co-offenders would be heard, sophistication and maturity of the offender, prior record, prospects for community protection, and likelihood of rehabilitation given the facilities of the juvenile court.

Methods

Data on all 206 waiver motions filed between March 1978 and December 1983 were collected from the Juvenile Court files of a large metropolitan county in northern California (population c. 900,000). Blacks, with 7.5 percent of the population, and Hispanics, with 7.2 percent, constitute the largest minorities. The community's labor force depends on government employment and service occupations. Information on the type of sentence was obtained from both the District Attorney's office and the California Youth Authority.

Variables

Because the analysis is accomplished in two stages, the dependent variable in the first stage—the outcome of the waiver hearing—becomes the independent variable in the second. The waiver hearing results in either (1) a finding that the youth is fit for adjudication in juvenile court; (2) a finding that the youth is unfit and is remanded to adult court for trial; or (3) a dismissal of the waiver petition in return for a negotiated plea. Demographic, legal, and organizational variables are treated as independent variables in the first stage and as covariates in the second. The dependent variable in the second stage is the severity of the sentence (none, supervision, county time, CYA, or Prison).

The demographic variables used were determined by the information available in court files. These included gender, race (dichotomized into white and minority categories), parents' marital status, number of children in family, age, and birth order. No reliable indicator of socioeconomic status was available.

The legal variables included seriousness of the alleged offense, number of prior court appearances on criminal petitions, nature of the most serious prior offense, previous juvenile court dispositions, supervision status of the youth at the time of the alleged offense, and type of 707 motion filed. Offenses were grouped into three broad categories: (1) property offenses and victims crimes, (2) personal offenses, and (3) aggravated personal offenses. These categories also were used in coding the nature of prior offenses: the most serious prior offense on the record was coded. The number of prior court appearances was an interval measure of delinquent history and court experience. Previous juvenile court dispositions include no previous treatment, supervision, minimum-security county incarceration (one-year maximum), and state-level incarceration at the California Youth Authority (with jurisdiction in some cases to age 25). Petitions filed against youth who were already under court supervision at the time were noted.

Organizational variables included the probation officer's recommendation (fit or unfit for juvenile court), the use of a negotiated plea, and the year in which the motion was filed. The year of filing was a proxy for organizational experience with the new law.

Results

The results are presented in two segments, mirroring the two-stage analysis described above. In the first section, the discriminant function analysis is discussed and the demographic, legal, and organizational variables influencing the waiver decision are identified. The second section describes the results of the analysis of covariance, which tested for differences in sentencing patterns between juvenile and adult court and analyzed the different contributions of the demographic, legal, and organizational variables to sentence severity.

Summary of Results

In the discriminant analysis, the model developed predicted the waiver decision in 59 percent of the cases. The more effective equation distinguished youth found fit from those found unfit for adjudication in juvenile court. The second discriminated those whose remand petitions were dropped from those who were found fit. The most important predictors of unfitness were largely those set forth in the legislative guidelines for the waiver decision: a previous commitment to the CYA, being charged with an aggravated personal offense, a large number of prior offenses, and (unexpectedly) the waiver motion being filed in recent years. A filing date of 1979 signaled a shift to more "unfit" recommendations by probation officers and an increase in the use of the waiver motion as a bargaining device. Within the juvenile court, variables distinguishing those whose waiver petitions were dropped from those who were found fit included being charged with a property offense, the waiver being filed in recent years when its filing served as a bargaining device, and being female. Those found fit were more apt to be first offenders who apparently declined to plea bargain. Race was the only demographic variable of some importance in the first function (members of minorities were more likely to be found unfit) and gender the only variable of note in the second (females were more apt to have their waiver petitions dropped). The relatively minor impact of demographic variables may be due to preselection bias and to the correlation of race with offense type.

The analysis of covariance suggested that the two courts differed both in sentence severity and in the criteria used in sentencing. In adult court, current offense is the overriding predictor, with plea bargaining a mitigating factor; in juvenile court, the current offense is outweighed by the number and nature of prior offenses and by prior treatment.

References

Fagan, Jeffrey, Martin Forst, and T. Scott Vivona (1987) "Racial Determinants of the Judicial Transfer Decision: Prosecuting Violent Youth in Criminal Court." *Crime and Delinquency* 33 (2):259-86.

Feld, Barry (1987) "The Juvenile Court Meets the Principle of the Offense: Legislative Change in Judicial Waiver Statutes." *Journal of Criminal Law and Criminology* 78 (3):471-533.

Hamparian, Donna M., Linda K. Estep, Susan M. Muntean, Ramon R. Priestino, Robert G. Swisher, Paul L. Wallace, and Joseph L. White (1982a) *Major Issues in Juvenile Justice Information and Training: Youth in Adult Courts: Between Two Worlds.* Columbus, OH: Academy for Contemporary Problems.

———— (1982b) *Major Issues in Juvenile Justice Information and Training: Youth in Adult Courts: Between Two Worlds—West Region.* Columbus, OH: Academy for Contemporary Problems.

Name of Student _____

Student ID # _____

Course Section # _____

Date _____

1. Design an experiment. Be sure to identify both an independent and a dependent variable.

   _____

   _____

   _____

   _____

2. Also, be sure to indicate how you plan to check on the following:

   a. Temporal order (x occurs in time before y)

   _____

   _____

   _____

   _____

   _____

   _____

   b. Covariance (changes in x occur with changes in y)

   _____

   _____

   _____

   _____

   _____

   _____

   c. Spuriousness (other possible causes of y cannot be controlled)

   _____

   _____

   _____

   _____

   _____

Raising the Minimum Drinking Age: Some Unintended Consequences of Good Intentions

Lonn Lanza-Kaduce and Pamela Richards
Justice Quarterly
Vol. 6, No. 2, pp. 247–262, June 1989

Introduction

Young drivers are disproportionately involved in alcohol-related traffic accidents and fatalities (see National Highway Transportation Safety Administration 1983; Wagenaar 1983). In an effort to combat the bloodletting on the highways, many states recently raised the minimum drinking age to 21.

Unfortunately, it is difficult to know whether raising the minimum drinking age has had the effect that lawmakers intended. Most research on the topic has relied on epidemiological evidence, but we know that during the past decade there has been a general, gradual decline in drinking and driving (Insurance Institute for Highway Safety 1987). Reductions in alcohol-related traffic accidents could be due to raising the drinking age, but they also may reflect changes in drinking and driving patterns that are unrelated to the legal drinking age.

It is difficult to sort out these problems with epidemiological data. Unfortunately, little information about drinking and driving has been obtained directly from respondents in the target population. This paper presents results from a self-report study of young people who were affected by changes in the legal drinking age. We use a naturally occurring experiment to gauge how different legal drinking ages are related to patterns of drinking and driving among 19-year-olds.

The Conceptual Framework

In this paper we will rely on the framework for social policy research proposed by Mayer and Greenwood (1980). Its special value lies in reminding us that policies such as raising the minimum drinking age can have unintended as well as intended consequences. . . . [L]egal intervention took place in Florida on July 1, 1985, when the state raised its minimum drinking age from 19 to 21 for anyone born on or after July 1, 1966. Nineteen- and 20-year-olds born before that date were "grandfathered in" under the previous legal drinking age of 19. Consequently, in the spring of 1986 some 19-year-olds were legal drinkers and others were not.

We assume that the primary policy objective of raising the drinking age is to reduce the frequency of youthful drinking and driving and/or the level of impairment of youthful drinking drivers. Raising the drinking age could have these intended consequences in two major ways: (1) by deterring underage drinkers through fear of sanction (a classical deterrence rationale) and/or (2) by restricting their opportunity to drink (a variant of an incapacitation rationale). In either event the frequency of drinking should drop when the legal drinking age is increased. This change in turn should alter drinking and driving patterns.

As Mayer and Greenwood's framework suggests, unintended and latent consequences may flow either from changing the law itself or from achieving the law's intended objective. We will examine the following consequences that may result from raising the minimum drinking age: (1) whether the legal change leads to derivative law breaking, (2) whether the change engenders a sense of injustice, and (3) whether the social context of drinking is altered by raising the minimum drinking age.

Methods

Sample

We conducted telephone interviews with the sample in April 1986, nine months after Florida raised its minimum drinking age from 19 to 21. The sample consisted of all students enrolled at a state university who were born in either June or July 1966, and for whom accurate telephone numbers could be obtained. Of the resulting 468 students, we were unable to locate 108 (23%) after at least three calls. Twenty-nine (6%) refused to participate, leaving us with a sample size of 331 (71%). Of these respondents, 154 were born in June and 171 were born in July. The difference in the size of the groups is due to an extra day in July and to a slightly higher attrition rate for those born in June.

Respondents born in June are our control group because they were unaffected by the change in the minimum drinking age. The experimental group consists of respondents born in July, for whom drinking was declared illegal. Although students could not be assigned randomly to one of the two conditions, the two groups should be substantially equivalent. Some of the survey items confirm their similarity.

We measured frequency of drinking and driving by asking respondents how often they had used alcohol and then had driven in the preceding month. The question was asked separately for beer, wine, and liquor. We measured impairment by asking respondents how much beer, wine, and/or liquor they had drunk the last time they drank and drove. The number of cans, bottles, glasses, or mixed drinks was summed.

If changing the drinking age is to affect drinking and driving, it must deter drinking and/or restrict the opportunity to drink so that individuals drink less. We measured frequency of drinking by asking respondents to report how often they had drunk beer, wine, and/or liquor in the preceding month.

We examined four types of unintended consequences. The first was derivative crime, for which we constructed three variables. We asked respondents whether they had ever used a fake identification to buy alcohol. We also asked whether they had ever used someone else's identification to buy alcohol. Response cate-gories for both items were yes (1) or no (0). To measure criminal associations with unfamiliar persons, we asked how often someone other than family members or friends bought alcohol for the respondent. Response alternatives were almost never (0), sometimes (1), and often (2).

The second unintended consequence we examined was whether the law would foster a sense of injustice. We used 13 survey items to operationalize the commensurability, comparability, and competence dimensions of the sense of injustice as discussed by Matza (1964). Commensurability refers to the legitimacy attributed to the law. Comparability taps whether respondents feel discriminated against because they do not enjoy the rights and privileges given those with adult status. Competence pertains to the technical proficiency and moral authority of the legal agents responsible for the law. In this case we focused on police (the rule enforcers) and legislators (the rule makers).

Our third unintended consequence was the social context of drinking. Using a response format of never or almost never (0), sometimes (1), or often (2), we asked how often respondents drank in a series of locations and with a variety of companions.

Our fourth concern was whether changes in the drinking age would produce differences in drinking norms and behaviors between legal and illegal drinkers. We included eight items, using a disagree (0), neutral (1), and agree (2) format to learn whether underage drinkers held more permissive norms. . . . We also included eight items to indicate *abusive drinking*.

Results

Raising the minimum drinking age appears to have no effect on the drinking and driving reported by this sample. We found no significant differences between the legal and the illegal 19-year-old drinkers in how often they drink and drive, or in the level of impairment when they drink and drive. This finding clearly contradicts research conclusions derived from the epidemiological study of traffic accidents and fatalities (for a review, see General Accounting Office 1987).

Conclusion

These data suggest raising the minimum drinking age may not have the effect on youthful drinking and driving that policy makers desire. In this sample, illegal drinkers drink and drive with the same frequency as legal drinkers. Earlier we noted that epidemiological data show an apparent relationship between raising the drinking age and alcohol-related traffic accidents. Could this relationship be spurious? It would be spurious if general social changes in the past few years have reduced the general frequency of drinking and driving, and have prompted states simultaneously to raise minimum drinking ages. Ross (1984) and Andenaes (1978) reached similar conclusions about the impact of other drunk driving laws in Scandinavia, and such an effect seems possible here.

References

Andenaes, J. (1978) "The Effects of Scandinavia's Drinking-and-Driving Laws." *Scandinavian Studies in Criminology* 6:35-53.

General Accounting Office (1987) "Drinking-Age Laws: An Evaluation Synthesis of Their Impact on Highway Safety." Washington, DC: General Accounting Office.

Insurance Institute for Highway Safety (1987) "Drinking and Driving Down Sharply in U.S. during Last 13 Years." News Release, January 14. Washington, DC: Insurance Institute for Highway Safety.

Matza, D. (1964) *Delinquency and Drift.* New York: Wiley.

Mayer, R.P. and E. Greenwood (1980) *The Design of Social Policy Research.* Englewood Cliffs, NJ: Prentice-Hall.

National Highway Traffic Safety Administration (1983) "Facts on Alcohol and Highway Safety." Washington, DC: U.S. Department of Transportation.

Ross, H.L. (1984) *Deterring the Drunk Driver: Legal Policy and Social Control.* Revised edition. Lexington, MA: Lexington Books.

Wagenaar, A.C. (1983) *Alcohol, Young Drivers, and Traffic Accidents.* Lexington, MA: Lexington Books.

Name of Student _____

Student ID # _____

Course Section # _____

Date _____

Based on your reading of the Lanza-Kaduce and Richards research, which uses a naturally occurring experiment, design a similar experiment on drinking behavior using college students at your university. While you cannot study the sense of injustice students feel because of the change in drinking age from 19 to 21, you can look at changes in behavior (if any) between those who are old enough to drink legally and those who are underage and therefore drink illegally. Given those observations, you should be able to get a sense of how students feel about the current legal drinking age.

Lanza-Kaduce and Richards asked questions about how much beer, wine, and/or liquor a person drank the last time they drank and drove as well as other questions about drinking and driving. Refer to the abstracted reprint of the article to develop questions for your survey. In addition, use the following 13 items (see questions 5–8) that the authors used to address the issues of commensurability, comparability, and competence.

1. Using a student population at your college or university, describe the steps you would follow to set up a research design similar to that of Lanza-Kaduce and Richards.

2. What population would constitute your control group in this experiment?

_____

_____

_____

_____

3. What population would constitute your experimental group?

_____

_____

_____

_____

4. What steps can you take in selecting your sample to match these control and experimental groups as closely as possible?

_____

_____

_____

_____

_____

_____

_____

Use the questions in items 5–8 as models or examples for creating your five questions about beer drinking attitudes in question 9.

5. Questions designed to measure commensurability:

   1. Drinking is a matter of personal choice and shouldn't be outlawed for someone my age.

   2. The laws against underage drinking should be obeyed.

   3. I approve of a legal drinking age of 21.

6. Questions designed to address the issue of comparability:

   1. Someone who is old enough to be drafted or to get married is old enough to drink.

   2. Older adults have more drinking problems than do people my age.

7. Questions designed to address the issue of competence of police:

    1. Police ought to worry about criminals, not underage drinkers.

    2. Police generally do their jobs well.

    3. Police don't obey the law any better than the rest of us.

    4. Police use their authority unfairly.

8. Questions designed to address the issue of competence of legislators:

    1. Legislators try to do a good job.

    2. Legislators will do anything to get elected.

    3. Legislators play God when it comes to legislating morality.

    4. Legislators break their own laws.

9. Develop five questions to include in your survey that address attitudes about drinking beer, wine, and/or liquor and driving. Use the questions in items 5–8 as models or examples. Explain why you believe each question will help assess attitudes either for or against drinking and driving.

    1. Question:

    _____

    _____

    Explanation:

    _____

    _____

    _____

    _____

    2. Question:

    _____

    _____

    Explanation:

    _____

    _____

    _____

    _____

3. Question:

    _____

    _____

    Explanation:

    _____

    _____

    _____

    _____

4. Question:

    _____

    _____

    Explanation:

    _____

    _____

    _____

    _____

5. Question:

    _____

    _____

    Explanation:

    _____

    _____

    _____

    _____

The Effect of Dropping Out of High School on Subsequent Criminal Behavior

Terence P. Thornberry, Melanie Moore, and R. L. Christenson
Criminology: An Interdisciplinary Journal
Vol. 23, No. 1, pp. 3–18, February 1985

Introduction

The relationship between school failure and criminal behavior is a recurrent theme in theories of delinquency. Eventual dropouts have been found to have considerably higher rates of delinquency during high school than do graduates (e.g., Elliott and Voss, 1974; Polk, Adler, Bazemore, Blake, Cordray, Coventry, Galvin, and Temple, 1981), a finding consistent both with conventional wisdom and most theories of delinquency. However, what is not clear either theoretically or empirically is the effect that dropping out of high school has on subsequent criminal behavior. Indeed, for this relationship two basic models of delinquency, strain theory and social control theory, offer rather divergent predictions.

In strain theory (Cohen, 1955; Cloward and Ohlin, 1960), the middle class environment of the school is viewed as a major source of frustration and alienation for lower class youth. To alleviate their frustration, these students withdraw their legitimacy from middle class norms and turn to delinquency as a source of success, status, and approval. Thus, for lower class students strain theory views school and its attendant failure as a major cause of criminal activity. On the other hand, in his formulation of social control theory, Hirschi (1969) posits that delinquency arises when the person's bond to conventional society is weakened. Individuals who are attached to conventional others and committed to conventional institutions are strongly bonded to society and hence are unlikely candidates for crime. Since school is ". . . an eminently conventional institution" (Hirschi, 1969: 110), social control

theory views it as a major source of bonding which should reduce delinquent activity.

Strain and control theories, therefore, offer divergent assessments of the relationship between school and delinquency, especially for lower class youths. In the former school is a source of failure and frustration which increases delinquent conduct; in the latter it is a source of social control which decreases delinquent conduct.

Based on these divergent viewpoints, strain and control theory present contradictory predictions concerning the effect of dropping out of high school on subsequent criminal involvement. According to strain theory, because dropping out eliminates the source of frustration brought about by failure in the school, criminal conduct should decline sharply following dropout. According to control theory, however, because dropping out reduces institutional control, criminal behavior should increase.

The most influential investigation of the relationship between dropping out and delinquency, Elliott and Voss's panel study (1974), is clearly supportive of strain theory. Elliott and Voss followed 2,617 subjects from the ninth grade until "the usual date for graduation from high school" (Elliott, 1978: 457) and hypothesized that ". . . the act of leaving school should reduce school-related frustrations and alienation and thereby lower the motivational stimulus for delinquency" (Elliott, 1978: 454). To test this hypothesis they compared rates of official delinquency for high school graduates and dropouts. The rates for dropouts were both higher and increased more rapidly than those for graduates throughout the high school years. Indeed, for the dropout group delinquency was highest just before leaving school and then, regardless of the age at which the student dropped out, declined sharply. Thus, dropping out of school was followed by a clear reduction in delinquent activity. Elliott and Voss conclude that these results ". . . support the basic proposition that the school is the critical social context for the generation of delinquent behavior" (Elliott and Voss, 1974: 124).

Other researchers examining the relationship between dropping out and subsequent criminal activity have produced similar results. In a pilot study to the one just described, Elliott (1966) also found that delinquency declined after students dropped out of high school. Mukherjee (1971), using data from the Philadelphia birth cohort of 1945, replicated the basic finding of Elliott and Voss. He found delinquency rates to be higher while subjects were in school as compared to the postschool period. But for high school dropouts, over two-thirds of those who had juvenile arrest records were no longer delinquent once they dropped out, and only 7.0% of the delinquent dropouts committed their first offense after dropping out (Mukherjee, 1971: 87). Finally, LeBlanc, Biron, and Pronovost (1979) also reported that delinquency declined for dropouts once they left high school.

Although . . . [these results] support strain theory's hypothesis, the strength of that support is limited by two methodological considerations. First, the observations in all four studies were completed by the time the subjects were nineteen years of age, an exceedingly short follow-up period. Second, the relationship between dropping out and delinquency behavior observed in these studies could be severely contaminated by the influence of the age distribution of crime. Following a steady upward trend during the early teenage years, criminal behavior exhibits a precipitous drop after age sixteen or seventeen (see for example Wolfgang, Thornberry, and Figlio, in press, chapter 4). Since most dropouts leave school at these same ages, the ensuing reduction in criminal activity coincides quite closely with a reduction expected from the age distribution alone. Therefore, in assessing the relationship between these variables, it is essential to control explicitly for the influence of age.

Research Problem

The present study reevaluates the relationship between these variables to provide a clear assessment of the divergent predictions that can be derived from strain and control theories. The design replicates that of Elliott and Voss as closely as possible and at the same time attempts to remedy methodological problems of previous studies. Three methodological factors are considered:

1. The observation period is extended to cover the early adult years as well as the period immediately following the act of dropping out. Thus both short-term and long-term effects of dropping out of high school are examined.
2. In light of the massive dampening effect that age has on criminal conduct after age sixteen, the association between dropping out of high school and later crime is assessed in relativistic terms. Specifically, analysis poses the question of whether dropping out of high school alters (i.e., whether it increases or decreases) the general downward trend in criminal involvement expected at these ages.
3. Finally, the relationship between dropout status and subsequent criminality is tested within major demographic subgroups and when the influence of postschool experiences are controlled. For the former, race and social status of origin are introduced into the analysis. For the latter, Elliott and Voss's design is again followed and marital status and employment status are held constant to see how postschool experiences mediate the effect of dropping out on subsequent crime.

Methodology

The present study reevaluates the association between dropout status and later criminal involvement, examining both short-term and long-term effects and controlling for the influence of both age and postschool experiences. To do so, it utilizes longitudinal data from a 10% sample of the Philadelphia birth cohort of 1945. The cohort consists of all males (n = 9,945) born in that year who resided in Philadelphia from at least the age of ten to the age of eighteen (Wolfgang, Figlio, and Sellin, 1972). The members of the 10% sample were the focus of a follow-up study that extended the observation period to age twenty-five. For the entire sample (n = 975) complete arrest histories are available and, in addition, attempts were made to interview all members of the sample. Successful interviews were conducted with 567, or 62%. Given this response rate the necessity of weighting the data for nonresponse was carefully assessed and the effect of nonresponse was found to be negligible on correlational analyses and on the estimation of significance levels (Wolfgang et al., in press; Singer, 1977). Thus while the attrition rate is fairly substantial, its consequences on drawing inferences from these data appear to be relatively minor. Moreover, the disadvantages of attrition are clearly offset by the fact that the cohort design traces criminal careers of dropouts and graduates from the beginning of high school until the age of twenty-five.

Variables for Analysis

The measure of the independent variable, dropout status, is based on responses to interview items in which each subject reported his educational attainment. Subjects are divided into high school dropouts, those who report completing less than twelve years of schooling, and high school graduates, those who report completing twelve or more years. For most analyses dropouts are further divided into groups based on the age at which they left high school.

The dependent variable, criminal involvement, is measured by the number of times each subject was arrested. These data are arrayed in annual intervals so that criminal involvement both before and after dropout can be compared.

For reasons mentioned above, four additional variables are included in analysis. Race is a dichotomous variable with the sample divided into white and black subjects. Social status of origin is also a dichotomy in which subjects are divided into white- and blue-collar categories based on the U.S. Census classification scheme. The occupation for this classification is that of the subject's father while the subject was in high school. Marital status is based on responses to

interview items in which each subject described his marital history. Finally, unemployment is based on an interview item in which each subject traced his employment history from high school until the time of the interview. Unemployment is defined as any period of time the person was not employed, a full-time student, or in the armed services. Due to incomplete unemployment or educational histories, analyses, including these variables are based on a sample size of 555.

Results

Regardless of how the analysis was conducted, one ineluctable conclusion emerged: dropping out of high school is positively associated with later criminal activity. Unlike . . . [others], we do not find an immediate dampening effect of dropping out on criminal involvement. Indeed, for two of the three age-at-dropout groups, criminal behavior increased in the year following departure from school. Moreover, dropping out of high school was also found to have a positive long-term effect on criminal behavior. Throughout the early twenties dropouts have consistently higher rates of arrests than do graduates and it is not until the mid-twenties that the rates for the two groups begin to converge. These findings are also observed for minority group subjects and for those from blue-collar backgrounds, the groups of particular interest to strain theory. Finally, dropout status was also found to have a significant positive effect on crime when the postschool experiences of marriage and employment are controlled. In general, therefore, results of this analysis are quite consistent with the theoretical explanations of social control theory; dropping out has a positive effect on subsequent arrest even when age and postschool experiences are controlled.

References

Cloward, Richard A. and Lloyd E. Ohlin
    1960   Delinquency and Opportunity: A Theory of Delinquent Gangs. Glencoe, IL: Free Press.
Cohen, Albert K.
    1955   Delinquent Boys. New York: Free Press.

Elliott, Delbert S. and Harwin Voss
  1974 Delinquency and Dropout. Lexington, MA: Lexington.

Elliott, Delbert S.
  1966 Delinquency, school attendance, and school dropout. Social Problems 13: 307-14.
  1978 Delinquency and school dropout. In Leonard D. Savitz and Norman Johnston (eds.), Crime in Society. New York: Wiley.

Hirschi, Travis
  1969 Causes of Delinquency. Berkeley: University of California Press.

LeBlanc, Marc, Louise Biron, and Louison Pronovost
  1979 Psycho-social development and delinquency evolution. Mimeograph, University of Montreal.

Mukherjee, S.K.
  1971 A typological study of school status and delinquency. Unpublished doctoral dissertation. Philadelphia: University of Pennsylvania.

Polk, Kenneth, Christine Adler, Gordon Bazemore, Gerald Blake, Sheila Cordray, Garry Coventry, James Galvin, and Mark Temple
  1981 Becoming Adult: An Analysis of Maturational Development from Age 16 to 30 of a Cohort of Young Men. Final Report of the Marion County Youth Study. Eugene: University of Oregon.

Singer, Simon I.
  1977 The effect of non-response on the birth cohort follow-up survey. Unpublished. Center for Studies in Criminology and Criminal Law. Philadelphia: University of Pennsylvania.

Wolfgang, Marvin E., Robert M. Figlio, and Thorsten Sellin
  1972 Delinquency in a Birth Cohort. Chicago: University of Chicago Press.

Wolfgang, Marvin E., Terence P. Thornberry, and Robert M. Figlio
  In press From Boy to Man—From Delinquency to Crime: Followup to the 1945 Philadelphia Birth Cohort.

Name of Student _____

Student ID # _____

Course Section # _____

Date _____

Based on the abstracted reprint of the Thornberry et. al. article entitled "The Effect Of Dropping Out Of High School On Subsequent Criminal Behavior," published in *Criminology: An Interdisciplinary Journal*, complete the following exercise.

A sociological/criminological research firm called Social Sciences Research, Inc., has asked you to serve as a consultant on a project related to changes in attitudes about dropping out of school and delinquency. As part of your work on the project, you are charged with the responsibility of surveying college students to determine what attitudes they currently have about dropping out and delinquency. To survey the students, you will need to develop a set of hypotheses, identify independent and dependent variables, and indicate the type of sampling technique appropriate for the project.

As a second step, you will actually survey five students from your class at two different times, using questions 1–5 (demographic questions) and 55–67 (crime and delinquency questions) in the survey shown in Appendix A. The second administration of the survey should occur at least one week after the first administration.

1. Hypothesis:

    _____

    _____

    _____

    _____

    _____

2. Variables:

    a. Identify an independent variable from those among the questions used in the exercise.

    _____

    _____

    _____

    b. Identify the dependent variable from those among the questions used in the exercise.

    _____

    _____

    _____

3. Sampling Technique:

    _____

    _____

    _____

4. Results of Surveys:

    a. First Administration:

    b. Second Administration:

5. Conclusions related to attitudes about dropping out and delinquency:

Ethnicity, Geography, and Occupational Achievement of Hispanic Men in the United States

Ross M. Stolzenberg
American Sociological Review
Vol. 55, No. 1, pp. 143–154, 1990

Introduction

Sociological interest in U.S. Hispanics has burgeoned, and much has been written about this rapidly growing ethnic group (Massey 1981; Borjas and Tienda 1985; Portes and Truelove 1987). Although Hispanics are disproportionately concentrated in low socioeconomic status occupations, occupational differences between Hispanic and non-Hispanic men have not been studied in detail (Tienda 1983a, b; Neidert and Farley 1985). Thus, my first concern in this paper is to examine those differences and investigate the connection between them and Hispanic–non-Hispanic differences in schooling, English language fluency and other work related characteristics of individuals.

My second concern is the hypothesis that the peculiar geographic distribution of American Hispanics substantially affects Hispanic-non-Hispanic occupational inequality. Prior research claims considerable effect of Hispanics' geographic location on their employment outcomes (Sanders and Nee 1987), and a long line of research relates occupational inequality to the distribution of minorities across geographic areas (Fossett and Swicegood 1982; Stolzenberg and D'Amico 1977). But the validity of these arguments has been hotly debated, and it remains unclear whether Hispanic-non-Hispanic occupational differences are generally and substantially affected by the unique geographic distribution of Hispanics.

My final concern is the occupational impact of the ethnic substructure of American Hispanics. Recent studies (Bean and Tienda 1987) stress the significance of differences among Hispanic ancestry groups, suggesting that if ethnicity per se affects employment of Hispanics, those effects should also be evident for Hispanic subgroups.

Background and Hypotheses

Geographic differences between American Hispanics and non-Hispanics are stark: in 1980, 31 percent of the U.S. Hispanic population lived in California, compared to 9 percent of the non-Hispanic population. About half of all Hispanics were concentrated in California and Texas, compared to 14 percent of the non-Hispanic population. Finally, four-fifths of all Hispanics resided in seven states compared to 35 percent of non-Hispanics (U.S. Bureau of the Census 1982, Table 1).

This paper tests two hypotheses: (1) Hispanic-non-Hispanic occupational inequality is substantially explained or affected by Hispanic-non-Hispanic differences in place of residence, Hispanic subgroup membership, and/or individual characteristics such as schooling and English language fluency. (2) Occupational differences among different Hispanic subgroups are substantially explained or affected by differences in place or residence, ethnic subgroup membership and/or individual characteristics such as schooling and English language fluency. Testing these hypotheses is complicated by the strong association between Hispanic subgroup membership, place of residence, and individual worker characteristics.

Data

Data are drawn from the Survey of Income and Education (SIE), which was fielded in 1976 by the U.S. Bureau of Census (1978), with a national response rate of 95.4 percent for approximately 160,000 sampled households. The SIE provides detailed information on English language ability, Hispanic ethnicity, Hispanic subgroup membership, country of birth, years of schooling, and other social, economic, and demographic factors. Large numbers of Hispanic respondents were obtained by oversampling low-income persons. Separate samples were drawn in each state, thereby enhancing coverage of states with large Hispanic concentrations. The present analysis is restricted to those nine states in which the SIE collected data on at least 200 Hispanics in the experienced civilian labor force (ECLF): New York, New Jersey, Florida, Texas, Colorado, New Mexico, Arizona, Nevada, and California. In 1980, these states included 81 percent of the Hispanic population of the U.S. (U.S. Bureau of the Census, 1982). The final sample contains 2,272 Hispanic and 17,087 non-Hispanic white men. Weighting of sample cases to reflect sampling probabilities prevents states with disproportionately large samples of Hispanics (e.g., Nevada) from having a disproportionate influence on the outcomes of analyses in which data from all nine states are pooled. The absence of adequate-sized samples from some states with substantial Hispanic populations (e.g., Illinois) restricts generalizability somewhat. However, these nine states included 88 percent of all U.S. Cubans, 85 percent of U.S. Mexicans, and 72 percent of mainland Puerto Ricans (U.S. Bureau of the Census 1982).

Specific variables used in this analysis are as follows:

Education (ED) is the number of years of schooling completed by the respondent. To allow non-linear effects, ED^2 is also included.

Potential years of labor experience (EX) is years of age minus years of school minus six. To allow non-linear effects, EX^2 is also included.

Foreign birth (FORBOR) is a dummy variable

set equal to one if the individual was born outside the U.S., and zero otherwise.

English language fluency (SPKENG) is measured on the following scale (1) speaks no English; (2) speaks English "not well—just a few words"; (3) speaks English "not well—more than a few words"; (4) speaks English "well"; (5) speaks English "very well"; and (6) native speaker of English was raised in a home where English was the usual language spoken.

Hispanic subgroup in the SIE is classified into five categories: Cuban, Mexican, Puerto Rican, Central or South American, and Other Spanish.

Race is classified into three categories: white, black, and other.

Occupation Three separate measures of occupation are used: (a) Duncan's socioeconomic index (SIE) is the basic dependent variable; (b) To measure differences in occupational payrates, each respondent's occupation is indexed by the natural logarithm of mean earnings reported by men in the occupation who worked 50 to 52 weeks per year in the 1970 Census; and (c) To measure occupational differences in opportunities for steady employment, each occupation is indexed by the proportion of male incumbents who were employed 50 to 52 weeks in the 1970 Census, the Census immediately preceding the SIE.

Analytic Strategy

The analytic strategy used here is two-way analysis of covariance (ANCOVA) (Johnson 1972), which is applied separately for each of the three dependent variables.

ANCOVA is used to test for and estimate group differences in basic model coefficients and intercepts. Finally, coefficient and intercept estimates are used to adjust the mean of OCC [occupation] in each group for group differences in means of independent variables. If coefficients differ across groups, then adjusted means are calculated by regression standardization. . . .

Summary and Conclusions

Results suggest that much of the occupational inequality between Hispanic and non-Hispanic white men is explained by differences in schooling and English language fluency. Findings are most consistent with this conclusion when occupation is measured by SIE, and less so when measured by weeks worked and earnings levels. However, closer scrutiny of findings suggests a pattern that might be called conditional occupational assimilation. If Hispanic men speak English "very well" and have completed at least 12 years of school, then their occupational achievement is close to that of white non-Hispanic men in the same geographic area with similar English fluency and schooling. However, at lower levels of English language proficiency and schooling, the occupations of Hispanics are inferior to the occupations of linguistically and educationally similar white non-Hispanic men. This pattern is suggested by the results based on all three occupational measures, but is most evident in analyses of occupational pay levels: the crude difference is a 26 percent advantage for non-Hispanics, but drops to 14 percent when comparisons are limited to those with poor English and eight years of school, and falls to 7 percent for high school graduates who speak English very well.

My analysis of ethnic subgroup effects found that Cuban origin or ancestry has a moderate positive effect on Hispanic occupational SIE, net of geographic location and basic model variable effects.

References

Bean, Frank D. and Marta Tienda. 1987. *The Hispanic Population of the United States.* New York: Russell Sage Foundation.

Borjas, George J., and Marta Tienda. 1985. "Introduction." Pp. 1-24 in *Hispanics in the U.S. Economy,* edited by G. Borjas and M. Tienda. Orlando: Academic Press.

Fossett, Mark and Gray Swicegood. 1982. "Rediscovering City Differences in Racial Occupational Inequality." *American Sociological Review* 47: 681-9.

Massey, Douglas. 1981. "Dimensions of the New Immigration to the United States and the Prospects for Assimilation." *Annual Review of Sociology* 7: 57-85.

Neiderdt, Lisa and Reynolds Farley. 1985. "Assimilation in the United States: An Analysis of Ethnic and Generation Differences in Status and Achievement." *American Sociological Review* 50:840-50.

Portes, Alejandro and Cynthia Truelove. 1987. "Making Sense of Diversity: Recent Research on Hispanic Minorities in the United States." *Annual Review of Sociology* 13: 359-85.

Sanders, J. and V. Nee. 1987. "Limits of Ethnic Solidarity in the Enclave Economy." *American Sociological Review* 52: 745:767.

Stolzenberg, Ross M. and Ronald D' Amico. 1977. "City Differences and Nondifferences in the Effect of Race and Sex on Occupational Distribution." *American Sociological Review* 42: 937-50.

Tienda, Marta. 1983a. "Nationality and Income Attainment Among Native and Immigrant Hispanic Men in the United States." *Sociological Quarterly* 24: 253-272.

———. 1983b. "Market Characteristics and Hispanic Earnings: A Comparison of Natives and Immigrants." Social Problems 31:59–72.

U.S. Bureau of the Census. 1978. "Consumer Income: Household Money Income in 1975, by Housing Tenure and Residence, for the United States, Regions, Divisions, and States, (Spring, 1976 Survey of Income and Education)." Series P-60, No. 108. Washington, D.C.: U.S. Government Printing Office.

———. 1982. Census of Population: 1980, *Supplemental Report,* PC80-S1-7, "Persons of Spanish Origin by State: 1980." Washington, D.C.: U.S. Government Printing Office.

Name of Student _____

Student ID # _____

Course Section # _____

Date _____

The Stolzenberg data are derived from 1976 sources and claim to include 88 percent of all Cuban Americans, 85 percent of Mexican Americans, and 72 percent of native Puerto Ricans.

1. How might the 1980 Mariel Boatlift of Cubans have affected the validity of Stolzenberg's research?

_____

_____

_____

_____

_____

_____

_____

_____

2. What could be done to improve the validity of this study?

_____

_____

_____

_____

_____

3. How might Stolzenberg's operationalization of the concept "race" as White, Black, or other effect his results in a study of Hispanics? What is an alternative way to operationalize the concept "race"?

_____

_____

_____

_____

_____

_____

_____

_____

Technologies of Observation

Have you ever been stopped while walking through a mall and asked a series of questions about some deodorant, breakfast food, or product packaging? Or have you ever been asked at the conclusion of a semester to evaluate the performance of one of your teachers? If you have, then you have participated in a *survey.*

A survey is usually thought of as a means of collecting a great deal of aggregate data in a very brief period of time. But the term *survey* also may be used to refer to information obtained in more qualitative interviewing strategies. To differentiate between formal, structured, questionnaire-type surveys and more nominal-level interviews, we will refer to the former as *questionnaire-based surveys* and the latter as *interviews.*

QUESTIONNAIRE-BASED SURVEYS

Questionnaire-based surveys are especially useful when working with representative samples (see Chapter 3). One of the major strengths of this type of survey is that it allows the researcher to examine a large sample of subjects, and when the sample is representative of some group, the research findings can be generalized to large populations.

A questionnaire should be developed to fulfill a specific research need or to address a particular research question. Many naive researchers construct questionnaires that have not been adequately conceptualized and operationalized. Such haphazard attempts—no matter how well intentioned—are seldom very useful in terms of generating meaningful findings and conclusions. The most common error inexperienced researchers

make is not asking the right questions or asking the right questions so imprecisely that they become fatuous. These sorts of flaws in research can be avoided during the design stage if the investigator is thoughtful and careful. We will discuss this in greater detail later in this chapter when talking about survey construction.

In some questionnaire-based surveys, respondents may answer written questions that they *self-administer* after reading all included instructions. In other questionnaire-based surveys, respondents answer questions asked by a researcher who administers the survey, explains the instructions, and is present in the event that the subject has questions of his or her own. Questionnaires may be distributed in a variety of ways: hand delivered, mailed, picked up at some organizational meeting, and so on. A *cover letter,* describing the research and inviting the subject to participate, typically accompanies a questionnaire.

Cover Letters

Cover letters usually are written on official university or organization letterhead to assure the potential subject of true institutional affiliation. Basically, the purpose of the cover letter is to introduce the subject to the researcher and the research project and to legitimate both. The letter should be sufficiently enticing to persuade the respondent to complete the survey. Cover letters typically strive to explain the importance of each subject's opinion and the research value of having his or her completed survey. Cover letters also usually state that there are no right or wrong answers to any questions and that all answers will remain anonymous and confidential.

Self-Administered Questionnaires

Self-administered questionnaires are given to respondents with the expectation that each person will be able to read and understand the questions, possesses the knowledge and willingness to answer them, and will take the time to do so. Self-administered questionnaires may be completed by individuals who are alone or in groups.

Mailed Questionnaires

A mailed questionnaire provides the researcher with a means of contacting a large number of respondents over an extensive geographic area, in a fairly expedient and inexpensive manner. With this type of questionnaire, each respondent answers the questions and returns the survey only if he or she has been convinced of its importance and is sufficiently motivated to do so. In order to motivate respondents in mailed surveys, researchers must write interesting and convincing cover letters.

One of the most difficult aspects of a mailed questionnaire is obtaining a large enough return rate to make the study meaningful. Response rates from an initial mailing may be well below 50 percent. However, this rate can and must be improved with follow-up mailings; some researchers use as many as three follow-up mailings.

In order to avoid unnecessary mailing costs and duplication of completed surveys, the researcher must develop some means of checking who has and has not returned a survey. Some researchers place an inconspicuous code number on the return envelope near the zip code. By checking envelopes containing returned surveys against a master mailing list, the researcher can avoid sending follow-up surveys to these people. Since the code number is on the outside of the envelope, the survey itself can be removed before the envelope is checked against the list, thus maintaining anonymity.

Advantages to Questionnaires

Collecting data through a questionnaire strategy has a number of significant advantages. First, the questionnaire-based survey is economical. It yields a great deal of information, or bits of data, in a short time period, and because it is mailed to subjects, it can cover a broad geographic area. Second, given the anonymity it provides, some people are likely to be more truthful answering a self-administered questionnaire than they would be responding to other types of surveys (Sudman & Bradburn, 1981). A third advantage to the questionnaire is that it can be completed at whatever pace the subject chooses. In other words, if the phone rings, shopping or homework needs to be done, or any other distraction or interruption occurs, the questionnaire may be put aside until time allows for its completion. This is not possible with some other data-gathering strategies, such as a researcher-administered questionnaire or an interview in which the investigator remains until the questionnaire or interview has been completed.

Disadvantages to Questionnaires

Of course, questionnaire-based surveys have several disadvantages, as well. Among the most serious is the potential limitation on data because of the restrictions such surveys place on the depth of questioning. Because the questions are formally structured and written on the page, no deviation or follow-up questioning is possible (besides those questions that were considered at the time the questionnaire was originally developed). Another disadvantage to the questionnaire is that it must be relatively short in order to assure that most subjects will complete the entire thing. As a result, questionnaires lack the depth of coverage possible with other means of data gathering, such as face-to-face interviews, which often exceed an hour to complete and may last six or eight hours. Although some questionnaires are quite lengthy, usually, they are kept relatively brief.

INTERVIEWS

Interviews frequently are conceived as "conversations with a purpose" (Berg, 1989, p. 13). That purpose is to gather information, or, as with questionnaires, bits of data. The research interview is a much underestimated device for gathering data. Most students inaccurately believe that because they have been asking and answering questions all their lives, conducting an interview should be a simple task. In truth, the interviewer cannot simply ask questions in the same manner one would in a normal conversation.

One important reason for this distinction is founded on what Erving Goffman (1967) terms *evasion tactics* and *deference ceremonies,* or avoidance rituals. In normal conversation, you might utter some word, phrase, or statement that invokes the other party's need to avoid this area. Usually, the other party will offer some audible or visual cue that he or she does not want to discuss this area. In exchange, you will *defer* and demonstrate an intrinsic respect for the other party by moving the conversation away from the sensitive area. Berg (1989, p. 27) explains that in these deference ceremonies, there is the "unspoken expectation that this respect will be reciprocated in some later communicational exchange."

Such a deference exchange in a research interview is untenable. Frequently, the very information that the respondent is attempting to avoid is the information sought in the research. The key factor in an interview is *control*. The conversation must at all times be under the control of the interviewer. This is not to suggest that the interviewer should be callous and unfeeling. Rather, the interviewer must develop strategies to maintain control and facilitate the smooth transition from one question to the next. To do so involves learning ways of temporarily deferring but later returning to sensitive areas (see Berg, 1995).

Types of Interviews

The inexperienced researcher may assume that every interview is the same, which is quite inaccurate. Some sources classify interviews as those that are *directive* and those that are *nondirective* (Abrahamson, 1983). Other sources use terms such as *formal* and *informal* (Fitzgerald & Cox, 1987). Denzin (1978), Babbie (1989), Gorden, (1987), and Berg (1995) provide three major categories of interviews: *standardized* (formal or directed),

unstandardized (informal or nondirective), and *semistandardized* (guided-semistructured).

Standardized Interviews

A standardized interview uses a formal, structured interview schedule, in which questions are asked the same way with each subject: precisely as worded in the schedule, in exactly the order in which the questions appear. The objective is to standardize the stimulus so that responses will be comparable (Babbie, 1989; Berg, 1995). In addition to a standardized schedule of interview questions, a formal interview is usually prearranged, so that both the interviewer and subject are aware that an interview is to occur.

While standardized interviews offer the advantage of asking questions that are readily comparable among subjects during analysis, interviews have several disadvantages. First, the requirement to adhere rigidly to the order and phrasing of questions in the interview schedule can potentially damage the interviewer's rapport with the subject. For example, neither the interviewer nor the subject can digress from the question series, as ordered in the interview schedule. This restriction will inhibit the subject from freely discussing information (albeit relevant to the study questions) that does not immediately relate to the question being asked. Further, the subject will be prevented from digressing to topics he or she might find personally gratifying to discuss but that are not relevant to the study.

Second, because the questions are developed entirely outside the interview process, they can seem artificial. If the subject senses this, it may affect how he or she sees the interviewer and the articulated purpose for the interview. If the situation becomes too artificial, the subject may be inclined to avoid speaking truthfully or completely about important areas for the research.

In brief, the potential disadvantage of the structured interview is the potential loss of information. Nuances of conversation that might have proven important, that might have yielded otherwise unanticipated areas of investigation, or that might have been simply serendipitous discoveries will have been lost. The principal advantage of the structured interview, like the questionnaire-based survey, is standardization of stimuli and, consequently, responses.

Unstandardized Interviews

In contrast to the strict rigidity of the standardized interview, the unstandardized interview does not use a formal schedule of questions. The unstandardized interview usually begins with a question that is intended to orient the respondent to the general area of research interest. Beyond that orienting question, which is usually conceived of in advance, the interviewer must adapt, develop, and generate questions and probes appropriate to the given interview situation.

Unstandardized interviews are extremely useful during the course of *field research* and are frequently used to augment researchers' observational notes. The use of unstandardized interviews in field work allows researchers to better understand the situations, people, and events that they observe and to access valuable information that might otherwise be missed.

The principal disadvantage of unstandardized interviews is their inability to offer comparability between subjects. In other words, because the same set of stimuli has not systematically been provided to every subject, their responses are not necessarily analytically comparable.

Semistandardized Interviews

Midway between the extremes of the standardized and the unstandardized interview is the semistandardized interview. This style of interviewing uses a series of predetermined questions that are systematically asked of each respondent exactly as written on an interview schedule. However, in a semistandardized interview, the researcher may periodically deviate from the order of questioning and may even digress from the scheduled questions entirely. This digression allows the interviewer to pursue information far beyond what is provided by the answers to prepared standardized questions. Digression also allows the interviewer to create a more fluid informational exchange during the interview, thereby increasing rapport and the quality of responses.

The chief advantage of the semistandardized interview is its flexibility. The interviewer has more freedom to elicit greater knowledge and information from the respondent than is provided by the rigid, standardized interview structure. Nonetheless, the researcher is still able to analyze the responses to the scheduled questions, which are systematically comparable.

CONSTRUCTING QUESTIONNAIRES AND INTERVIEW SCHEDULES

The development of questionnaires and interviews begins in a similar manner. First, the researcher must decide on the nature of his or her research and whether it will be better served by a questionnaire or an interview. Second, the researcher must create a list of all the broad categories of interest to the study. For example, assume the researcher is interested in studying spouse abuse and, in particular, abused women. The broad research categories for such a survey might include the following:

1. Demographics
2. Basic family background information
3. History of victimization (outside the family)
4. History of victimization (inside the family)
5. Friendship and social patterns
6. Knowledge about spouse abuse
7. Perceptions of self-esteem and efficacy

Next, the researcher must develop questions that are relevant to each category and that have been operationalized to represent and measure concepts appropriate for the research. (Operationalization was discussed in Chapter 1.) The purpose of these questions will be to elicit information corresponding to the subjects' views and attitudes.

In effect, as the researcher creates questions to measure concepts related to each broad category, he or she is developing a draft of the instrument. The basic structure of each question will be determined based on decisions made by the researcher. Clearly, the decision to develop a questionnaire, rather than an interview schedule (or vice versa), makes an initial determination about the structure of the questions. Surveys are usually characterized by the use of *closed-ended*, or *forced-response* questions, whereas interviews typically use *open-ended* questions.

Closed-Ended, or
Forced-Response, Questions

A closed-ended question offers several choices of answers to the respondent. These answers are those that the researcher believes are the likely choices, but the option "other" is often included to provide for alternatives. The question and corresponding answers must all be carefully and clearly worded to assure that the subject understands them and can identify a response from those provided. Closed-ended questions are used regularly in questionnaire-based surveys and sometimes in interviews, as well.

The obvious advantage to closed-ended questions is the ease with which they can be coded. They can be computerized effortlessly, without the time-consuming creation of logs of corresponding numbers and categories. The corresponding disadvantage, however, is that the subject must fit his or her response into one of the options provided. Thus, the researcher forces the subject (sometimes imprecisely) to identify an answer from among the alternatives predetermined by the researcher, not the subject. Hence, the label *forced response* is sometimes applied to closed-ended questions.

Open-Ended Questions

Opened-ended questions are designed to provide subjects with the latitude of responding with the greatest amount of fluidity and personal discretion. For example, if a researcher were to ask a sample of college students what constitutes "date rape," they might respond with a variety of characteristics, such as forced sexual contact, forced vaginal penetration, unwanted genital touching, taking sexual advantage of an intoxicated partner, sexual contact preceded by violence, and so on. In other words, the researcher can expect a lexicon of responses, reflecting various nuances of how college students see and understand date rape. Later, after receiving the subjects' answers, the researcher can categorize and subsequently analyze these various responses.

Open-ended questions are most useful when investigators are interested in learning how certain groups of people think about given issues.

Interviews are largely composed of open-ended questions, although several closed-questions may also be included. When open-ended questions are used in questionnaires, the usual intent is to elicit brief statements and not lengthy, complete explanations about certain events. Conversely, in interview schedules, open-ended questions are the norm and may be followed by a number of probes that will draw out full descriptions of certain events or issues.

Coding open-ended questions used in questionnaires is somewhat more difficult than coding closed-ended responses. Since questionnaire responses are usually brief, they are likely to be categorized and the categories numerically coded in a process sometimes referred to as *data reduction*. In this process, nominal data are transformed into numerical codes, making them more comparable with the data obtained from closed-ended responses.

When used in interviews, open-ended questions are coded using some variation on content analysis (Berg, 1995). When using content-analytic strategies, the nominal and textual character of the data may be preserved and displayed.

ETHNOGRAPHY

So far, this chapter has described several similarities between two major techniques of data collection: questionnaire-based surveys and interviews. As we move on to discuss *ethnography,* we will see a number of vivid contrasts. Surveys and interviews can be conducted virtually anywhere, administered by the respondent or researcher, and completed at virtually any hour of the day. But ethnographic research, by definition, can only be conducted when and where the phenomenon under consideration naturally occurs.

Ethnographic research is sometimes referred to as *natural scientific research* (Denzin, 1978) or simply *field research* (Berg, 1995; Guy et al., 1987). Even though definitions of ethnographic research vary somewhat, one element common to all is that ethnography "places the researchers in the midst of whatever it is they study" (Berg, 1989, p. 52). Some textbooks label as "ethnographic" any research that takes the investigator into the field or natural setting. This type of research can be contrasted with that in which an investigator identifies a sample of subjects and artificially brings them into his or her study through the use of questionnaires or interviews. Ethnographic research moves the investigator into the natural setting that his or her potential subjects inhabit. The subjects then come to the researcher, who works in their setting in a fluid and reflexive manner.

The Ethnographic Record

James Spradley (1979) suggests that a wide variety of items can be used effectively when conducting ethnographic research: photographs, recordings (audio and video), relevant newspaper and magazine articles, interviews, surveys, and, of course, direct observations. In effect, any documentation of the phenomenon under investigation should go into the ethnographic record.

Note that many textbooks limit their discussions to *field research* and *observations in field research*. There is nothing intrinsically wrong with this; surely, many of the data collected in field studies or ethnographies are observational. Yet the types of data included in field studies should not be restricted. A wide variety of material may be useful and relevant to the study of certain phenomena. Nonetheless, one major means of gathering data in the field is observation.

Observations in Field Settings

Observation is usually a central means of collecting data in ethnographic studies. Observations may vary in their degree of structure and reflect the kinds of settings or types of events, people, and behaviors under investigation. One researcher may enter the field with a very clear focus and goals for his or her research, whereas another may enter the field with virtually no aim other than to discover how inhabitants of the setting live, work, and play together. Researchers may also immerse themselves, or "culturally soak" (Ellen, 1984), by participating in the ongoing situations they are investigating.

A classic example of an ethnographic study that uses observation as a major data-gathering technique is Laud Humphreys's (1970, 1975) analysis of homosexual encounters in a public bathroom. Humphreys used a bathroom in a California public park as his research setting. Serving as a lookout and voyeur, or "watch queen," Humphreys observed various sexual interactions between men in the bathroom. Humphreys' research led to the social scientific acceptance of homosexual activities as a lifestyle and behavioral choice, rather than a biological dysfunction.

Many textbooks credit the *Chicago School* (the sociology department at the University of Chicago during the 1920s through early 1940s) with spawning observational research strategies. The nature of observational research is to place oneself in a setting in a manner that will (1) allow the researcher to visually observe as much interaction between parties as possible or (2) provide the researcher access to participate in interactions among parties without seriously disrupting the process.

In the first case, the researcher's role is called the *nonparticipant observer,* and in the second case, the *participant observer.* Each of these perspectives or researcher roles offers a slightly different view of the setting. The nonparticipant observer is free to devote all his or her attention to observing the interactions, events, and processes under investigation. The participant observer must split his or her time between strictly observing and actually participating. The advantage of being a nonparticipant observer is obtaining a potentially more comprehensive description of observable details. The advantage in being a participant observer is that not only does the researcher observe and record the event, but he or she also experiences the emotions and interests of the people under study.

UNOBTRUSIVE RESEARCH

Much of the research conducted by social scientists relies on direct contact with subjects, whether observing them in their natural setting, interviewing them in a convenient location, or having them complete some sort of questionnaire. This type of contact with subjects is described by many research textbooks as being *intrusive* in subjects' lives.

Given the questioning that usually occurs in research about the validity of results and reliability of data, we might ask whether intrusion in some manner taints or biases the eventual analytic results.

An alternative to this intrusive approach to collecting data is *unobtrusive,* or *nonreactive,* data collection. To a large extent, all unobtrusive strategies use a variation of observation. In this case, however, the researcher observes various traces of human activity and behavior (Abrahamson, 1983; Berg, 1995; Shaughnessy & Zechmeister, 1990). *Traces* refer both to the accumulation of various by-products left by people, whether intentionally or inadvertently, and to the erosion caused by people or natural phenomena (i.e., weathering). Through traces, researchers can observe what factors motivate people to behave in certain ways, how people structure their daily lives, how different cultural or political ideologies affect people's behavior, and so forth.

Textbook descriptions of unobtrusive measures sometimes conjure in the minds of readers images of detectives using clues and bits of physical evidence to solve complicated crimes. In fact, this is not unlike the use of unobtrusive measures in research. However, you don't need to be Sherlock Holmes to conduct unobtrusive social scientific research. A number of strategies can be used to conduct unobtrusive research. Webb et al. (1966, 1981), Berg (1989, 1995), and to a large measure Shaughnessy and Zechmeister (1990) establish three major categories: archival strategies, accretion measures, and erosion measures.

Archival Strategies

Archives can be defined as any "running record" (Webb et al., 1981), regardless of the location or means of housing the record. Archives include birth and death certificates kept in a local courthouse; books and documents shelved in a library; videotapes displayed in a video-rental store; admission, disposition, and discharge records stored in a hospital computer; and even rows of tombstones in a graveyard. Records may be maintained by individuals, public institutions, private corporations, governments, and even social organizations. Hence, archives may be either public or private, easy or difficult to access.

For example, incident reports and initial complaint reports are usually held in municipal police departments and can be accessed easily. Reports of sexual assaults and crimes involving juveniles are usually held in these same police departments, but access may be restricted or denied to researchers. Nonetheless, all these files represent a kind of public archive.

Private archives may be represented by personal libraries, or private collections of documents held by various institutions, including libraries. Private archives may also include diaries and autobiographies, letters, home movies/videos, and various artistic endeavors (e.g., drawings, sketches, doodles). When these various documents occur naturally, without prompting by an investigator, they are called *unsolicited documents.* In other situations, documents may be the products of requests or solicitations by investigators, in which case they are called *solicited documents.*

An example of an unsolicited private document might be the daily journal or diary of a serial killer on death row. Information such as this might be very useful to an investigator interested in understanding what serial killers think about or perhaps what motivates them. An example of a solicited document might also be a diary written by a serial killer but one that an investigator requested the inmate to create. The specific difference between an unsolicited and solicited document, therefore, is whether it was self-initiated or created at the behest of a researcher.

Using archival records has a number of advantages. First, archival records can usually be accessed with relatively little expense and difficulty. They are a source of data that is immediately available to the investigator, one that doesn't require survey construction, pilot tests, or similar concerns. Second, archival documents are nonintrusive, which means there is no chance of research reactivity or potential biasing effects when conducting archival research. Third, the use of archival data along with data collected by other techniques (e.g., surveys, observations, interviews) can augment and validate analyses and findings.

Researchers must, of course, be mindful of several disadvantages when working with archival data, the most serious of which is the possibility of omissions or misleading inclusions.

Webb et al. (1981) refer to problems regarding selective deposits and selective survival. *Selective deposits* refer to documents that have possibly been edited or altered in some manner. *Selective survival* describes documents in which portions are missing, rendering the documents incomplete. Regardless of whether these alterations to archival documents have occurred intentionally or inadvertently, researchers must carefully consider the biases and potential informational gaps that might result.

Accretion and Erosion Strategies

When researchers examine the physical artifacts and traces of human activity in a field setting, these items provide measures of accretion or erosion. *Accretion* is the building up or accumulation of materials and products, and *erosion* is the wearing away or deterioration of materials.

Accretion Measures

Ecological concerns have increased rapidly in recent years. Because of this concern, the examination of certain types of human traces may be advantageous and also provide clues to contemporary social culture. In this case, *traces* refer to items that people have disposed of: garbage. There is, in fact, a national movement in the United States to recycle various items such as glass, paper, cardboard, plastic, and metals, which requires separating them into designated containers. The materials collected through recycling provide a wealth of potential unobtrusive data.

Over 30 years ago, Sawyer (1961) employed a similar version of "garbageology" to examine rates of liquor sales in Wellesley, Massachusetts, a so-called dry town (i.e., no liquor stores were permitted). Sawyer obtained estimates of liquor sales by sifting through the garbage at the town dump and counting the number of discarded liquor bottles.

It would be interesting (and somewhat cleaner) to replicate such a study today by examining the contents of recycling containers. We could investigate which neighborhoods or communities consume what proportion of beer, wine, and hard liquor. We might even be able to identify certain ethnic or religious clusters of people

through their alcohol consumption. For example, in communities in which disproportionate amounts of kosher wines have been identified, we might have uncovered a cluster of Jewish families. In short, the examination of alcohol bottles disposed of in recycling containers could yield a number of interesting findings.

Erosion Measures

Erosion measures include evidence that indicates selective wear or use on some object or material. In most research, erosion measures, like accretion measures, are used along with other techniques for corroboration.

Erosion measures provide interesting documentation occurrences in natural settings. In one well-quoted study, Edward Shils examined erosion at the Chicago Museum of Science and Industry (Berg, 1989, p. 98; Webb et al., 1981, p. 7). In his study, Shils learned that the vinyl tiles around an exhibit of live, hatching chicks had to be replaced approximately every six weeks, whereas the tiles around other exhibits went unchanged for years. A comparative examination of the rates of tile replacement throughout the museum produced rough estimates of how attractive the visiting public found certain exhibits.

The actual difference between accretion and erosion measures is not always clear cut. In some cases, what one researcher might identify as an *accretion* measure might be called an *erosion* measure by another researcher. For example, in the previous discussion of the naturally occurring accretion of disposed alcohol containers, we could argue that since the containers were originally filled with alcoholic beverages and are now empty, they are an erosion measure. To some extent, then, this designation is a matter of perspective, and whether the measure is called an accretion or erosion measure amounts to unnecessary terminological hairsplitting.

Another interesting perspective involves the use by some researchers of both naturally occurring and more controlled measures of accretion or erosion. In this type of case, the investigator arranges a situation in which some accretion or erosion measure that he or she has created can be measured along with any naturally occurring measures. For example, Friedman and Wilson (1975) placed dots of glue between adjacent pages at different intervals throughout textbooks before students purchased them for a given course. At the conclusion of the semester, the researchers collected the books and examined them.

First, they examined each glued pair of pages in each text and recorded how many there were and which had been separated. Next, the researchers noted the frequencies and locations of passages that students had underlined. These underlined segments provided the researchers with a natural accretion measure, which could be compared along with the controlled erosion measure: the glued pages. What the researchers found was quite surprising: Analysis of both the naturally occurring and controlled measures suggested that students more often read the first several chapters than the remaining chapters of their textbooks.

The use of various unobtrusive measures provides a rich and interesting source of data. The kinds of unobtrusive measures available to researchers are limited only to their imagination. As a stand-alone data set, a single unobtrusive measure may be questionable, in some cases, but when used with other data-collection strategies, each technique tends to strengthen the other. This procedure is referred to as data *triangulation.*

TRIANGULATION

The term *triangulation* was originally used in geographic-surveying activities, map making, navigation, and military applications. In these fields, triangulation involves using three known points or objects to draw sighting lines toward an unknown point or object. Usually, the three sighting lines intersect, forming a small triangle called the *triangle of error.* The best estimate of the true location of the new point or object is the center of the triangle, assuming that the three lines are about equal in error. Although sightings can be done with two lines intersecting at one point, a third line permits a more accurate estimate of the location of the unknown point or object.

Triangulation was first used in the social sciences as a metaphor describing a form of *multiple operationalism* or *convergent validation* (Campbell, 1956; Campbell & Fisk, 1959). In this context, triangulation largely was used to describe multiple data-collection technologies designed to measure single concepts or constructs (data triangulation). However, Denzin (1978, p. 292) introduced an additional metaphor, *lines of action,* which characterizes the use of multiple data-collection technologies, multiple theories, multiple researchers, multiple methodologies, or combinations of these four elements of research activities.

If your instructor asked all the students in your class to look out the window and describe what they saw, the results might be quite diverse. For instance, one person might see a "large" tree; another, a "tall, oaklike" tree; a third, a "spreading, green, shade" tree; and a fourth, a "pin-oak" tree. In short, each person might see a slightly different facet of the same tree, yet their descriptions would all share some basic essence: a tree. If we took these observations together, we would be better able to visualize what the students saw: in this case, a tall, green, spreading, pin-oak tree.

So it is with triangulation. When the researcher uses multiple lines of action, he or she manages to improve the final results. Doing so increases the validity of a research project by demonstrating that similar conclusions have been obtained when using diverse lines of action. Findings that are largely bound to a single method may be difficult to accept and not taken very seriously. Method-bound results may be artifacts of a given technique and not true findings. While it is unlikely that multiple lines of action will result in identical findings, multiple lines of action should offer sufficient overlap and similarity to make the findings quite convincing, as demonstrated by the example of the pin-oak tree.

REFERENCES

Abrahamson, M. (1983). *Social research methods.* Englewood Cliffs, NJ: Prentice-Hall.

Babbie, E. (1989). *The practice of social research.* Belmont, CA: Wadsworth.

Berg, B. L. (1989). *Qualitative research methods for the social sciences.* Boston: Allyn and Bacon.

Berg, B. L. (1995). *Qualitative research methods for the social sciences* (2nd ed.). Boston: Allyn and Bacon.

Campbell, D. T. (1956). *Leadership and its effects upon the group.* Columbus, OH: The Ohio State University Press.

Campbell, D. T., & Fisk, D. W. (1959, March). Convergent and discriminant validation by the multivariate-multimethod matrix. *Psychological Bulletin, 56*, 81–105.

Denzin, N. (1978). *The research act.* New York: McGraw-Hill.

Ellen, R. E. (1984). *Ethnographic research.* New York: Academic Press.

Fitzgerald, J. D., & Cox, S. M. (1987). *Research methods in criminal justice.* Chicago: Nelson-Hall.

Friedman, M. P., & Wilson, R. W. (1975). Application of unobtrusive measures in a study of textbook usage by college students. *Journal of Applied Psychology, 60,* 659–662.

Goffman, E. (1967). *Interaction rituals.* New York: Anchor Books.

Gorden, R. L. (1987). *Interviewing* (4th ed.). Chicago: Dorsey Press.

Guy, R. F., Edgley, C. E., Arafat, I., & Allen, D. E. (1987). *Social research methods.* Boston: Allyn and Bacon.

Humphreys, L. (1970). *Tearoom trade.* Chicago: Aldine.

Humphreys, L. (1975). *Tearoom trade: Impersonal sex in places* (enl. ed.). Chicago: Aldine.

Sawyer, H. G. (1961). "The meaning of numbers." Paper presented at the Association of Advertising Agencies.

Shaughnessy, J. J., & Zechmeister, E. B. (1990). *Research methods in psychology.* New York: McGraw-Hill.

Spradley, J. P. (1979). *The ethnographic interview.* New York: Holt, Rinehart & Winston.

Sudman, S., & Bradburn, N. M. (1981). *Asking questions: A practical guide to questionnaire design.* San Francisco: Jossey-Bass.

Webb, E., Campbell, D. T., Schwartz, R. D., & Sechrest, L. (1966). *Unobtrusive measures: Nonreactive research in the social sciences.* Chicago: Rand McNally.

Webb, E., Campbell, D. T., Schwartz, R. D., Sechrest, L., & Grove, J. B. (1981). *Nonreactive measures in the social sciences.* Boston: Houghton Mifflin.

Gender and Delinquency in White-Collar Families: A Power-Control Perspective

John Hagan and Fiona Kay
Crime and Delinquency
Vol. 36, No. 3, pp. 391–407, July 1990

Introduction

The concept of white-collar crime is entrenched in the public vernacular, although we have neither an accepted definition nor established explanation of this phenomenon (Gibbons, 1979:62–64). In this context, it may seem presumptuous to expand our inquiry to white-collar delinquency. Yet the expansion of criminological research to include the study of adolescents has greatly advanced our understanding of criminogenesis (Hirschi and Rudisill, 1976), largely because of the part socialization is assumed to play in adult criminality (Toby, 1974) and because adolescents are more accessible for research than adults. These points may apply as much or more to the topic of white-collar crime. This set of premises motivates the following study of class and gender variations in youthful violations of patents and copyrights through the copying of audio- and videotapes and computer software.

Operationalizing White-Collar Delinquency

The ambiguities and contradictions of white-collar illegalities are such that the *New York Times* recently published two stories in the same edition, one that warned and possibly discouraged its readers from "pirating" computer software (Lewis, 1989), and another which informed and likely encouraged its readers to acquire newly designed devices to copy audiotapes (Fantel, 1989). The contradiction probably was unnoticed, but the latter story nonetheless began with a mildly apologetic and perhaps not entirely facetious suggestion:

Among the higher animals and human beings, larceny seems to be an innate trait held in check by social conditioning. But inhibitions fail, and the primal impulse asserts itself when it comes to tape recording. Even decent folk, who refrain from pocketing silver spoons, think nothing of taping copyrighted music (Fantel, 1989:27).

Yet this Everyperson's version of Tolstoy's lament (that "the seeds of every crime are in every one of us") may be as misleading as it is revealing: for these violations of patents and copyrights, as widespread as they might be, are probably not distributed randomly across the population. They likely are committed more often by males than by females, and they may also be committed more often by the rich than the poor.

The latter possibility, of course, raises the specter of white-collar illegality. This brings into play a primary feature of white-collar crime: the position or status of the perpetrator. Equally primary features are that the behavior causes social injury and is liable to penal sanction. However, the sanction may be more a matter of legal theory than prosecutorial practice, as clearly is the case with patent and copyright violations for personal pleasure. What is more relevant here is the legal proscription. Meanwhile, white-collar crimes are sometimes also restricted by definition to include activities undertaken in association with work. Patents and copyrights are, of course, a part of the world of work, but their violations need not be in association with occupation.

We propose that the copying of audio- and videotapes and computer software by adolescents have necessary and sufficient characteristics of a broader genre we call white-collar delinquency. These violations of patents and copyrights cause social injury in the form of lost income and profit, they are threatened with penal sanctions (i.e., as indicated on audiocassette containers, in the lead-ins to film videos, and on the packaging of computer software), and they are a growing part of the information economy, as well as Western youth culture. But: is the expropriation of these copyrighted cultural commodities class-linked? And: is this activity otherwise socially patterned and explainable? Power-control theory answers affirmatively.

A Power-Control Perspective on White-Collar Delinquency

Power-control theory (e.g., Hagan, Gillis, and Simpson, 1985:1154–56; Hagan, 1989: chap. 6) encourages consideration of the conditions under which adolescents are free to deviate from social norms. It assumes that both the presence of power and the absence of control contribute to this freedom. For most common forms of delinquency, it is suggested that males are freer to deviate than females; and for some common forms of delinquency, it is suggested that the freedom to deviate will be directly related to class position.

Special attention is given in power-control theory to two kinds of power, or relations of dominance, that channel restrictions on a freedom to deviate that we all might otherwise pursue with equal abandon: (a) the controls exercised or experienced by parents in relation to others in the workplace, and (b) the controls exercised by parents in relation to their children. We already have considered the tastes for risk and feelings of freedom from normative and legal constraints that may be evoked by high positions of class power and dispersed through youth culture. We turn next, then, to the role of familial controls in transmitting effects of gender on white-collar delinquency.

The Sample: Crestwood Heights Revisited

An obvious reason that little research has been done on white-collar delinquency is that children of highly placed white-collar families form a small part of the population who are more difficult than the children of more typical families to sample for the purposes of survey research. However, to effectively investigate the role of powerful class positions on illicit behavior, it is necessary to stratify samples along class lines and oversample from among the most powerful class segments of the population. Yet few studies have singled out white-collar families for the purposes of survey research. An exception is a study of the affluent Canadian community called Crestwood Heights (Seeley, Sim, and Loosely, 1956), the setting for an important part of the research reported below.

The Seeley study was undertaken during the post–World War II affluence of the early 1950's, a period that may rival the final decade of the twentieth century in its preoccupation with material wealth. Crestwood Heights, known locally as Forest Hills, was (and is even more so today) a very appropriate place to consider matters of material wealth and power. Located within the city of Toronto, the boundaries of Crestwood Heights define the wealthiest political jurisdiction in Canada.

We returned to Crestwood Heights to collect a part of the sample for this study. We initially did so through the files of a provincial agency that records assessed home values and enumerates eligible voters. These records made it possible to identify persons living in homes assessed above threshold property value who are also parents of adolescent children. Property in this community is not assessed at current market value, so it was necessary to estimate the meaning of a threshold established for inclusion in the sample: This value is well above a half million 1989 U.S. dollars.

In the winter and spring of 1988, respondents were contacted by mail and asked to return questionnaires either by mail or in person. (In this part of the research design, mothers as well were asked to complete a survey instrument, although these responses are not analyzed here.) This part of the sample included 328 respondents. This represents a conservatively estimated response rate of just over 55%, which was achieved over a 9-month period with four follow-up reminders. Because there was a significant margin of error in the enumeration list indication of ages of adolescents in these families, and because we insisted that the adolescents be between 14 and 18, we believe a more accurate and still conservative estimation of our response rate is over 60%. The average family income in this part of the sample was over $100,000 a year.

The second part of our sample was drawn from three schools in an adjoining area of the Metropolitan Toronto that is quite heterogeneous in class composition. The school youth were selected through a probability sampling of classes. Invitations to participate during lunch periods were distributed in randomly selected 9th- through 12th-grade classes. The school sample included 562 students, with a response rate of 67.2%.

A choice of popular album tapes was offered as an inducement to participate in both parts of the study, resulting in a combined sample of 890 students and a response rate of over 60%.

Measurement

A central concept in this study is, of course, class position. This concept is a source of uncertainty in the study of white-collar illegality, in part because of confusion that probably was inadvertently introduced by Sutherland (1983:7) when he wrote that a white-collar crime is a "crime committed by a person of respectability and high social status." . . . Although Sutherland often implied much more, status today is understood as a social-psychological concept that refers to the perceived relative position of an individual in a hierarchy of respect. . . .

[I]n the current study we used a relational conception of class (see Wright, 1980; Hagan and Parker, 1985; Hagan et al., 1985), based on employment and the authority relations parents occupy in their work. The criteria for the class categories we applied are set out in Table 1 and are based on the work experiences of *both* mothers and fathers (cf. Hagan et al., 1987), as reported by their adolescent children.

Respondents were assigned to categories in the above taxonomy using conditional transformation in the SPSSX software package. Transformations were made in sequence for each category in the taxonomy, so that cases that satisfy specified criteria were included, and cases that did not meet the criteria were passed on to the next command structure. In the multivariate analyses, employed workers were treated as the omitted comparison category. Gender was treated as a dummy variable, with sons coded 1.

The remaining endogenous variable in the power control model of youthful violations of

TABLE 1   Criteria for Class Categories

CLASS	EMPLOYMENT RELATION	AUTHORITY RELATION	DISTRIBUTION (IN PERCENTAGES)
Employers	Employer	Employs	24.0 (215)
Petite bourgeoisie	Self-employed	None	5.9 (53)
Managers	Employee	Unsupervised manager of subordinates	13.7 (123)
Supervisors	Employee	Supervised supervisors of subordinates	2.4 (291)
Employed workers	Employee	Supervised subordinate	20.1 (190)
Surplus workers	Unemployed	None	3.9 (35)

NOTE: *N*s in parentheses

patents and copyrights built on earlier work (see Hagan et al., 1987; 1988) and included measures of parental relational and instrumental control, risk preferences, perceived risks, and white-collar delinquency. Each concept is measured as a summed scale. . . .

Discussion and Conclusions

A power-control perspective on white-collar delinquency is not fully satisfying, but it does provide useful insights into aspects of white-collar crime that to this point have not been well understood or studied. One way of making this point is to note some disjunctures between social scientific and journalistic considerations of contemporary white-collar crime.

Two themes frequently emphasized in journalistic exposes are the prognostic signs of indiscretion in the early lives of those later found responsible for white-collar crimes, and the absence of need as a motivation for these crimes. Consider the involvement of Richard Nixon in perhaps the best known of contemporary white-collar crimes, Watergate. These crimes were committed in the absence of need, as signified by one of the largest electoral victories in American history; and early signs of events to follow continue to be uncovered in multivolume Nixon biographies, one of which recently reported a break-in of the Duke Law School Records Office by the later President for an early look at his term marks. Power-control theory speaks to these issues: (a) by pointing to exogenous conditions (i.e., class position and gender) that increase freedom (rather than the need) to deviate, and (b) by emphasizing socialization experiences (e.g., weak parental controls) that intervene in and in their own right influence processes that increase the likelihood of white-collar delinquency.

Two aspects of white-collar crime and delinquency that are neglected in our research involve the roles of access to machinery, technical knowledge, and peers in the causation of white-collar delinquency. Male and employer class adolescents may have better access and know more about the techniques that are necessary for patent and copyright violations and other forms of white-collar delinquency, and the knowledge and motivation of these activities may be promoted within adolescent peer groups, especially among males. Yet it also should be noted that the machinery and motivation needed for some of these activities is minimal, as illustrated by the audiotape copying capacity available in most "ghetto blasters" and "boom boxes." Of the three components of our scale of patent and copyright violations, copying audiotapes actually correlates most strongly with employer class position.

References

Fantel, Hans. 1989. "Tape-Copying Decks Improve Their Act." *New York Times,* July 9 sec. 2, p. 27. Copyright © 1990 by The New York Times Company. Reprinted by permission.

Gibbons, Don. 1979. *The Criminological Enterprise.* Englewood Cliffs, New Jersey: Prentice-Hall.

Hagan, John. 1989. *Structural Criminology.* New Brunswick, NJ: Rutgers University Press.

Hagan, John, A.R. Gillis, and John Simpson. 1985. "The Class Structure of Gender and Delinquency: Toward a Power-Control Theory of Common Delinquent Behavior." *American Journal of Sociology* 90:1151-78.

———. 1987. "Class in the Household: A Power-Control Theory of Gender and Delinquency." *American Journal of Sociology* 92:788-816.

———. 1988. "Feminist Scholarship, Relational and Instrumental Control and a Power-Control Theory of Gender and Delinquency." *British Journal of Sociology* 39:301-36.

Hagan, John and Patricia Parker. 1985. "White Collar Crime and Punishment: The Class Structure and Legal Sanctioning of Securities Violations." *American Sociological Review* 50:302-16.

Hirschi, Travis and David Rudisill. 1976. "The Great American Search: Causes of Crime: 1876–1976." Pp. 11–15 in *Annals of the American Academy of Political and Social Science.* Salem, NH: Ayer.

Lewis, Peter. 1989. "Cracking Down on Computer Pirates." *New York Times,* July 9, p. 10.

Seeley, J., R.A. Sim, and E. Loosley. 1956. *Crestwood Heights.* Toronto: University of Toronto Press.

Sutherland, Edwin. 1983. *White Collar Crime: The Uncut Version.* New Haven: Yale University Press.

Toby, Jackson. 1974. "The Socialization and Control of Deviant Motivation." Pp. 85-100 in *Handbook of Criminology,* edited by D. Glaser. Chicago: Rand McNally.

Wright, Erik Olin. 1980. "Varieties of Marxist Conceptions of Class Structure." *Politics and Society* 9:299–322.

Name of Student _____

Student ID # _____

Course Section # _____

Date _____

1. Identify six variables you could use to conduct a study on delinquency.

    1. _____

    2. _____

    3. _____

    4. _____

    5. _____

    6. _____

2. Now, operationally define each variable. Be certain to indicate what indices can be used to measure each operationalized variable.

    1. _____

    _____

    _____

    _____

    _____

    _____

    2. _____

    _____

    _____

    _____

    _____

    3. _____

    _____

    _____

    _____

    4. _____

    _____

    _____

_____

_____

5. _____

_____

_____

_____

_____

6. _____

_____

_____

_____

_____

3. Using the operationalized variables, create a survey that could be used in a study of delinquents from white-collar families. Be sure to include demographic questions relating to subjects' white-collar status.

_____

_____

_____

_____

_____

_____

_____

_____

_____

_____

_____

_____

_____

_____

_____

_____

_____

The Consequences of Professionalism among Police Chiefs

Robert M. Regoli, John P. Crank, and Robert G. Culbertson
Justice Quarterly
Vol. 6, No. 1, pp. 47–67, March 1989

Introduction

Police chiefs are perhaps the most influential policy makers within their departments. They are responsible for the agency's day-to-day operation; more important, the agendas established during their tenure set the style of police service for the community (Bordua and Reiss, 1966; Wilson, 1968). The chief's power to influence the course of police services arises from two sources: the chief makes procedural decisions on the implementation of policy as well as substantive decisions concerning the allocation of departmental resources and the extent and type of law enforcement that will be practiced (Brown, 1981). The chief's perception of the "proper" police function can lead to enforcement policies that are reactive and community-based or to policies that are aggressively proactive, with crime-prevention programs and universal enforcement of law. Thus police chiefs' attitudes (and the factors affecting them) may have far-reaching implications and effects (Nees, 1986).

Police chiefs' attitudes have been influenced by the police professions movement. Reform among police has been integral to the historical development of American law enforcement (Fogelson, 1977); this movement has affected and often has guided the tenor and style of police services (Mauss, 1975). Issues such as lateral entry, college degree requirements, specialized police functions, and civilian review boards have generated controversy and confrontation (Brown, 1981; Sherman and National Advisory Commission on Higher Education, 1978).

Methods

Data Production

Data were derived from questionnaire responses by 574 of 771 Illinois police chiefs (74.4 percent). We generated the list of chiefs by complete enumeration of Illinois police jurisdictions, using information from official publications of the Illinois Department of Law Enforcement. Following procedures established by Dillman (1978), we mailed a survey questionnaire to the chief of each jurisdiction. Three days after the survey was mailed, we sent a postcard prompt as a reminder and a thank-you to all chiefs. One month later, we sent a second mailing to officials who had not responded to the first mailing. Then, 30 days later, we sent a third survey packet by certified mail to the officials who had not responded to our first two requests.

Measurement of Variables

We measured professionalism using Snizek's (1972) modification of Hall's (1968) Likert-formatted inventory. Factor analysis was used to estimate the extent to which Snizek's (1972) professionalism factor structure is replicated in the present sample of chiefs.

Findings

Our findings are presented in two sections. The first section is a descriptive analysis of our sample of Illinois police chiefs, in which we discuss their level of professionalism, their job satisfaction, their self-perceptions regarding work relations, and their attitudes toward aspects of professionalization. In the second section we assess the interrelationships among the variables. Specifically we report on the impact of professionalism on police chiefs' job satisfaction, work relations, and professionalization.

Sample Characteristics

Our first concern is with the characteristics of professionalism among Illinois police chiefs. We are curious to learn whether police chiefs are generally professional and whether they rank higher on some dimensions of professionalization than on others.

Police chiefs display the highest level of professionalism on IACP-REFERENT [use of the professional organization the Illinois Association of Chiefs of Police as a professional referent]. They are more likely to support professional police organizations both by reading professional journals and by attending professional meetings. Their agreement with the items forming this dimension only slightly exceeds CALLING, their belief in the intrinsic value of police work. PUBLIC SERVICE ranks third, following by AUTONOMY and SELF-REGULATION.

Second, we will report on chiefs' responses to service-related outcomes. We are concerned with the extent to which chiefs are satisfied with their employment, their perceptions of their work relations, and attitudes toward aspects of professionalism.

Chiefs are generally a satisfied lot. The midpoint of the job satisfaction scale (between "satisfied" and "dissatisfied") is 2.5; the value 4 indicates the highest response, or "very satisfied." In six of the job satisfaction categories, the chiefs' average scores fall between "satisfied" and "very satisfied." Chiefs score highest on ASSIGNMENT, followed by WORKING HOURS, SAFETY, JOB CONDITIONS, JOB TRAINING, PROMOTION CHANCES, JOB SECURITY, and SALARY.

Next we examine chiefs' work relations. Relations are coded in the same metric as job satisfaction. The midpoint of the distribution is 2.5; a response of 4 indicates the highest level of response. Chiefs' perceptions of the quality of their work relations are uniformly high. In every instance the average response is between "satisfied" and "very satisfied." Only relations with SERGEANTS stands out as slightly lower.

The Impact of Professionalism on Service-Related Variables

In this section we use multiple regression techniques to establish the impact of chiefs' professionalism on the various job-related categories. The five dimensions of professionalism [REFERENT, PUBLIC SERVICE, CALLING, AUTONOMY, and SELF-REGULATION] are regressed on each item within each category. We generated standardized regression coefficients to establish the impact of each dimension of professionalism on each item.

Job Satisfaction

What is the effect of a chief's level of professionalism on the eight criteria of job satisfaction?

Generally, no clear pattern of relationships emerge among the dimensions of professionalism and the criteria of job satisfaction, although several significant regression coefficients are shown. Three dimensions of professionalism affect significantly three or more of these criteria. AUTONOMY emerged as the most consistent predictor of job satisfaction. It attains significance in four instances: ASSIGNMENT, SAFETY, PROMOTION CHANCES, and JOB SECURITY. IACP-REFERENT attains statistical significance on three dimensions of job satisfaction: ASSIGNMENT, WORKING HOURS, and JOB TRAINING. CALLING also is significant in three instances: ASSIGNMENT, JOB CONDITIONS, and JOB SECURITY. PUBLIC SERVICE and SELF-REGULATION are the weakest overall predictors of job satisfaction.

Interestingly, PUBLIC SERVICE is related negatively to SAFETY: Chiefs who believe in the indispensability of the police to society also are more concerned with their personal SAFETY. The negative relationship between PUBLIC SERVICE and SAFETY addresses the link between the service orientation of the police and the safety that they provide to the public.

Work Relations

Next we examine the impact of professionalism on two areas of work relations: community and department relations.

First we look at chiefs' perceptions of their community relations. AUTONOMY, SELF-REGULATION, and CALLING significantly influence relations with the CAUCASIAN PUBLIC. The more professional chiefs believe that they have better relations with their constituency than do chiefs who score lower on professionalism. Next we look at selected dimensions of department relations: relations with LIEUTENANTS AND ABOVE, SERGEANTS, BLACK OFFICERS, CAUCASIAN OFFICERS, and CIVILIAN PERSONNEL. The most consistent predictor of department relations is SELF-REGULATION, which significantly affects relations with CIVILIAN PERSONNEL, BLACK OFFICERS, CAUCASIAN OFFICERS, and the CAUCASIAN PUBLIC.

CALLING also emerges as an important predictor of work relations. It exhibits significant effects on four areas of work relations: SERGEANTS, CIVILIAN PERSONNEL, CAUCASIAN OFFICERS, and the CAUCASIAN PUBLIC. Neither IACP-REFERENT nor PUBLIC SERVICE affects a chief's work relations; AUTONOMY is significant only in one instance, for relations with the CAUCASIAN PUBLIC.

Attitudes toward Aspects of Professionalism

With respect to ACCREDITATION, three dimensions of professionalism make significant contributions: IACP-REFERENT, PUBLIC SERVICE, and SELF-REGULATION. It is noteworthy that these dimensions affect attitudes toward criteria of professionalization in opposite directions. PUBLIC SERVICE, for instance, is related negatively to ACCREDITATION. In other words, the more professional chiefs are less disposed to weak accreditation.

When we turn to EDUCATION, the only significant predictor is PUBLIC SERVICE. This relationship runs counter to what we predicted: police chiefs who believe in the indispensability of the police function are less likely to favor increased formal education for their personnel. Thus we note once more that PUBLIC SERVICE is related negatively to an important police service outcome.

For TRAINING, two significant predictors stand out: IACP-REFERENT, and SELF-REGULATION. Finally, we see that DEDICATION and SELF-REGULATION influence SPECIALIZATION. The more dedicated chiefs are more likely to support the presence of specialized units in their departments. Chiefs who favor internal SELF-

REGULATION of the police, however, are less likely to support SPECIALIZATION. Increase in specialized squads fosters decentralization of the command structure and thus undermines chiefs' authority. Thus, chiefs who support colleague control are suspicious of relatively autonomous units; such units may be either insulated from their control or capable of resisting or overriding their influence.

When we examine the variance explained for each criterion of professionalization, professionalism predicts ACCREDITATION (R^2 = .136) most strongly followed by TRAINING (R^2 =.056), SPECIALIZATION (R^2 =.045), and EDUCATION (R^2 = .027). Each of these R^2 values is statistically significant; in each instance, however, only a small amount of variance is explained.

Of the eight significant predictors of professionalism, three are negative. We reach the anomalous conclusion that the more professional chiefs support some criteria of professionalization and reject others.

References

Bordua, David L. and Albert J. Reiss, Jr. (1966) "Command, Control, and Charisma: Reflections on Police Bureaucracy." *American Journal of Sociology* 72:68–76.

Brown, Michael K. (1981) *Working the Street: Police Discretion and the Limits of Reform.* New York: Russell Sage.

Dillman, Don A. (1978) *Mail and Telephone Surveys: The Total Design Method.* New York: Wiley.

Fogelson, Robert M. (1977) *Big City Police.* Cambridge: Harvard University Press.

Hall, Richard (1968) "Professionalization and Bureaucratization." *American Sociological Review* 33: 92–104.

Mauss, Armand L. (1975) *Social Problems as Social Movements.* Philadelphia: Lippincott.

Nees, Harold H. (1986) "Police Use of Discretion: A Comparison of Community, System, and Office Expectations." Ph.D. dissertation, University of Colorado at Denver.

Sherman, Lawrence W. and the National Advisory Commission on Higher Education for Police Officers (1978) *The Quality of Police Education.* San Francisco: Jossey-Bass.

Snizek, William E. (1972) "Hall's Professionalism Scale: An Empirical Reassessment." *American Sociological Review* 37: 109-12.

Wilson, James Q. (1968a) *Varieties of Police Behavior.* New York: Atheneum.

Name of Student _____

Student ID # _____

Course Section # _____

Date _____

1. Create five *Likert-formatted* questions that could be used to assess the concept "police professionalism."

   1. _____

   _____

   _____

   _____

   _____

   2. _____

   _____

   _____

   _____

   _____

   3. _____

   _____

   _____

   _____

   _____

   4. _____

   _____

   _____

   _____

   _____

   5. _____

   _____

   _____

   _____

   _____

2. Create five *forced-answer* questions that could be used to assess the concept "police professionalism."

   1. _____

   _____

   _____

   _____

   _____

   _____

   2. _____

   _____

   _____

   _____

   _____

   _____

   3. _____

   _____

   _____

   _____

   _____

   _____

   4. _____

   _____

   _____

   _____

   _____

   _____

   5. _____

   _____

   _____

   _____

   _____

   _____

3. Create five *open-ended* questions that could be used to assess the concept "police professionalism."

   1. _____

   _____

   _____

   _____

   2. _____

   _____

   _____

   _____

   3. _____

   _____

   _____

   _____

   4. _____

   _____

   _____

   _____

   5. _____

   _____

   _____

   _____

4. The Regoli, Crank, and Culbertson article used a mailed questionnaire-based survey, which was sent to a sample of police chiefs derived through a listing of Illinois police jurisdictions using information from official publications of the Illinois Department of Law Enforcement.

   a. How could you redesign this study to include a different sampling technique?

   _____

   _____

   _____

   _____

   _____

   _____

b. What alternative data-collection strategy might be substituted for mailed questionnaire-based surveys?

Drinking in the Dorms: A Study of the Etiquette of RA-Resident Relations

Earl Rubington
The Journal of Drug Issues
Vol. 20, No. 3, pp. 451–462, 1990

Introduction

Residential assistants (hereafter referred to as RAs) are the enforcement agents who are supposed to control drinking in the dorms. This paper examines how RAs define, interpret, and respond to infractions of college drinking rules. It focuses on social conditions which alter the definition and exercise of the RAs' authority.

RAs are clients of the organization which employs them. Similarly, they live in the very organization which asks them to exercise authority. In addition, proximity can increase the frequency, duration, and intensity of contacts with residents. These aspects of their situation make RAs' definition and enforcement of drinking rules problematic. Research on role-conflicts of prison guards, probation officers, foremen, and counselors in therapeutic communities show how changes in contacts with "client" alters control agents' status (Jacobs, 1977; Roethlisberger and Dickson, 1946; Rubington, 1965; Spencer, 1983). And these changes over time also change the way agents define and enforce rules. This exploratory study examines how changes in contact with residents and in RAs' status change the way RAs define, interpret, and respond to infractions of campus drinking rules. It suggests that an etiquette of RA-resident relations evolves over time and that this etiquette becomes the basis for solving mutual problems that may come up in the course of the enforcement of residence hall drinking rules.

Setting and Method

The Main Street Campus (the names of persons and places are fictitious) of City University (CU) is located in a commercial and residential section of Metro City. This study deals primarily with RAs who live and work in West Hall and East Hall. East and West were selected for study because they both house freshmen who are under the legal drinking age, they have men and women living on alternate floors, and they have different floor layouts. West Hall RAs live on an open corridor in the form of a square where thirty-two residents all live in double rooms. East hall RAs live at one end of a long corridor where thirty-five freshmen live in doubles, triples, and quads. The corridor generally is punctuated by one or more fire doors. This study is based on interviews with East Hall's residence director and eight of its RAs, with West Hall's residence director and nine of its twelve RAs, and with five RAs from other residence halls.

The Drinking Rules

The legal drinking age in the state at the time of this study was twenty. People who have yet to attain their twentieth birthday are enjoined from purchasing, serving, or consuming alcoholic beverages. Anyone who purchases or serves alcoholic beverages to alcoholic "minors" is likewise liable for criminal prosecution. In addition, city ordinance forbids both open containers in public, as well as drinking in public. CU agrees to uphold state statutes and tells RAs both in official documents, as well as in training sessions and orientations, that RAs must enforce state liquor laws.

In addition to these state laws and city ordinances, CU has its own rules and regulations on possession, consumption, and service of alcoholic beverages. Students under twenty cannot possess, serve, or consume alcoholic beverages. Students of legal drinking age can possess, serve, and consume alcoholic beverages, but only in their own rooms. No drinking is allowed in common areas such as hallways, stairwells, elevators, lounges, cafeterias, and bathrooms.

Evolution of the Etiquette

Changes take place over the academic year in contacts RAs have with residents of the whole building, as well as the residents on their own floor. The changes lead to status changes and ultimately, for some, changes in the definition and enforcement of drinking rules. Through a process of mutual socialization, RAs and residents evolve an etiquette for handling rules on drinking.

At school's start freshmen residents assign RAs to the master status of policeman (Becker, 1963; Hughes, 1945). This assignment makes many RAs personally uncomfortable. The passage of time, however, offers considerable opportunity to live down the stereotype and the negative feelings attached to it. In effect, as R-11 explains below, the RA goes from being the incumbent of a status and an authority figure to becoming a person in his or her own right.

> R-11: Freshmen think all RAs are alike. At the beginning of the year, they think you're out to restrict their freedom. After they get to know you, they change their attitudes. There are certain trouble-makers who may have a thing about RAs. But when residents get to know you on a personal basis, they find out that RAs are people. As they get to know you, they break down. And you're able to become more flexible. I started strict, then I found it gradually breaking down. You get close to them, you get to know them.

In a social environment that generates a high frequency of violations, RAs come to see that excessive application of sanctions only cheapens their value. Thus, RAs reduce sanctions as much as possible while at the same time developing a set of specific conditions for their applications. And these conditions arise, in time, out of the nature of RAs' duties, as well as the range

of social contacts they sustain in the course of residence hall life. When RAs are on duty, for example, they make their rounds over the entire building. At all other times, they are on call, but largely at the service of residents of their own floor. Thus, in the slow shift from status to personal contacts, they are much more likely to know more about residents of their own floors in contrast to residents of the entire building. Personal knowledge makes for differential enforcement of the drinking rules. As the excerpts below indicate, RAs sanction residents of their own floors differently from the way they sanction residents of other floors.

> R-6: You use your discretion. I treat guys on my floor different from the rest of the building. I treat my guys good. I know them better than anyone else. This quarter I've noticed there's more smoking than drinking. When they drink, they become loud and violent. When they smoke pot, they're mellow, quiet; they just hang out. I tell them I smell smoke, suggest they stuff towels in the door, spray Glade. The residents were shocked to find that I let 'em smoke. All the other RAs bust residents for smoking pot. My floor has less vandalism this quarter, probably because the residents have been smoking pot instead of drinking. If some of my guys are going to have a punch party, they tell me. I let them know who's on duty. I advise them to keep it quiet.

> R-23: I am less formal when I approach residents on my floor, more formal when I approach residents on other floors. With residents of other floors, I identify myself as an RA, I explain rules to them, then I make my request. With residents on my own floor, all I need to say is: "You know what you're doing."

A reciprocal of differential enforcement of rules on the home floor is that residents can repay their own RA by breaking the rules on other floors. When the RA is not around, residents may be expected to stray from the housing rules. However, when the RA is around, residents who want to stray can take themselves to other floors. Two women RAs independently of each other said in separate interviews that the residents of their floors were "not angels." By this they meant that their residents did get into trouble on other floors, not on theirs. These RAs learned of the trouble by reading about it in the log or else by having other RAs tell them about it. Getting into trouble on other floors is a way of showing respect for one's RA as well as saving face.

With time, then, RAs and residents arrive at mutual accommodations. Out of their collective experience with taking specific roles in situations of social control (that is, the enforcer and the one subject to rule enforcement), they constitute an agreement for how they will "work the rules."

Summary and Conclusions

In effect, RAs teach residents how to break drinking rules. Residents learn discretion in situations of social control. When an RA sees a student drinking in his or her room with the door open or walking in the hallway with a beer in hand, the RA suggests that the student drink in his or her room behind closed doors. Students with a "good attitude" accept the suggestion good-naturedly and retire to their rooms immediately. If in the future they never go out in the hallway with a beer in hand and always keep their door closed when drinking, they have learned "discretion."

Finally, the version of responsible drinking which RAs preach and sometimes teach by example has little to do with moderating or limiting amounts. Rather, it stems from one of the implicit norms of urban life. This is the norm of MYOB ("mind your own business") in a double sense. This norm requires discretion in deviance. Residents mind their business when drinking if they do so behind closed doors, keeping their voices and their stereos down. In so doing they do not disturb their neighbors nor come to the attention of RAs.

References

Becker, H.S.
  1963   *Outsiders,* New York: The Free Press.
Hughes, E.C.
  1945   Dilemmas and Contradictions of Status, *Amer. J. Soc.,* 50:353-359.
Jacobs, J.
  1977   *Stateville: The Penitentiary in Mass Society,* Chicago: University of Chicago Press.
Roethlisberger, F.J. and W.J. Dickson
  1946   *Management and The Worker,* Cambridge: Harvard University Press.
Rubington, E.
  1965   Organizational Strains and Key Roles, *Adm. Sci. Quarterly,* 9:350-369.
Spencer, J.E.
  1983   Accounts, Attitudes, and Solutions: Probation Officer-Defendant Negotiations of Subjective Orientations, *Soc. Probs.,* 30:570-581.

Name of Student _____

Student ID # _____

Course Section # _____

Date _____

1. Using the interview schedule that follows, conduct interviews with five undergraduate students in your class (your section or another section). You may want to tape record their answers. Be certain to explain that these brief interviews are confidential and that the students will remain anonymous. Also explain that these interviews are for a *class project and not genuine research.* If you tape the interviews, be sure to transcribe both questions and answers exactly as you hear them. Remove these sheets and transcribe your answers in the space provided. (Make copies of these sheets, as needed.)

Interview Schedule

a. First, I want to get some general information about you. What category of student are you (e.g., freshman, junior, etc.)?

   Subject #1 _____

   Subject #2 _____

   Subject #3 _____

   Subject #4 _____

   Subject #5 _____

b. How old were you on your last birthday?

   Subject #1 _____

   Subject #2 _____

   Subject #3 _____

   Subject #4 _____

   Subject #5 _____

c. Do you live in a residence dorm or off campus?

   Subject #1 _____

   Subject #2 _____

   Subject #3 _____

   Subject #4 _____

   Subject #5 _____

d. Do you ever have parties in your dorm room (substitute *house* or *apartment,* as appropriate)?

   Subject #1 _____

   Subject #2 _____

   Subject #3 _____

   Subject #4 _____

   Subject #5 _____

e. Is there ever any drinking of alcoholic beverages at these parties?

   Subject #1 _____

   Subject #2 _____

   Subject #3 _____

   Subject #4 _____

   Subject #5 _____

    f.   Do you ever drink any sort of alcoholic beverages in your room (substitute *house* or *apartment,* as appropriate) when there isn't a party going on?

Subject #1* _____

Subject #2* _____

Subject #3* _____

Subject #4* _____

Subject #5* _____

* If "yes," see "Probe Questions" that follow.

Probe Questions (ask only if answer to [f] is "yes")

    g.   What do you usually do when having these drinks?

Subject #1 _____

_____

Subject #2 _____

_____

Subject #3 _____

_____

Subject #4 _____

_____

Subject #5 _____

_____

    h.   Do you ever listen to loud music when drinking in your room (substitute *house* or *apartment,* as appropriate)?

Subject #1 _____

Subject #2 _____

Subject #3 _____

Subject #4 _____

Subject #5 _____

    i.   Have you ever gotten into trouble while you were drinking? (If "yes," ask: Could you tell me about that?)

Subject #1 _____

_____

Subject #2 _____

_____

Subject #3 _____

_____

Subject #4 _____

_____

Subject #5 _____

2. Using the answers to these interview questions, explain whether Rubington's general findings about "MYOB" drinking patterns are consistent with your investigation.

_____

_____

_____

_____

_____

_____

_____

_____

_____

_____

3. Compare your assessments with those of others in your class.

_____

_____

_____

_____

_____

_____

_____

_____

_____

_____

_____

Assessing Age and Gender Differences in Perceived Risk and Fear of Crime

Randy L. LaGrange and Kenneth F. Ferraro
Criminology: An Interdisciplinary Journal
Vol. 27, No. 4, pp. 697–718, November 1989

Introduction

The literature on fear of crime has grown substantially in the past two decades. Among the many descriptive analyses of sociodemographic correlates of fear, the most persistent findings are that women and older persons are highly afraid of crime (Braungart et al., 1980; Clemente and Kleiman, 1976; Cook and Cook, 1976; Lee, 1982; Mullen and Donnermeyer, 1985; Ollenburger, 1981; Ortega and Myles, 1987; Warr, 1984). Fear of crime among older persons has sparked the greatest research interest and public concern, perhaps because of the apparent paradox that older persons are more fearful but generally experience fewer incidents of victimization than other age groups (Lindquist and Duke, 1982). Ever since Harris (1975) reported that 23% of persons aged 65 and older rated fear of crime as their most serious personal problem in a nationwide poll, fear of crime and its implications for the life satisfaction and general well-being of older persons have become serious gerontological issues. As Warr (1984:681) observes, most articles about fear of crime perfunctorily begin with "lurid stories about elderly citizens barricaded in their homes." The high level of fear among older adults has been so widely communicated that professionals, politicians, and the public commonly accept it as truth.

Increasingly, however, research on fear of crime is being closely scrutinized. Several critics maintain that conceptual cloudiness and inappropriate methodologies minimize the usefulness of many empirical findings (DuBow et al., 1979; Ferraro and LaGrange, 1987; Garofalo and Laub, 1978; Lawton and Yaffe, 1980). Indeed, Warr (1984) claims that the term "fear of crime" has been so loosely used that it ceases to have any clear meaning or utility in scientific research. Although the relationship between gender and fear of crime has not been seriously questioned, the belief that older persons are exceptionally fearful has been challenged. Recent evidence indicates that the prevalence and intensity of fear among older persons have been overestimated (Jeffords, 1983; LaGrange and Ferraro, 1987; Yin, 1982).

Problems of Measurement

Ferraro and LaGrange (1987) indicate that measures of crime risk are often mistaken for measures of crime fear (e.g., Wiltz, 1982). Questions that ask respondents how safe they think they are from crime or what the likelihood is of their being victimized by crime are asking people to estimate their risk of being victimized, not how afraid they are of being victimized. Judgment of risk and feelings of fear are two distinct perceptions. Simply because people think they are unlikely to be crime victims does not mean they are unafraid of crime, nor does a heightened sense of perceived risk automatically translate into heightened feelings of fear. And equal levels of perceived risk do not generate equal levels of fear among all people. Warr (1984) has demonstrated that a "differential sensitivity to risk" exists across sociodemographic groups which, he suggests, could explain why women and older persons are more afraid of being victimized. In sum, substituting measures of perceived risk or crime concern for measures of fear reduces measurement validity and confounds proper interpretation of findings.

The second problem is that several widely used measures of fear of crime do not measure fear of "crime," or at least do not measure it well. The National Crime Survey (NCS) asks the question, "How safe do you feel or would you feel being out alone in your neighborhood at night?" The related General Social Survey (GSS) question is, "Is there any place right around here—that is, within a mile—where you would be afraid to walk alone at night?" The two questions are routinely used as indicators of fear of crime. There are several serious flaws, however, with these types of measures: (1) the reference to crime in each question is implied rather than explicit, (2) single-item indicators of theoretical constructs are more error prone than multiple-item indicators, and (3) single-item indicators of fear of crime are insensitive to variation in fear of different types of crime. Certain offenses, such as serious violent crimes, are inherently more fear provoking than others. Moreover, the scenario of walking alone at night, included in both the NCS and the GSS questions, appears overly ominous and likely to evoke exaggerated levels of fear. Although serious personal victimization occurs disproportionately in public places, such as in parks or on the streets (Hindelang et al., 1978), the "routine activities" of most people do not include walking alone on the streets at night (Cohen and Felson, 1979).

This study attempts to provide new insight into several familiar questions: Is fear of crime really higher among women and older persons? Are certain types of crime more fear provoking than others, and for whom? Are perceived risk of crime and fear of crime empirically distinct perceptions of crime? If so, how do these perceptions vary by age and gender? A few researchers have provided useful information on some of these questions (Warr, 1984; Warr and Stafford, 1983), but much additional work is necessary, especially because researchers continue to use the NCS and GSS measures as purported measures of fear of crime (e.g., Liska et al., 1988).

Methods and Measures

Data for this study are from a social survey conducted in the fall of 1987. Residents from a southeastern metropolitan area of the United States with a population of 120,000 were randomly contacted by telephone and interviewed on a variety of issues. The sampling frame was the most recently published telephone book. The telephone numbers of commercial, governmental, political, and religious establishments were omitted, thereby limiting the survey to residential numbers. The sampling procedure is best described as a systematic sample with multiple random starts. For analytic purposes, the sample is a probability sample approximating the simple random design.

The interviews were conducted on four evenings to increase the probability of reaching people at home. Out of 700 random calls, contact was made with 418 residents and interviews were completed with 320 residents, which represented a refusal rate of 30%. The ages of the respondents range from 18 to 86 years, and the median age was 40. Women and whites are slightly overrepresented in the final sample: 60% of the completed interviews were with women and 86% were with whites (approximately 75% of the population in the survey are white and 23% are black). On other important sociodemographic characteristics (age, educational attainment, dwelling type, percentage renting), the sample appears representative of the local area.

References

Braungart, Margaret, Richard Braungart, and William Hoyer
    1980   Age, sex, and social factors in fear of crime. Sociological Focus 13:55-66.
Clemente, Frank and Michael B. Kleiman
    1976   Fear of crime among the aged. British Journal of Criminology 22:49–62.
Cohen, Lawrence E. and Marcus Felson
    1979   Social change and crime rate trends: A routine activity approach. American Sociological Review 44:588-608.

Cook, Fay L. and Thomas D. Cook
  1976 Evaluating the rhetoric of crisis: A case study of criminal victimization of the elderly. Social Science Review 50: 632–646.

DuBow, Frederic, Edward McCabe, and Gail Kaplan
  1979 Reactions to Crime: A Critical Review of the Literature. Washington, D.C.: National Institute of Law Enforcement and Criminal Justice.

Ferraro, Kenneth F. and Randy L. LaGrange
  1987 The measurement of fear of crime. Sociological Inquiry 57:70–101.

Garofalo, James and John Laub
  1978 The fear of crime: Broadening our perspective. Victimology 3:242–253.

Harris, Louis
  1975 The Myth and Reality of Aging in America. Washington, D.C.: National Council on Aging.

Hindelang, Michael J., Michael Gottfredson, and James Garofalo
  1978 Victims of Personal Crime: An Empirical Foundation for a Theory of Personal Victimization. Cambridge, Mass.: Ballinger.

Jeffords, Clifford R.
  1983 The situational relationship between age and the fear of crime. International Journal of Aging and Human Development 17:103–111.

LaGrange, Randy L. and Kenneth F. Ferraro
  1987 The elderly's fear of crime: A critical examination of the research. Research on Aging 9:372–391.

Lawton, M. Powell and Sylvia Yaffe
  1980 Victimization and fear of crime in elderly public housing tenants. Journal of Gerontology 35:768–779.

Lee, Gary
  1982 Sex differences in fear of crime among older people. Research on Aging 4:284–298.

Lindquist, John H. and Janice Duke
  1982 The elderly victim at risk: Explaining the fear-victimization paradox. Criminology 20:115–126.

Liska, Allen E., Andrew Sanchirico, and Mark D. Reed
  1988 Fear of crime and constrained behavior specifying and estimating a reciprocal effects model. Social Forces 66:826-837.

Mullen, Robert E. and Joseph E. Donnermeyer
  1985 Age, trust, and perceived safety from crime in rural areas. Gerontologist 25:237–242.

Ollenburger, Jane C.
  1981 Criminal victimization and fear of crime. Research on Aging 1:101–118.

Ortega, Suzanne T. and Jessie L. Myles
  1987 Race and gender effects on fear of crime: An interactive model with age. Criminology 25:133–152.

Warr, Mark
  1984 Fear of victimization: Why are women and the elderly more afraid? Social Science Quarterly 65:681–702.

Warr, Mark and Mark Stafford
  1983 Fear of victimization: A look at the proximate causes. Social Forces 61:1033–1043.

Wiltz, C.J.
  1982 Fear of crime, criminal victimization and elderly blacks. Phylon 43:283–294.

Yin, Peter
  1982 Fear of crime as a problem for the elderly. Social Problems 30:240–245.

Name of Student _____
Student ID # _____
Course Section # _____
Date _____

Answer the following questions based on your reading of the LaGrange and Ferraro article.

1. What reasons support LaGrange and Ferraro's use of a telephone interview to collect their data?

_____
_____
_____
_____
_____

2. What are some of the disadvantages/problems with this method in general?

_____
_____
_____
_____
_____

3. Design and carry out a telephone survey on students' fear of crime at your college or university.

   a. Identify the hypotheses you will test. Including the variables gender, age, and major, create three hypotheses that indicate what differences, if any, you expect with regard to these variables when correlated with fear of crime.

   (1) Gender

   _____
   _____

   (2) Age

   _____
   _____

   (3) Major

   _____
   _____

   b. Next, determine a sampling technique for your telephone survey. Select a systematic random sample of 10 student names and telephone numbers from the most recent student telephone directory available. Describe in detail the specific steps taken to select this systematic sample.

_____

_____

_____

_____

c. Call each student in your sample. Using the survey questions in Appendix A, collect demographic data using questions 1–16 and fear-of-crime data using questions 68–77. Duplicate the form below for use with each subject.

Subject # _____

Demographic Questions   Fear-of-Crime Questions

(1) _____   (68) _____

(2) _____   (69) _____

(3) _____   (70) _____

(4) _____   (71) _____

(5) _____   (72) _____

(6) _____   (73) _____

(7) _____   (74) _____

(8) _____   (75) _____

(9) _____   (76) _____

(10) _____   (77) _____

(11) _____

(12) _____

(13) _____

(14) _____

(15) _____

(16) _____

Effects of Interview Mode on Self-Reported Drug Use

William S. Aquilino and Leonard A. Lo Sciuto
Public Opinion Quarterly
Vol. 54, pp. 362–395, 1990

Introduction

Telephone interviewing has increased in popularity relative to personal interviewing due to cost savings, efficiency, and the availability of computer-assisted methods to speed data collection and processing (Groves, 1983; Klecka and Tuchfarber, 1978). Compared to face-to-face interviewing, telephone surveys are cheaper, have shorter data collection periods, and lend themselves to closer monitoring of interviewer performance, thus enhancing quality control during data collection. The utility of the telephone survey has been demonstrated in marketing, political polling, health, and numerous forms of attitudinal research. Herzog and Rodgers (1988), for example, found almost no difference in response distributions obtained from telephone and personal interviews in a survey of older Americans' political attitudes, health, well-being, and life satisfaction. Telephone approaches have been shown to produce reliable and valid results for relatively non-threatening interview topics. Much less is known, however, about the efficacy of telephone surveys for highly threatening interview topics, such as sexual behavior, criminality, and the use of illicit drugs. Surveys on these topics have relied almost exclusively on costly and time-consuming face-to-face interviewing. This research addressed the question: To what extent does the validity of sensitive surveys differ by mode of interview? Specifically, is there a difference between face-to-face surveys using self-administered questionnaires (SAQs) and telephone surveys in their estimates of lifetime and current use of tobacco, alcohol, marijuana, and cocaine?

Literature Review

Response rates typically vary between telephone and face-to-face interview modes. Experimental comparison of interview modes for the National Health Interview Survey (NHIS) yielded overall response rates of 80% for the telephone and 96% for the personal survey (Groves, Miller, and Cannell, 1987). Groves and Kahn (1979) reported a Random Digit Dial (RDD) response rate of 59% in their national survey (including all unanswered telephone numbers in the denominator of the response rate equation), compared to 75% in the personal interview. Exclusion of the unanswered numbers raised the telephone rate to 70%.

Telephone surveys tend to have higher break-off rates (Groves and Kahn, 1979) and higher refusal rates (Jordan, Marcus, and Reeder, 1980) than personal surveys. The collection of household composition data early in the call, to determine eligibility and respondent selection, may increase refusals (Hauck and Cox, 1974). Telephone nonresponse occurs disproportionately among minorities, the less affluent, less educated, and among older respondents (Freeman et al., 1982; Groves, Miller, and Cannell, 1987; O'Neil, 1979). Nonresponse may vary by race and ethnicity. Blacks tend to be disproportionately inaccessible in telephone surveys (Weaver, Holmes, and Glenn, 1975); this is especially true for younger, lower income, and male black respondents.

Bias in Drug Use Estimates

Drug use surveys are subject to response set bias, most notably socially desirable responding

Source: William S. Aquilino and Leonard A. Lo Sciuto, *Public Opinion Quarterly,* Vol. 54, copyright © 1990 by the University of Chicago Press. Reprinted by permission.

in the face of threatening survey items (Mensch and Kandel, 1988). Use of illicit drugs, such as marijuana and cocaine, and heavy versus social drinking are assumed to be socially undesirable behaviors for the majority of respondents. To the extent that social desirability affects responses, and respondents feel threatened by such interview questions, one would expect underreporting of drug use to be the largest threat to the validity of drug use surveys (Bradburn et al., 1978). The more socially unacceptable the substance, the greater the underreporting should be. Sudman and Bradburn (1974) maintained that the higher the threat, the more influential the interview milieu on respondents. There is reason to suspect, then, that the more threatening the topic, the more potential there is for survey characteristics, such as interview mode, to affect tendencies toward socially desirable responding. The central question of this paper, then, is: Will a switch from face-to-face to telephone survey modes affect the validity of population estimates of drug use, i.e., result in lower estimates of drug use?

Design of the Personal Survey

Anonymity

For all but tobacco, answers to drug use questions were recorded by respondents on self-administered answer sheets; interviewers read the instructions at the start of each drug sequence, and at the respondent's request, read the question aloud, while the respondent completed the answer sheet. Respondents were told that interviewers would not see their answers on the self-administered sheets. Answer sheets were sealed in an envelope in the respondent's presence, upon completion of the interview.

Data Collection

A sample of New Jersey's civilian, noninstitutionalized household population aged 18–34 years was developed. The multistage area probability design yielded a total sample of 4,571 residential addresses. Advance letters were sent to selected households in the sample. The letter explained the purpose of the survey, confidentiality procedures, and the voluntary nature of participation. All screening and interviewing was done in-person. During screening, household members were listed by age and first name, and one respondent per household was selected from the eligible 18–34-year-olds using tables developed by Kish (1965). When definite refusals were obtained, one refusal conversion attempt was made, with reassignment to another interview where possible.

Design of the Telephone Survey

The overriding concern in designing the telephone survey was comparability to the personal survey. Thus, it was paramount that the telephone survey attempt to (1) achieve high screening and interview response rates, (2) minimize item nonresponse, (3) preserve question content and meaning, and (4) guarantee confidentiality to respondents.

In order to maximize response rates, we decided to conduct a telephone survey averaging no more than 25 minutes. It was clear that only a subset of the personal interview sequences could be used, since administering the entire NHSDA questionnaire over the phone would have required well over an hour. We decided to ask the complete sequence of items about a smaller number of drugs: tobacco, alcohol, marijuana, and cocaine (including crack). These drugs were selected because they are relatively prevalent in the population, they have potential for abuse, they represent both legal and illegal substances, and they form a continuum from relatively nonthreatening (smoking, social drinking) to threatening (heavy drinking, marijuana use, cocaine use) questions.

Data Collection

The Waksberg procedure (Waksberg, 1978) of Random Digit Dialing (RDD) was used to draw the telephone sample. The Waksberg procedure was adopted to maximize the proportion of residential households contacted during the screening, thus reducing survey costs and field period length. Our goal was the completion of at least 2,000 interviews with respondents 18- to 65-years-old. (This paper reports substantive results for 18- to 34-year-olds only, the same age group available in the face-to-face survey.)

Results

Mode Differences in Sample Characteristics

One source of demographic differences between RDD and area probability sampling is RDD's exclusion of nontelephone households. Blacks and other minorities were much more likely than whites not to have telephones. Respondents without telephones were also much more likely to be unemployed, have less than a high school education, and have lower incomes. Telephone status correlated with respondents' race and economic status, both important predictors of drug use.

Mode Differences in Self-Reported Drug Use

Four substances of high use-prevalence were chosen for these analyses: tobacco (cigarette smoking), alcohol, marijuana, and cocaine. In analyzing drug data, responses from both surveys were pooled into one data set, with mode of interview added to the pooled data set as a categorical variable. Demographic characteristics were entered as control variables in the analyses. Race-of-interviewer effects also were explored, but were found to be unrelated to the interview mode and respondent race.

Discussion

. . . [A] justifiable conclusion for white [subjects] is that the telephone survey yielded results comparable to face-to-face estimates across all drug groups. Where telephone estimates for whites were significantly lower—for the current use of alcohol and drunkenness—the percentage differences between modes were small. The RDD sample also reproduced the demographic profile for whites found in the personal mode. The dearth of mode effects for whites is especially noteworthy given the large sample sizes (over 1,300 cases) and therefore relatively high power to detect differences.

The conclusions for blacks are very different. The telephone survey introduced a significantly higher SES profile for blacks. After controlling for SES and other demographic characteristics, the telephone survey resulted in substantially lower estimates of blacks' current alcohol consumption and marijuana use, compared to the face-to-face results. The telephone interviews also suggested more and larger racial differences in drug use than the personal survey. By telephone, black alcohol and marijuana use was significantly lower than whites' in nearly all categories. The personal survey indicated almost no racial differences in marijuana use, and few racial differences in the amount of recent alcohol consumption. The personal survey indicated no significant racial differences in cocaine use; the telephone estimates suggested that blacks were significantly less likely than whites to have ever used cocaine, or to have used it more than ten times. We recognize that neither provides a fully accurate description of black drug use or demographic characteristics. Minority men were substantially underrepresented in the surveys, accounting for only one-third of the respondents in both modes.

Mode Effects by Drug Categories

Differences between telephone and personal survey estimates were not found for tobacco use, the least threatening of the four drug groups. This is consistent with mode comparison literature on health surveys and other less threatening topics (Herzog et al., 1983; Herzog and Rodgers, 1988; Groves, Miller, and Cannell, 1987). Mode effects (for blacks) were more evident as the sensitivity of the questions increased, with the strongest differences for recent and heavy drinking and marijuana use. Contrary to expectations, however, the findings were not as clear for cocaine as for the other three drug groups.

Although the telephone surveys furnished consistently lower cocaine use estimates for blacks than did the personal survey, the mode differences were not significant. This was somewhat surprising since questions on cocaine should be at least as sensitive as questions on marijuana use.

References

Bradburn, N. M., S. Sudman, E. Blair, and C. Stocking (1978)
"Question threat and response bias." Public Opinion Quarterly 42:221–234.

Freeman, H., K. Kiecolt, W. Nicholls, and J. M.
Shanks (1982)
"Telephone sampling bias in surveying disability."
Public Opinion Quarterly 46:392–407.

Groves, R. M. (1983)
"Implications of CATI: Costs, errors, and organization of telephone survey research." Sociological Methods and Research 12:199–215.

Groves, R. M., and R. L. Kahn (1979)
Surveys by Telephone: A National Comparison with Personal Interviews. New York: Academic Press.

Groves, R. M., P. V. Miller, and C. F. Cannell (1987)
"Differences between the telephone and personal interview data." In O. Thornberry (ed.), An Experimental Comparison of Telephone and Health Interview Surveys. Vital and Health Statistics, series 2, no. 106. DHHS Pub. No. (PHS)87-1380. Washington, DC: Public Health Service.

Hauck, M., and M. Cox (1974)
"Locating a sample by random digit dialing." Public Opinion Quarterly 38:253–260.

Herzog, A. R., and W. L. Rodgers (1988)
"Interviewing older adults: Mode comparison using data from a face-to-face survey and a telephone resurvey." Public Opinion Quarterly 52:84–99.

Herzog, A. R., W. L. Rodgers, and R. A. Kulka (1983)
"Interviewing older adults: A comparison of telephone and face-to-face modalities." Public Opinion Quarterly 47:405–418.

Jordan, L., A. Marcus, and L. Reeder (1980)
"Response styles in telephone and household interviewing: A field experiment." Public Opinion Quarterly 44:210–222.

Kish, L. (1965)
Survey Sampling. New York: John Wiley.

Klecka, W. R., and A. J. Tuchfarber (1978)
"Random digit dialing: A comparison to personal surveys." Public Opinion Quarterly 42:105–114.

Mensch, B. S., and D. B. Kandel (1988)
"Underreporting substance use in a national longitudinal youth cohort: Individual and interviewer effects." Public Opinion Quarterly 52:100–124.

O'Neil, M. (1979)
"Estimating the nonresponse bias due to refusals in telephone surveys." Public Opinion Quarterly 43:218–232.

Sudman, S., and N. Bradburn (1974)
Response Effects in Surveys: A Review and Synthesis. Chicago: Aldine Publishing.

Waksberg, J. (1978)
"Sampling methods for random digit dialing." Journal of the American Statistical Association 73:40–46.

Weaver, C., S. Holmes, and N. Glenn (1975)
"Some characteristics of inaccessible respondents in a telephone survey." Journal of Applied Psychology 60:260–262.

Name of Student _____

Student ID # _____

Course Section # _____

Date _____

1. What are some of the methodological problems a researcher must confront when using a telephone survey?

   _____

   _____

   _____

   _____

   _____

2. Construct a letter of explanation for an imaginary survey. The letter should explain the purpose of the survey, the confidentiality procedures, and the voluntary nature of participation. Remember, this letter is a key element in convincing potential subjects to take part in the project.

   _____

   _____

   _____

   _____

   _____

   _____

   _____

3. Construct two survey instruments: one for a face-to-face interview and one for a telephone survey. Each instrument should contain six demographic questions and five questions on each of the following topics: tobacco use, alcohol use, marijuana use, and cocaine use.

Face-to-Face Survey

Demographic Questions

1. _____

_____

_____

2. _____

_____

_____

3. _____

_____

_____

4. _____

_____

_____

5. _____

_____

_____

6. _____

_____

_____

Tobacco Use Questions

1. _____

_____

_____

2. _____

_____

_____

3. _____

_____

_____

4. _____

_____

_____

5. _____

_____

_____

Alcohol Use Questions

1. _____

_____

_____

2. _____

_____

_____

3. _____

_____

_____

4. _____

_____

_____

5. _____

_____

_____

Marijuana Use Questions

1. _____

_____

_____

2. _____

_____

_____

3. _____

_____

_____

4. _____

_____

_____

5. _____

_____

_____

Cocaine Use Questions

1. _____

_____

_____

2. _____

_____

_____

3. _____

_____

_____

4. _____

_____

_____

5. _____

_____

_____

Telephone Survey

Demographic Questions

1. _____

_____

_____

2. _____

_____

_____

3. _____

_____

_____

4. _____

_____

_____

5. _____

_____

_____

6. _____

_____

_____

Tobacco Use Questions

1. _____

_____

_____

2. _____

_____

_____

3. _____

_____

_____

4. _____

_____

_____

5. _____

_____

_____

Alcohol Use Questions

1. _____

_____

_____

2. _____

_____

_____

3. _____

_____

_____

4. _____

_____

_____

5. _____

_____

_____

Marijuana Use Questions

1. _____

_____

_____

2. _____

_____

_____

3. _____

_____

_____

4. _____

_____

_____

5. _____

_____

_____

Cocaine Use Questions

1.

2.

3.

4.

5.

4. a.   What are some of the ethical concerns that must be considered when conducting a face-to-face survey?

    b.   How do these compare with the ethical concerns that must be considered when conducting a telephone survey?

Power in Hospitals: Implications for the Validity of Data

Barbara Haley
Journal of Applied Sociology
Vol. 6, pp. 65–76, 1989

Introduction

The position of the social scientist who conducts research in hospital settings is a delicate one. In that setting, the tensions generated by power relationships can have major consequences for the successful implementation of a research design. The very survival of a project to completion may depend on the investigator's understanding of and accommodation to a persistent feature of that setting, the impulse to acquire or maintain control of major aspects of the setting.

Overview of the Emergency Room Study

We entered in a medium sized university hospital, located in the Deep South, with a broad research problem. The Head Administrator instructed us to answer the following question regarding the emergency room (ER) patients: "Why are they here?" He posed this question because the ER was the major mode of entry for indigent patients into the hospital. His interest was based on a concern for the financial health of the institution. This facility is also the public county hospital. At the time, the indigent patients consumed services worth approximately $1 million per month that were unreimbursed from any source. The academic issues were several: (1) How important is distance in seeking emergency care in the South? (2) To what extent are the characteristics of patients who seek clinic care in the ER different from other ER patients? (3) What policies will address the problems of institutions who serve the medically indigent as well as the needs of the indigent patients themselves? The project operated under severe budget constraints, which

made the support and cooperation of many of the hospital staff indispensable.

The overall research strategy was to interview all patients who were undergoing treatment during 196 randomly selected interviewing periods. If a patient was deemed to be too sick to be interviewed or was a child, an accompanying adult was approached. No attempt was made to obtain an interview if a patient arrived in very serious condition. Coinciding with our efforts, the physicians rated the patients regarding the type of care received viz. clinic care or other kinds of care. This information was to be merged with information in the hospital records and questionnaires.

Our preparation included plans to measure the extent of patient dumping into the ER. Dumping is the practice of rejecting a potential patient for non-medical reasons (usually financial) and sending that person elsewhere for treatment, usually the county hospital ER (Korcok, 1985). This measurement effort included designing and revising of the patient triage sheets, negotiating with the Head Nurse to supply appropriate training for the triage nurses, and negotiating with the Director of Admissions to supply training for the admitting clerks who would enter this information into the hospital computer. The computer systems manager agreed to our request to create a data field in the computer for them to use. The effort to measure dumping failed for reasons to be explained below.

Cooperation of Lower Level Workers

The social researcher in a hospital setting faces a paradox. On one hand, the approval of data collection by head administrators is necessary (Weiss, 1971). On the other hand, a head administrator cannot do much more than guarantee physical access to the facility. Once access is secured, the researcher is in a position much like other lower participants in complex organizations. Just as the patient is dependent on a wide variety of ancillary health workers, so too does the quality and completeness of research data collected there depend on this cooperation. As Mechanic (1968) has observed, it is not unusual for lower participants in complex organizations to assume and wield power and influence not associated with their formally defined positions. In sociological terms, they have considerable personal power, but no authority. Dissatisfied or uninformed lower personnel can do much to hinder the work of an organization.

Accordingly, the researcher must recognize the necessity of cultivating the approval of the lower ranking personnel of the purpose and methods of the data collection effort.

Lower level personnel are overwhelmingly female, and the traditional norms of sociability, supportiveness, and sympathy among women usually prevail. For these reasons, the recruitment of research assistants who understand and can conform to these norms is essential. In our case, the members of the research team were exclusively female. Although we had not consciously planned to have all women, we were pleased by the fortuitous outcome of our recruitment effort. Most of the team intuitively recognized our dependence on the nurses and supported women's working norms.

The other source of power for lower level participants that are identified by Mechanic (1968) are (a) location and position, (b) effort and interest, and (c) expertise. The former may also be readily used to enhance an acceptance of a research project. Our interviewers obtained acceptance by being highly visible. The nurses lounge became our headquarters when long waits between interviews were required. Visibility, coupled with longevity and dedication to a research design that included randomly selected interviewing periods, had a marked effect on the acceptance of the project.

Medical Politics

A knowledge of hospital politics is a helpful ingredient to successful research in the setting. In our case, an internal struggle over medical control of the ER was the source of a problem in eliciting the active cooperation of the surgery residents in the ER. Specifically, one of our goals was to measure the amount of primary or clinic care delivered in the ER. Those most qualified to make this measurement were the physicians themselves. We originally believed that obtaining the approval and support of the physician who was in charge of the ER would be sufficient in generating support from the rest of the physicians. This assumption was correct for the medical staff but not for the surgical staff. When we met with the surgical staff to request their cooperation we were rebuffed. They told us that cooperation would be impossible due to their concern that this kind of activity might cause them to be party to a law suit. Later inquires revealed that the surgeons had lately lost control over who would be the medical chief of the ER. Still smarting from their loss of turf, they routinely opposed the policies that were supported by the current incumbent.

The Emerging Power of Computer Systems Managers

The multiple hierarchical structure of the large urban hospital traditionally has been dual: professional and administrative. The "cleavage between the interests" of administration and medical staff has long been recognized (Duff and Hollingshead, 1968:48). We observed a third, emergent structure during the course of the research. It consists of the computer systems managers and their support personnel. The power of this hierarchy rests on the dependence of the other hierarchies on the information it controls. We see the data processors as a third hierarchy rather than an extension of the administration hierarchy, for inquiries into the relationship between our systems manager and the regular administrative departments (e.g., medical records) showed that considerable tensions existed. We observed that the systems manager was attempting to dictate the structure of work that used computer support. For example, he set deadlines for other departments, instead of tailoring his functions to their tasks.

The extent to which computer systems managers can influence the agenda of social researchers in hospital settings was amply demonstrated during our project. Our systems manager purged computerized patient records that were essential to the project. He made deliberate programming errors that made our measurement of dumping largely unreliable.

Conclusions

The barriers to obtaining quality data in hospitals are many. As with most complex organizations, the most formidable are interpersonal. In this setting, lower level workers, systems managers, and medical politics are sufficiently powerful to diminish the validity of data or even destroy the data itself. The researcher who dares to venture into the hospital setting needs to appreciate its sociopolitical environment. A lack of awareness of its imperatives can cost the researcher many additional hours of labor or cause the untimely demise of a research project. Obtaining the approval of a hospital's head administrator is not enough. Alliances must be formed and approval obtained from sources that are less than obvious to the untutored newcomer.

References

Duff, Raymond S., and August B. Hollingshead
   1968   *Sickness and Society*. New York: Harper
           and Row.
Korcok, Milan
   1985   "Patient Dumping: The Ignoble Face of
           American Medicine." *Canadian Medical
           Association Journal*. Vol. 132:1064–1071.
Mechanic, David
   1968   *Medical Sociology: A Selective View*. New
           York: Free Press.
Weiss, Carol, H.
   1971   "Using Research in the Policy Process:
           Potential and Constraints." *Policy Studies
           Journal*. Vol. 4:224–227.

Name of Student _____

Student ID # _____

Course Section # _____

Date _____

1. Conduct a three-hour observation of a public hospital ER waiting room. Be sure that during the course of the observation, you make notes on the following:

    a. Positions of lower-level workers who run ER

    b. Date of observation

    c. Time of observation

    d. Location of observation

Field Notes (attach additional pages as needed):

_____

_____

_____

_____

_____

_____

_____

_____

_____

_____

_____

_____

_____

_____

_____

_____

_____

_____

_____
_____
_____
_____
_____
_____

2. If you wanted to conduct a more extensive study of the ER, from whom would you need to gain support?

_____
_____
_____
_____
_____
_____
_____
_____
_____
_____

3. How might your style of dress or appearance contribute to or detract from your ability to gain acceptance from ER staff workers?

_____
_____
_____
_____
_____
_____
_____
_____
_____
_____

4. What other factors might negatively impact a study of power and authority relationships in the ER?

_____

_____

_____

_____

_____

_____

_____

_____

_____

_____

5. How did the ER staff respond to your presence, and what did you do to gain acceptance?

_____

_____

_____

_____

_____

_____

_____

_____

_____

Self-Concept as an Insulator against Delinquency

Walter C. Reckless, Simon Dinitz, and Ellen Murray
American Sociological Review
Vol. 21, pp. 744–746, 1965

Introduction

This study is concerned with sixth-grade boys in the highest delinquency areas in Columbus, Ohio, who have not become delinquent. What insulates an early teen-age boy against delinquency? Is it possible to identify certain components that enable young adolescent boys to develop or maintain non-delinquent habits and patterns of behavior in the growing up process?

Methodology

In order to study the non-delinquent boy, all 30 sixth-grade teachers in schools located in the highest white delinquency areas in Columbus were asked to nominate those white boys in their school rooms who would not, in their opinion, ever experience police or juvenile court contact. Treating each nominee separately, the teachers were then requested to indicate their reasons for the selection of a particular boy. Of the eligible students, 192, or just over half were selected and evaluated by their teachers as being "insulated" against delinquency. A check of police and juvenile court records revealed that 17 (8.3 percent) of those nominated had some type of law enforcement record, and these boys were eliminated from further consideration. Repeated neighborhood visits failed to locate 51 others. In the remaining cases both the boy and his mother were interviewed.

The 125 "good" boys comprising the final sample were given a series of four self-administered scales to complete. These included in somewhat modified form, (1) the delinquency proneness and (2) social responsibility scales of the Gough California Personality Inventory, (3) an occupational preference instrument, (4) and one measuring the boy's conception of self, his family, and other interpersonal relations. At the same time, though not in the presence of the nominee, the mother or mother-surrogate was interviewed with an open-ended schedule to determine the boy's developmental history, his patterns of association, and the family situation.

Findings

An analysis of the scores made by these 125 nominees on the delinquency vulnerability (De) and social responsibility (Re) scales seemed to justify their selection as "good" boys. Out of a possible total (De) score of 54, scores ranged from a low of 4 to a high of 34 with a mean of 14.57 and a standard deviation of 6.4. This mean score was significantly lower than that of school behavior problem boys, young delinquents, or reformatory inmates investigated in other studies. In fact, the average De score of the sample subjects was below that obtained in all but one previous study using the same scale.

For a twelve year old group, the nominees scored remarkably high on the social responsibility scale. The mean Re score for the group was 28.86 with a standard deviation of 3.60 and a range of 12 to 40 out of a possible 42 points. This mean score was appreciably higher than that achieved by school disciplinary cases, delinquents, and prisoners tested in other studies.

The correlation between the two sets of scores was –.605, indicating a significant and negative relationship between delinquency vulnerability and social responsibility as measured by these instruments.

Nominee perceptions of family interaction also appeared to be highly favorable. As noted in a previous paper, the 125 families were stable maritally, residentially, and economically. There appeared to be close parental supervision of the boys' activities and associates, an intense parental interest in the welfare of the children, and a desire to indoctrinate them with non-deviant attitudes and patterns. This parental supervision and interest seemed to be the outstanding characteristic of the family profiles. It extended over the entire range of their sons' activities—from friendship patterns, leisure activ-ities, and after school employment to movie attendance and the performance of well-defined duties at home.

Conclusions

"Insulation" against delinquency on the part of these boys may be viewed as an ongoing process reflecting an internalization of non-delin-quent values and conformity to the expectations of significant others. Whether the subjects, now largely unreceptive to delinquent norms of con-duct, will continue to remain "good" in the future remains problematic. The answer to this ques-tion, it is felt, will depend on their ability to main-tain their present self-images in the face of mounting situational pressure.

Name of Student _____

Student ID # _____

Course Section # _____

Date _____

1. This study used a modified version of a sociometric rating scale to determine whom teachers believe are "good" boys. Once these boys were identified, Reckless and his associates pursued several other means of assuring these boys were good. As a class exercise, attempt a more traditional version of a sociometric test. Below, list the names of the three people in your class whom you like the most. Place them in descending order of your preference (e.g., you like number 1 the most; number 2, second most; and so forth).

   Person 1 _____

   Person 2 _____

   Person 3 _____

2. Next, briefly explain what about each person makes him or her likable to you.

   Person 1 _____

   _____

   _____

   Person 2 _____

   _____

   _____

   Person 3 _____

   _____

   _____

3. Collect all the forms from the other students in the class, and tally the number of nominations for each name listed on the forms.

   _____

   _____

   _____

   _____

   _____

   _____

4. Next determine a status index for each student nominated. This is accomplished by dividing the number of votes tallied for a given nomination by the total number of students who voted. For example, assume that Bill, Bob, Jack, Barbra, and June all received nominations for positions 1 through 3 and that 44 students voted.

Position		
1	2	3
Bill (18)	Barbra (16)	June (17)
Barbra (16)	Jack (14)	Barbra (16)
Jack (10)	Bill (8)	Bob (6)
	Bob (6)	Jack (5)
44	44	44

Bill's position 1 status index would be 18/44, or .41; Barbra's would be 16/44, or .36; and Jack's would be 10/44, or .23. A similar status index can be calculated for each student in each position. Make these calculations for your own data.

_____

_____

_____

_____

_____

_____

_____

A Field Experiment on Insurance Fraud in Auto Body Repair

Paul E. Tracy and James Alan Fox
Criminology: An Interdisciplinary Journal
Vol. 27, No. 3, pp. 589–603, August 1989

Introduction

White-collar crime is an offense type that, despite much theoretical attention, remains a highly underresearched area of criminal behavior (see Duncan and Caplan, 1980). Much of this neglect is a function of society's greater concern over violent street crime and the usual forms of property crime, like burglary, larceny, or motor vehicle theft, despite growing evidence that certain forms of white-collar offending are ranked as more severe than many forms of street crime (Wolfgang et al., 1985). Although the average citizen may recognize cognitively the grave harm to society caused by white-collar offenses, he or she may not react as emotionally to the threat of such crimes compared with violent crimes. The criminal justice system, in turn, reflects this concern; law enforcement agencies, prosecutors, and the courts seem to devote the vast majority of their resources to responding to street crime and criminals.

Automobile Insurance Fraud

Reiss and Biderman (1980) have suggested that white-collar crimes are those that involve the use of the offender's position of power, influence, or trust for purposes of illegal gain. Alternatively, Braithwaite (1985) argues that white-collar crimes are acts committed by concealment or guile to obtain money or property or to obtain business or personal advantage.

In this article we focus on a particular form of white-collar crime—insurance fraud. Insurance is an economic venue characterized by a wide range of opportunities for white-collar offending. It is well known, for example, that a large percentage of arson fires are instigated by building owners in a fraudulent attempt to squeeze profits from their properties (see, e.g., Scondras and Cohn, 1979). Similarly, many reported automobile fires and thefts may actually be fraudulent disposals of vehicles by their owners to improve on diminished trade-in values (Fox, 1985) or to get out from under the burden of unaffordable car payments without having to default on a car loan.

Another opportunity for insurance fraud which has been largely ignored, but which represents an issue of prime consumer interest and public policy concern, involves automobile accident claims. It is not uncommon to hear stories about how auto body shops even kick back all or part of the insurance deductible to the car owner. The goals of such practices are to save the consumer some money or to increase the body shop's profit by displacing a disproportionate share of the repair cost onto the insurance company.

Study Method

In conjunction with the 1988 hearings to set automobile insurance rates for Massachusetts, the opportunity arose to conduct research on possible fraud in automobile body shop repair costs. Specifically, we designed a field experiment to measure the extent to which auto body repair shops in Massachusetts inflate the repair estimates for collision damage claims to insurance companies. The logic of the research involved obtaining estimates for body-damage repair costs for the same vehicle(s), under conditions when the damage was covered by insurance and when it was not.

We constructed and carried out a field experiment in which we manipulated or measured several variables—including whether the damage to the vehicle was covered by collision insurance, the extent of the damage to the vehicle, the location of the body shop, and the sex of the driver presenting the car for the repair estimate.

To obtain repair estimates, we rented from a major car rental agency four collision-damaged vehicles: two Buick Skylarks with moderate damage to the front and front fender areas, a Volvo 740GLE with rather superficial damage to the front bumper and rear quarter, and a Ford Tempo with substantial damage to the right side. All vehicles were 1987 models and were in safe operating condition. We engaged four drivers, two men and two women, all in their early twenties, to pose as the owners of the vehicles. For a 4-week period during August–September 1987, the drivers presented assigned cars to select body shops across Massachusetts to obtain estimates of collision repair cost.

Stratifying the state into seven geographic regions, we drew a random sample of 96 auto body shops, selected proportionate to resident population in each stratum. Specifically, one-half of the sample came from the Boston metropolitan area; one-quarter of the sample was spread over the four smaller metropolitan areas; . . . and the remaining quarter of the sample was divided equally between the southeastern rural counties . . . and the western rural counties. . . .

For sampling frames we used listings under the heading, "Automobile Body Repairing and Painting," in the set of 48 New England Telephone Yellow Pages for the state. We divided the directories into their respective metropolitan areas/counties, which produced multiple books for every region. . . . The selections were distributed across phone directories within each area proportionate to the number of auto body listings per phone book.

From each shop selected, we obtained estimates of repair costs for two cars, one of which was presented as being covered by insurance and the other of which was not. Two of our drivers

rotated assignments to the Buick Skylarks so that we could test the influence of the sex of the driver on the repair estimates and the interaction of this variable with the insurance coverage variable. The other two drivers remained with their assigned vehicles throughout the experiment.

The key experimental variable was whether the damage was covered or not covered by insurance. For the covered condition, the drivers told the body shop estimator that they had been in an accident and had collision coverage with a $300 deductible. Further, they reported that their insurance carrier . . . did not maintain drive-in claim centers and that they were told by their insurer to obtain and submit a written estimate.

The noninsured condition required a different scenario because it would seem implausible to have a late model car (the Volvo in particular) that was not covered for collision damage. The driver explained that he or she had purchased the car "as is" at a bank repossession sale "for a good price" and wanted the car fixed up like new. Thus, the damage would not be covered under the existing insurance policy.

Discussion and Conclusion

The experimental design used for this analysis permitted us to assess the influence of insurance coverage separate from the effects of extraneous factors. By focusing on within-shop differences, we controlled out the between shop variability from the estimates. Moreover, in one-half of the design we explicitly included the sex of the driver as a design factor.

The statistical results demonstrate unequivocally that repair estimates for vehicles presented as insured were higher than estimates obtained for noncovered collision damage. For all four cars, the differences in mean repair estimates between the covered and noncovered conditions were statistically significant. Further, the measured effects of insurance persisted regardless of the extent of damage, sex of driver, or location of the body shop. Averaged across observations, repair estimates under the insured condition were 32.5% higher than under the noncovered condition.

If the repair estimates we obtained were different, and if the differences were found to be a random function of such factors as sex of driver, make of vehicle, and the like, then the question of fraud would likely not arise, even if the differences were frequent or widespread. But when differences in repair estimates are found to be a direct result of whether the customer is covered under an insurance policy, then the issue of questionable behavior surely must be addressed. Thus, the residual cost noted above is a function of questionable practices on the part of body shops, practices that must be construed as fraud and that certainly represent an infringement on the rights of consumers to receive fair and equitable treatment.

This research has indicated that some members of an automobile collision repair industry engage in business practices that place a particular class of consumers at a disadvantage. These practices are clearly questionable and may be illegal. The consequence of these practices is that automobile insurance policy-holders in Massachusetts (those who have accidents and those who do not) are forced to pay higher insurance premiums than would be the case if repair estimate fraud did not exist. Given the cost of automobile insurance, the problem is nontrivial and requires the development of appropriate reforms.

References

Duncan, J.T. and Marc Caplan
    1980   White Collar Crime: A Selected Bibliography. Washington, D.C.: Government Printing Office.

Braithwaite, John
    1985   White collar crime. Annual Review of Sociology 11:1–25.

Fox, James Alan
    1985   Insurance rates spur auto thefts. Boston Herald, January 23.

Reiss, Albert J., Jr., and Albert Biderman
    1980   Data Sources on White-Collar Law-Breaking. Washington D.C.: U.S. Department of Justice.

Scondras, David and Mike Cohn
    1979   Profiles: A Manual for Arson Classification. Boston, Mass.: Urban Educational Systems.

Wolfgang, Marvin E., Robert Figlio, Paul Tracy, and Simon Singer
    1985   The National Survey of Crime Severity. Washington, D.C.: Government Printing Office.

Name of Student _____

Student ID # _____

Course Section # _____

Date _____

After reading the synopsis of the Tracy and Fox article on insurance fraud in auto body repair, answer the following questions and then design a field experiment, based on the following description.

1. What general hypothesis did Tracy and Fox design their field experiment to test?

    _____

    _____

2. Identify the independent variable in the study.

    _____

    _____

3. Identify the dependent variable in the study.

    _____

    _____

4. Identify the type of sampling technique used by Tracy and Fox.

    _____

    _____

    _____

    _____

    _____

    _____

    _____

    _____

    _____

    _____

5. You have been asked to serve as a consultant to a project that involves people who are homeless. The problem of homelessness has reached epidemic proportions in many large cities. As an approach to assisting people who are homeless, the city has developed SROs (Single Room Occupancy buildings): buildings designed to provide temporary living quarters for homeless individuals during the time in which they are trying to get on their feet. A large number of complaints have been made that the city agency designated to dispense the available SROs to the homeless has not been doing its job properly and in fact has discriminated against various types of individuals. As a consultant to this project, your assignment is to design a field experiment to

determine how decisions are being made by the agency designated to provide SROs to people who are homeless.

a.   Describe the general design of your study.

_____

_____

_____

_____

_____

_____

_____

_____

_____

_____

b.   What is the hypothesis?

_____

_____

_____

_____

_____

c.   What is (are) the dependent variable(s)?

_____

_____

d.   What is (are) the independent variable(s)?

_____

_____

e.   What is (are) the control variable(s)?

_____

_____

Data Organization and Analysis

The subject data organization and analysis can be examined from two broad perspectives: quantitative and qualitative. In order to answer a research question, the researcher should consider what methodological technique of data collection, organization, and analysis would best serve this purpose: quantitative or qualitative? The nature of the research question itself should suggest which strategy is most suitable.

By design, *quantitative* strategies employ an analysis that is numerical in nature. Typically, when quantitative data-analysis strategies are used, the data are ordinal-, interval-, and possibly ratio-level variables. Statistical tests are used to measure relationships and determine their significance. When using quantitative strategies, researchers often collect data from large numbers of individuals, making it difficult, if not impossible, to assess the data because of their vastness. In quantitative strategies, surveys are typically given to a large number of individuals or structured interview schedules with mainly closed-ended questions are used.

In addition to the standard data-collection techniques of surveys and interviews, numerous creative techniques have been employed in doing qualitative research. In the classic work *Unobtrusive Measures: Nonreactive Research in the Social Sciences,* Webb and colleagues (1966) describe a number of innovative techniques that can be used to collect data, including examples of studies that use assessments of erosion and accretion measures. The use of erosion measures is illustrated by a study (also mentioned in Chapter 4) comparing the rates of wear of floor tiles in front of different exhibits at the Chicago Museum of Science and Industry; the purpose of the study was to determine the popularity of various exhibits (Webb et al., 1966, pp. 36–37). The use

of accretion measures in quantitative analysis is illustrated by a study of the settings of radio dials in cars; the settings of cars brought into repair shops were recorded to determine the popularities of individual radio stations (p. 39). These are just two examples of the innovative data-collection techniques that can be employed in quantitative data collection.

Qualitative data-collection, organization, and analysis strategies are typically nonnumerical in nature. Data that are analyzed using qualitative strategies must usually be nominal-level variables (the lowest level of variables) (Bailey, 1982). Qualitative strategies often produce data that are of considerable depth but (because of the depth) include far fewer individuals than are typically included in quantitative strategies. In qualitative studies, structured interviews are used as well as techniques that incorporate nonobtrusive means of observation and data collection, such as field notes, artifacts, newspaper articles, and participant observation.

While there are a number of similarities between quantitative and qualitative strategies, there are also enough significant differences to warrant separate discussions of the two.

QUANTITATIVE DATA

Types/Sources

In quantitative research, there are two general types of data: primary data and secondary data. Each type can be described according to its source.

Primary data are original data, collected specifically to answer a research question or questions. They are often referred to as "raw data," since they have not previously been collected, analyzed, or interpreted.

In some instances, depending on the type of research question being asked, collecting primary data may be the only way to answer the question. For instance, a relatively new correctional technique called *electronic monitoring* is being selectively employed in various probation/parole jurisdictions. This technique uses an electronic bracelet to help monitor the whereabouts of an individual who is on probation or parole. To date, the impact that home incarceration of an individual has on his or her family members has not been sufficiently assessed. If a researcher was interested in determining that impact, he or she would have to collect primary data, since it is unlikely that any existing data base would provide the needed information. Likewise, a researcher attempting to replicate a certain study would need to collect primary data and compare them to those in the original study.

Secondary data were originally collected for another purpose but are also suitable for answering a current research question or questions. The researcher must determine whether existing data contain the information necessary to answer his or her new question. Because these data have already been collected, organized, analyzed, and interpreted, the use of secondary data can save a research staff countless hours of work as well as precious dollars.

A number of state and federal agencies regularly collect the data they need to compile statistics and produce reports. In addition to being used inhouse, these data sets are often made available to outside researchers who wish to analyze them for other purposes. For example, the U.S. Bureau of the Census collects a tremendous amount of information when it surveys the national population every 10 years. These data are made available to the public for use in a variety of research conducted outside the census bureau. The Bureau of Justice Statistics likewise makes available the data it collects on crime.

Getting Started

As Hagan points out, "Data analysis should be planned at the beginning of a project rather than at the end" (1993, p. 295). This is sound advice for all researchers, regardless of how much experience they may have. Knowing the type of data analysis that will be undertaken once the data have been collected will help direct the researcher in selecting what type of data are needed and in what form they should be collected.

When possible, an early step in data collection should be the *precoding* of responses to facilitate data entry and verification later. Precoding takes place after the questions have been developed. The precoding of questionnaires is directly related to the types of questions the researcher plans to ask. Closed-ended questions lend themselves to precoding. In fact, the codes can be listed right on the questionnaire, so that when the data are being entered into a file, the data-entry person needs only to follow the codes. When coding takes place after the questionnaire has been completed, a column on the right-hand side is left blank for this purpose.

Coding actually consists of assigning a numerical value to a particular answer to a question. For example, suppose a question asked an individual's gender. If the individual responded "female," that answer could be coded "0," and if the individual responded "male," that answer could be coded "1." If the question asked the respondent's year in college, the coding could be as follows:

Freshman = 1
Sophomore = 2
Junior = 3
Senior = 4
Graduate student = 5

For most closed-ended questions, this type of coding scheme is relatively easy to initiate.

What about questions that respondents fail to answer? The standard approach to this problem is to assign either a "9" or a "99" to each unanswered question to signify missing data. When the data are analyzed, the computer can be directed to ignore these entries and concentrate on the responses from individuals who did answer the questions. If a respondent failed to answer a majority of the questions, it would probably behoove the researcher to eliminate that response set from the analysis.

To document these kinds of coding decisions, the researcher must prepare a *codebook,* which is a detailed account of the questions, the codes assigned to the answers, and the format in which the codes appear. (If the data are secondary, they should come with a prepared codebook.) The format normally corresponds to the 80 columns found on a punch-type computer card. This practice is a carryover from the early days of data processing; cards are typically not used today. A file for a respondent may contain more than one "card" if the number of columns necessary for storing the data exceeds 80. When a respondent has more than one card, each should be labeled with the number of the respondent and a card number, as well.

Before the data are entered into a respondent's file, they are usually entered on a codesheet. A *codesheet* is a rectangular piece of paper, divided into 80 columns and 24 rows (usually). Coded data are recorded in appropriate locations on the codesheet, corresponding to question and answer numbers. Coding data at this stage greatly facilitates their entry into the computer file. At each step of the coding and data-entry process, verification checks are made to ensure that the data entered accurately represent the original responses.

Once the data have been entered and verified, they are ready for analysis. Typically, the first run done is a *one-variable run.* This means that each question on the survey instrument is listed by the computer and the numbers for each response are presented. For example, using the gender question from above, the printout would show (1) how many respondents indicated they were female versus male, (2) what percentage of all respondents each figure represents, and (3) how many individuals responded to the question. Given this information for the entire survey, the researcher would have a general sense of the spread of responses on individual variables.

This printout also serves as another means of verifying the data. If the response for one of the questions seems out of character with the range of possible answers, the researcher will know to look for a coding or data-entry problem. Once he or she is satisfied with the correctness of the data, the researcher can run more sophisticated types of data analysis to address the research questions the study was undertaken to answer.

QUALITATIVE DATA

Qualitative research data come in a wide variety of types, including photographs, tape and video recordings, field notes, interviews, artifacts, drawings, books, and even newspaper and magazine articles. In this section, the discussion will be limited to the organization of *textual data.* A considerable amount of qualitative data either exists as text or can be transformed through description to some form of text.

Do not interpret the previous statement to suggest that photographic data, for example, must be reduced and limited to textual analysis. Certainly, examination of images, or *visual ethnography,* is an important and worthwhile type of data analysis (Dowdall & Golden, 1989; Schwartz, 1989). However, the authors believe that the largest amount of qualitative research currently being undertaken by social scientists in the United States involves textual data. Operating from this orientation, we will begin by considering how to organize textual data.

Organization

Organization of qualitative research characteristically means considering words—a great many words, at that. The basic underlying organizational scheme in any qualitative analysis is to reduce the amount of raw data without simultaneously losing content meaning. As Miles and Huberman (1984) express, researchers need methods for data management and analysis that are systematic and explicit. In other words, researchers need to arrange data in systematic ways that allow for quick location and retrieval of specific elements.

During the past 35 years, this desire for systematic arrangement and retrieval has evolved considerably. At one time, qualitative researchers created various "hard copy" *filing* or *indexing* systems to organize, store, and retrieve data. To do so involved making numerous copies of data records (e.g., interview transcriptions, letters, field notes) and organizing them in paper folders, piles, and even cardboard boxes. In turn, these folders, piles, and boxes were coded in some systematic manner to allow researchers to identify and index their contents. This identification procedure also allowed for various sorts of cross-referencing of topics.

Over the years, more and more qualitative researchers have moved away from paper-and-folder systems for coding and indexing and toward the use of computers. And as the technology has changed, so, too, has the vocabulary describing it. For example, the term *word crunching* (Dennis, 1984) has slowly crept into the vocabularies of many qualitative researchers to describe the reduction of data bulk and the use of computerized methods for accessing and retrieving textual data. Computer programs have been developed that specifically address or are dedicated to the organization and analysis of textual data. Some programs have been designed to perform content analysis, for instance (Stone et al., 1966), and others have been created to help in the development of grounded theory (Shelly & Sibert, 1985). Among the most popular types of dedicated qualitative programs are those designed to assist in the storing and analysis of ethnographic data (Seidel, 1984).

Many researchers, however, co-opt and adapt commercial data- and word-processing programs to suit their various qualitative-analytic needs. Today, most social scientists are at least sufficiently computer literate to use word-processing systems, which provide several significant tools. Most word-processing systems have an indexing function and a means of searching for terms or specific characters (see also later in this chapter). Word processors also facilitate text revision, such as quickly "cutting and pasting" (i.e., copying and moving) blocks of text; when desired, this text can be stored as a new electronic file or printed out as revised "hard copy." In short, word-processing systems offer innovative qualitative researchers a fairly versatile means of organizing and analyzing textual data.

Getting Started

The researcher begins the process of qualitative data analysis by preparing and organizing the data. If he or she has conducted interviews using a tape recorder, the first task will be to *transcribe* the interview tapes. Ideally, the researcher should transcribe the interview data directly into a computer, and the data should be transcribed verbatim. Quite literally, this means that if the subject makes a clicking sound with his or her mouth, the transcriber should indicate that such a sound was made. If a telephone rings in the background, the transcriber should indicate parenthetically that the phone rang. If a dog barks and can be heard on the tape, even this should be included in the transcription. The idea is to recreate the entire interview situation, not merely the verbal exchange between interviewer and subject.

Because transcription is a lengthy and sometimes tedious process (as well as expensive, if a transcriber is hired), extraneous sounds heard during an interview are ignored by some researchers. For expediency, the researcher may choose to eliminate anything that is not directly a question or an answer. In cases in which a consistent interview schedule has been used, the researcher may even transcribe shorthand versions of the questions and write out full representations of the answers. The guiding principle behind any of these possible arrangements is to preserve the most detail in the briefest possible form.

The researcher working with field notes should convert the shorthand jottings he or she made in the field to *full field notes*. (See Berg, 1995, for a description of full field notes.) Such full notes will likely have been prepared during the course of the investigation, so by the analysis stage of research, the data will largely have been entered and will be ready for coding and indexing.

When working with artifacts, photographs, drawings, or other nontextual data, the researcher needs to prepare a written account that describes these items in detail. This account can then be used as a textual record of the objects and artifacts.

Once material has been entered into a word processor, it can be indexed using the function provided by most systems. Indexed terms can be used to locate various classification categories, specific words, classes of key terms, and themes. Most indexing systems provide the dual capacity of identifying specific words where they appear in text or listing more general key terms or phrases on pages where material is present. For instance, in a page of text on drug use, marijuana and cocaine may be discussed in some detail. The researcher will likely identify the words *marijuana* and *cocaine* and might also key the page with the term *drugs,* even though this particular word is not literally shown on the page. This indexing process provides two benefits:

1. It allows the researcher to move to a slightly more abstract line of thinking during her or his analysis.
2. It provides a type of cross-referencing that will quickly allow the researcher to search for and retrieve discussions of related terms—for instance, in the example, any type of drug.

Using key words in indexing also allows the researcher to work with various analytic themes or classes of words, which facilitates intentionally listing thematic categories that represent specific concepts examined by certain questions. Indexing data in this way also makes it possible to locate structured questions from the instrument, as well as their corresponding responses. Answers to questions can be compared across subjects or aggregated to calculate the magnitude of a particular pattern of response.

REFERENCES

Bailey, K. D. (1982). *Methods of social research* (2nd ed.). New York: Free Press.

Berg, B. L. (1995). *Qualitative research methods for the social sciences* (2nd ed.). Boston: Allyn and Bacon.

Dennis, D. L. (1984). Word crunching: An annotated bibliography on computers and qualitative data analysis. *Qualitative Sociology, 7*(1/2),148–156.

Dowdall, G. W., & Golden, J. (1989). Photographs as data: An analysis of images from a mental hospital. *Qualitative Sociology, 12*(2), 183–213.

Hagan, F. (1993). *Research methods in criminal justice and criminology* (3rd ed.). New York: Macmillan.

Miles, M. B., & Huberman, A. M. (1984). *Qualitative data analysis: A sourcebook of new methods.* Beverly Hills, CA: Sage.

Schwartz, D. (1989). Visual ethnography: Using photography in qualitative research. *Qualitative Sociology, 12*(2), 119–154.

Seidel, J. (1984). The ethnograph. *Qualitative Sociology, 7*(1/2), 110–125.

Shelly, A., & Sibert, E. (1985). *The Qualog's user's manual.* Syracuse, NY: Syracuse University, School of Computer Information Science.

Stone, P. J., Murphy, D. C., Smith, M. S., & Ogilvic, D. M. (1966). *The general: A computer approach to content analysis.* Cambridge, MA: The MIT Press.

Webb, E. J., Campbell, D. T., Schwartz, R. D., & Sechrest, L. (1966). *Unobtrusive measures: Nonreactive research in the social sciences.* Chicago: Rand McNally.

Teenage Suicide: An Evaluation of Reactive Responses to Change and a Proposed Model for Proactive Accommodation/Adaptation

Dennis L. Peck and Kimberly A. Folse
Sociological Practice Review
Vol. 1, No. 1, pp. 33–39, June 1990

Introduction

Suicide is one of the major causes of death among teenagers (U.S. Bureau of the Census, 1989:79). It is also the focus of a frequently cited question: "Why did that individual commit suicide?" (Leenaars, 1988:17). And, despite more than two hundred years of analysis (Douglas, 1967), suicide remains a matter of vexation among analysts and the general public, especially when teenage persons resort to self-destructive behavior. Explanations for why self-inflicted death occurs are varied, drawing upon many points of view. Notes left by committers suggest that reasons for suicide as an ultimate solution vary.

A methodological issue relating to suicidal behavior is whether suicide notes do, in fact infer intent of the writer—a matter which has long been debated. Bernstein (1979), for example, was skeptical that suicide notes accurately portray suicidal intent. Jacobs (1967), Edelman and Renshaw (1982), and Peck (1983), on the other hand, argued that suicide notes provide an adequate basis for inferring attitudes toward and motives for acts of self-destruction, while Shneidman and Farberow (1957) and Leenaars (1988:8) argue that suicide notes and personal documents provide important evidence for discerning the ideation and affect of the writer. Suicide notes, according to Leenaars, inform the reader of "what it was like for them (committers) at the last moments of their life." Understanding the nature of suicide notes, Leenaars argues,

may by implication assist those interested in more effective suicide prevention.

Procedure

The teenage suicide notes used for this pilot project were collected from official Medical Examiner's case files and are part of a larger research project. The data reported represents a portion of this sample for which suicide notes were available. Therefore, no random procedure of selection is used. A selection of suicide notes (n = 19) provide categorical examples of notes written by teenagers just prior to committing suicide. Despite the small number of suicide notes, we have no reason to believe these teenage committers would differ dramatically from committers whose notes were filed elsewhere.

Data and Discussion

Suicide notes written by individuals 15 to 19 years of age at the time of death are employed to demonstrate the varied psychosocial states which contributed to the writers' suicidal behavior. These notes include expressions of love, discontentment, inadequacy, anger, remorse, self-pity, rejection, rebellion, and bereavement. Other expressions and general content refer to a specific crisis, stressor events, personal failure, and indicators of low self-esteem. What also emerges from the notes is the writer's belief that suicide may have an effect which could change, manipulate, or persuade others, a change which could not be affected in the everyday life of the individual. In the final analysis, however, the act of suicide may be described, from the perspective of the actor, as a response to unacceptable life conditions and lack of personal fulfillment.

Anger and Resentment of Authority Figures

These notes, written by teenagers, are characterized by the strong emotional anger of the writer. The first set of notes contain elements of anger and perhaps rebelliousness. An act of suicide, in some instances, is revenge directed and based on anger (Maris, 1985), or it may represent defiance directed toward authority figures similar to that described by Henry and Short (1954) and Peck (1983).

Dear Sir:

I wish to inform you that I have for some time been pondering suicide. My arrest and then general attitude of yourself and Sgt. _____ and one other Sgt. have made my choice. If you don't believe me, read the . . . journal for the 10th and 11th. I never informed my mother, if you wish to it is your choice.

Sincerely,

RHS

P.S. Get f——-!

Michael,

I hate you more than anything else in the world—you are a nothing and never will be nothing! I hate you more than that f—— Larry! Your a stone junkie at heart!

My name is Glenn _____ and I lived at _____ with my parents. I have attempted suicide because I could no longer take my father's sadistic nature. My mother was a "machine"—lacking in human emotions. This was the only way to get away from my parents.

Stress and frequency of daily "hassles" are known to contribute to temporary emotional instability (Rowlison and Felner, 1988). These include the death of a loved one, financial crisis, arguments, personal ineptitude, being jailed, and repeated failure. Thus, an assessment of indicators of personal well-being seems crucial for understanding motivations to engage in self-destructive behavior.

P.R.S.

I am very sorry—but the future holds for me only more trouble—I've tried my d—— to make good—but even working legally—people try to rip me off. I do not wish to hurt anyone.

Suicide as a Reaction to Rejection/Broken Relationship

Broken and strained interpersonal relationships often are cited as causes for acts of self-destruction. When comparing adolescent committers with older suicides, Maris (1985) found that interpersonal motivations involving relationships with parents, peers, and lovers is an important aspect of self-destructive behavior.

Dear Barb,

I only wish I understood, but I don't. I guess I still feel for you but don't know in what way. You understood me and understand what I am about to do.

Ted

Paula:

By the time you get this I will no longer be around. But just you remember one thing, that I love you with all my heart and I have always loved you. I am sorry that things did not work out as I wanted them too. My things, no one know but you knows where they are, will you take them please to remember me by! I love you and this is the only way out for me.

Love R.M.

Please do not come to see me being put away.

Rational Justification for Suicide

Battin (1982) suggested three nonimpairment criteria be used to evaluate suicide as a rational act, including: the ability to reason; a realistic world view; and adequacy of information. Two other criteria, identified by Battin as representing satisfaction of interests, include avoiding harm and achieving goals. Maris (1982) suggested that suicide contemplation is rational in that the thought process is intelligible, logical, and problem solving; however, the act itself may not be rational (Clements, Sider, and Perlmutter, 1983).

To be opened in the event of my death! This letter is being written previous to the event of my death. I would like very much for everyone who may have come to be affiliated with me in the previous years, or in the present to try and understand what I am about to say. First of all, I want you to know that I will have died a quiet and painless death. If I were to have continued living I would just be dying a little of myself everyday of my remaining life. I have decided to choose this alternative. There are many reasons why I have decided to leave this world, but the main reasons are my feelings about this world and my philosophies. Please try and understand that this was my best solution, and is what I have

been longing for. I realize that I have not been satisfied in this world, and I only hope that I might be in the next world to come. We all have to leave this present world at sometime in our life, and in a way I may have an advantage as I am able to say when and how I am to leave.

Cordially,

RMF

Failure Suicide: Reactions to Inadequacy

Repeated failure may lead to what has been defined as a fatalistic world view or feelings of hopelessness for the future (Peck, 1983), where hopelessness is the symptom of negative expectation for the future (Beck, Steer, and Garrison, 1985). This final set of suicide notes include elements of a fatalistic view of life, toward the current social environment, and orientation toward the future.

To Whom It May Concern:

I feel I am overwhelmed by grief. A grief that I neither fully understand nor can bear in the light that I had the sincerest intentions to amend but was refuted by the very thing that could have saved me from what you now observe. Realistically, however, it was my very failure if not impossible to accept. The fate has long been overdue. There is one thing worse than losing and that is never to have tried. I felt I tried the best I could with what I had to work with. Do not worry I am with God. I'm sorry for causing ___ and the police trouble.

Accommodation/Adaptation to Change Model: A Proposed Process of Suicide Prevention

Although these committers were young, they appear to be reactive to or unable to accommodate or adapt to change. These young individuals were incapable of control and were unable to engage in proactive behavior to gain control over their lives. This lack of control influenced, in part, their decision to commit suicide. According to Rowlison and Felner (1988), cumulative negative life change may lead to impaired functioning but such impaired functioning may also lead to the occurrence of more negative life events. The key to accommodation/adaptation to change is to move one out of a dysfunctional reactive mode into a functional proactive mode.

Conclusions

Because of the nonprobabilistic nature of our sample, the brief accounts reported here should not be viewed as representative of an entire population of teenage suicides. The intent is not to generalize these findings to other committer populations; rather, our purpose is to use the categories of suicide described above to demonstrate the hypothesized relationship between teenage suicide and a lack of accommodation/adaptation to change.

The reasons for suicidal behavior, as presented in the notes documented above, identify interpersonal and intrapersonal factors which affect the committers' efforts to control their lives, and influence the decision to engage in self-destructive behavior. While many committers apparently do not leave a written statement explaining this act, the content of these suicide notes suggests that committers may have recently experienced a series of stressor events. These findings, however, provide only a partial explanation of teenage suicide since the psy-chosocial states experienced by these youthful committers can also be used to explain non-deviant behavior.

References

Battin, Margaret P. 1982. *Ethical Issues in Suicide.* Englewood Cliffs: Prentice-Hall.

Bernstein, Michael. 1979. "The Communication of Suicidal Intent by Completed Suicides." *Omega: Journal of Death and Dying,* 9:175–182.

Clements, Collen D., Roger C. Sider, and Richard Perlmutter.. 1983. "Suicide: Bad Act or Good Intervention?" *Suicide and Life-Threatening Behavior,* 13:28–41.

Edelman, Ann M. and Steven L. Renshaw. 1982. "Genuine versus Simulated Suicide Notes: An Issue Revisited Through Discourse Analysis." *Suicide and Life-Threatening Behavior,* 12:103–113.

Jacobs, Jerry. 1967. "A Phenomenological Study of Suicide Notes." *Social Problems,* 15:60–72.

Leenaars, Anton A. 1988. *Suicide Notes: Predictive Clues and Patterns.* New York: Human Sciences Press.

Maris, Ronald W. 1985. "The Adolescent Suicide Problem." *Suicide and Life-Threatening Behavior,* 15:91–109.

Peck, Dennis L. 1983. "The Last Moments of Life: Learning to Cope." *Deviant Behavior: An Interdisciplinary Journal,* 4:13–32.

Rowlison, Richard T. and Robert D. Felner. 1988. "Major Life Events, Hassles, and Adaptation in Adolescence: Confounding in the Conceptualization and Measurement of Life Stress and Adjustment Revisited." *Journal of Personality and Social Psychology,* 55:432–444.

Shneidman, Edwin S. and Norman L. Farberow. 1957. *Clues to Suicide.* New York: McGraw-Hill.

U.S. Bureau of the Census. 1989. *Census Update, 1989.* Washington, D.C.: U.S. Government Printing Office.

Name of Student _____

Student ID # _____

Course Section # _____

Date _____

1. In the Peck and Folse article, each category of suicide includes a brief description of characteristics associated with notes of individuals in that category. Using these characteristics as a criteria for selection, sort each of the four fictitious suicide notes that follows into an appropriate category:

   (1) Anger/resentment of authority figures

   (2) Rejection/broken relationship

   (3) Rational justification

   (4) Failure/inadequacy

      a. Note #1: Category _____

      I can't stand my life as it is now. My boss is a moron who wants nothing better than to get me in the back room and harass me into having sex with him again. I feel so dirty. It's just like when I was younger and Uncle Joe would make me do things to him. I can't take it any more—I hope they both get AIDS!

      b. Note #2: Category _____

      Mom:

      I know I have let you and Dad down. I really tried to get better grades, but it just doesn't seem to work for me. I know that you and Dad have put all of your savings into my going to college. I can't come home knowing I have spent your money on nothing. I know you would never say anything about it, but I would always know in my heart that I have ruined your lives and my own. I love you and I hope you understand.

      c. Note #3: Category _____

      Donna,

      I thought I was over you. I probably would have been if you had not started sleeping with John. How could you and my own brother do this to me? I can't continue bumping into you on the street and living with John knowing what I know. I only hope something like this someday happens to you!

      d. Note #4: Category _____

      Sandy,

      I have been unable to make you fully understand me. Although I have tried, I don't think you really understand that I adore you. Yet, I realize that you could never love anyone like me. I know you will find happiness with someone some day. I can never foresee that in my own life and think this is the best answer for me. I'm sorry if this causes you to be upset, but I needed to let you know how I felt—just once.

2. The suicide notes in the article were all written by teens. How might suicide notes written by adults possibly be different? similar?

   a. Possible differences:

   _____

   _____

   _____

   _____

   _____

   _____

   _____

   _____

   _____

   b. Possible similarities:

   _____

   _____

   _____

   _____

   _____

   _____

   _____

   _____

   _____

   _____

   _____

   _____

Economic Antecedents of Mental Hospitalization: A Nineteenth-Century Time Series Test

George W. Dowdall, James R. Marshall, and Wayne A. Morra
Journal of Health and Social Behavior
Vol. 31, No. 2, pp. 141–147, 1990

Introduction

The 1973 publication of M. Harvey Brenner's *Mental Illness and the Economy* was viewed widely as a milestone in psychiatric epidemiology. In the foreword, Hollingshead called Brenner's application of economic statistical techniques to mental hospital admissions data "ingenious," but labeled his results "controversial," and predicated that they would need to be examined carefully (Brenner, 1973, pp. vi–viii). A comprehensive review of the literature in the sociology of mental health (Goldstein, 1979:395) credited Brenner with providing an impetus to researchers to study how larger socioeconomic forces shape mental illness. By examining the links among economic, social, and individual events, Brenner's research built on themes first emphasized by such founders of social science as Marx and Durkheim. Moreover, the research appeared to demonstrate that sophisticated models of important issues could be tested with mental health care utilization data, a large untapped but very promising resource (Leaf, 1985). Finally, Brenner's work became a datum in national discussions of economic and social policy (Brenner, 1976; 1984).

This paper employs what is recognized as the current standard for statistical analysis of time series data (Catalano et al., 1985); it studies admissions of people from a single community, using individual-level data that can be aggregated into theoretically meaningful units of time. The central question it tests—whether economic change provokes first hospital admissions—is based on individual-level data for every first admission to mental health care facilities in Buffalo, a large American urban center, from 1881 to 1891.

Methods

Admissions Data Set

A study (Dowdall, 1986; Dowdall and Golden, 1989) examining the social history of care for the mentally ill discovered that a full set of admissions registers existed for the three institutions that cared for the mentally ill in the Buffalo area (defined operationally as Erie County) in the 1880s.

The Buffalo State Asylum for the Insane published detailed yearly tables about its patient population (e.g., New York State, 1881). Its supervising (and, after 1890, governing) agency in Albany also published yearly data, used by Brenner (1973:25) in his analysis. By contrast, the Erie County Poorhouse published little about its inmates; a historian who wished to analyze its population was forced to examine original archival materials (Katz, 1983, 1986). The small Catholic asylum, the Providence Retreat, sent yearly figures to the state agency that oversaw the care of the mentally ill, but published only brief reports (Providence Retreat, 1896).

We coded the data for the present study from the original archival records of each institution. The data examined in this paper are limited to first admissions of residents of Erie County, New York. In view of the relative isolation of Buffalo in the 1880s, it is likely that these three institutions, as the sole source of psychiatric care in the region, provide a nearly complete record of mental hospital first admissions of Erie County residents.

Economic Activity Measures

It would be desirable to use an economic performance measure that reflects only local conditions (Catalano et al., 1985; Marshall and Dowdall, 1982). Unfortunately, however, extensive archival research yielded no adequate measures for the Buffalo area before 1914. Thus the present analysis uses the Ayres index, which Brenner employed for that most compelling of his findings: the association of economic conditions with admissions to the Utica State Hospital for the 57-year period from 1850 to 1907 (Brenner, 1973:47–57). The Ayres index, one of the oldest measures of the performance of the American economy as a whole, has been used widely as a measure of business cycles (Ameritrust, 1987).

Conclusions

These nineteenth-century findings, like those found for the Rochester area almost a century later (Catalano et al., 1985), show a remarkably similar lack of support for Brenner's hypothesis that economic fluctuations provoke mental hospital admissions. Thus the two studies that use sophisticated modeling, individual-level data for all psychiatric inpatient episodes, and theory-based measurement provide little support for the provocation hypothesis. The studies use conservative statistical techniques that probably estimate the lower boundary of the effect (Catalano et al., 1985). Yet the virtual absence of evidence in both the contemporary Rochester data and the nineteenth-century Buffalo data can be regarded only as nonsupportive of the provocation hypothesis.

Social researchers are trained to reach conclusions—the sharper, the more stimulating, and the more disquieting, the better. Although Brenner's conclusions must be regarded as sharp, stimulating, and disquieting, the method on which those conclusions are based has been criticized roundly (Catalano et al., 1985; Marshall and Dowdall, 1982; Marshall and Funch, 1979). Because Brenner's method is seriously flawed,

and because his findings depend heavily upon his use of flawed methods, we must call into question his conclusion that economic change has been the single most important source of mental hospital fluctuation in the United States over the past 120 years. The most sophisticated exploration of the provocation hypothesis (Catalano et al., 1985) casts doubt on its validity. The test conducted in this paper, based on data derived from the nineteenth-century records, also raises doubt about the validity of the hypothesis. Thus, both historical and contemporary evidence argue for abandonment of the provocation hypothesis.

References

Ameritrust. 1987. *American Business Activity from 1790 to Today.* 58th ed. Cleveland: Ameritrust.

Brenner, M. Harvey. 1973. *Mental Illness and the Economy.* Cambridge: Harvard University Press.

———. 1976. *Estimating the Social Costs of National Economic Policy: Implications for Mental and Physical Health.* Washington, DC: U.S. Government Printing Office.

———. 1984. *Estimating the Effects of Economic Change on National Health and Social Well-Being.* Washington, DC: U.S. Government Printing Office.

Catalano, Ralph A., David Dooley, and Robert L. Jackson. 1985. "Economic Antecedents of Help Seeking: Reformulation of Time-Series Tests." *Journal of Health and Social Behavior* 26:141–52.

Dowdall, George W. 1986a. "The Birth of the Buffalo Asylum: James Platt White and the Professionalization of Medicine." Presented to the American Association for the History of Medicine, Rochester, May 10th.

Dowdall, George W. and Janet L. Golden. 1989. "Photographs as Data: An Analysis of Images from a Mental Hospital." *Qualitative Sociology* 12: 183–213.

Goldstein, Michael S. 1979. "The Sociology of Mental Health and Illness." *Annual Review of Sociology* 3: 381–409.

Katz, Michael B. 1983. *Poverty and Policy in American History.* New York: Academic Press.

———. 1986. *In the Shadow of the Poorhouse.* New York: Basic Books.

Leaf, Philip J. 1985. "Mental Health Systems Research: A Review of Available Data." *American Behavioral Scientist* 28: 619–38.

Marshall, James R. and George W. Dowdall. 1982. "Employment and Mental Hospitalization: The

Case of Buffalo, New York, 1914–1955." *Social Forces* 60: 843–53.

Marshall, James R. and Donna P. Funch. 1979. "Mental Illness and the Economy: A Critique and Partial Replication." *Journal of Health and Social Behavior* 20: 282–89.

Providence Retreat. 1896. *The Thirty-Fourth Annual Report of the Providence Retreat for the Year 1895.* Buffalo: Courier.

Name of Student _____

Student ID # _____

Course Section # _____

Date _____

1. You will need to examine a local newspaper for this exercise. Consult issues from the past five years; for each year, use the month of November to represent fall, February to represent winter, May for spring, and August for summer. Locate the section of the newspaper that contains daily crime listings for the area. If the newspaper does not have a daily listing, review the crime coverage on the front page for this exercise. For the past five years, examine each day of the month for the four months listed. Using the following charts, plot the number of crimes reported.

Day of Month	November	1ST YEAR February	May	August
1				
2				
3				
4				
5				
6				
7				
8				
9				
10				
11				
12				
13				
14				
15				
16				
17				
18				
19				
20				
21				
22				
23				
24				
25				
26				
27				
28				
29				
30				
31				

2ND YEAR

Day of Month	November	February	May	August
1				
2				
3				
4				
5				
6				
7				
8				
9				
10				
11				
12				
13				
14				
15				
16				
17				
18				
19				
20				
21				
22				
23				
24				
25				
26				
27				
28				
29				
30				
31				

3RD YEAR

Day of Month	November	February	May	August
1				
2				
3				
4				
5				
6				
7				
8				
9				
10				
11				
12				
13				
14				
15				
16				
17				
18				
19				
20				
21				
22				
23				
24				
25				
26				
27				
28				
29				
30				
31				

4TH YEAR

Day of Month	November	February	May	August
1				
2				
3				
4				
5				
6				
7				
8				
9				
10				
11				
12				
13				
14				
15				
16				
17				
18				
19				
20				
21				
22				
23				
24				
25				
26				
27				
28				
29				
30				
31				

Day of Month	November	5TH YEAR February	May	August
1				
2				
3				
4				
5				
6				
7				
8				
9				
10				
11				
12				
13				
14				
15				
16				
17				
18				
19				
20				
21				
22				
23				
24				
25				
26				
27				
28				
29				
30				
31				

2. Based on your data, answer the following questions:

    a. What patterns, if any, are reflected by season?

Fall

_____

_____

_____

_____

Winter

_____

_____

_____

_____

Spring

_____

_____

_____

_____

Summer

_____

_____

_____

_____

    b. What patterns, if any, are reflected by year?

1st Year

_____

_____

_____

_____

2nd Year

_____

_____

_____

_____

3rd Year

_____

_____

_____

_____

4th Year

_____

_____

_____

_____

5th Year

_____

_____

_____

_____

c.   What patterns, if any, are reflected overall?

_____

_____

_____

_____

_____

_____

_____

_____

_____

d. What conclusions might be drawn about these relationships?

_____

_____

_____

_____

_____

_____

_____

_____

The Deterrent Effect of Capital Punishment in the Five Most Active Execution States: A Time Series Analysis

Scott H. Decker and Carol W. Kohfeld
Criminal Justice Review
Vol. 15, No. 2, pp. 173–191, 1990

Introduction

Capital punishment is an issue that has promoted analysis from scholars in a variety of disciplines. Virtually every social science (and many physical sciences and humanities as well) has contributed to the debate over the existence, effect, and imposition of the death penalty. Such study now appears to have reached a historical high, prompted no doubt by the recent certification of the death penalty by the U.S. Supreme Court and the executions that have subsequently been carried out.

Three areas of debate have received the most attention. First, the legal merits of capital punishment have been debated in the courts, in state legislatures, and by the public. These debates have been most concerned with procedural issues and have concentrated in particular on Eighth Amendment concerns regarding "cruel and unusual punishment." While some have sought to ground these arguments in a more substantive framework, the bulk of the security in this regard has focused on the issue of the way in which the penalty has been imposed. Typically, the discriminatory or nonpatterned application of the death penalty has been the principal concern of these studies (Kleck, 1981; Paternoster, 1983). Thus, questions about the nature of the victim, characteristics of the offender, and contribution of aggravating circumstances to the sentencing decision have been the hallmark of this approach.

As a second concern, many have debated the moral or ethical merits of the death penalty. This tradition is perhaps the oldest and most consistent theme in the analysis of the death penalty. Opponents have consistently emphasized that executions represent little more than legalized killing performed in the name of the state. As such, they argue, these practices are without moral justification (Amsterdam, 1977; Conrad, 1983). Proponents, on the other hand, have argued that the failure to impose this severe penalty represents a serious moral error; indeed, such arguments have emphasized that it is a moral injustice not to impose the death penalty. These arguments stem from the traditional retributionist contention that those such persons go unpunished, and injustice has been committed (Hook, 1961; Van den Haag, 1978).

Of all the debates, though, perhaps none has received more attention than the presumed deterrent effect of capital punishment on homicides. These deterrence studies have increased significantly in methodological and statistical rigor in the last decade. Earlier works employed the use of contiguous states as the basis for analysis. States with roughly similar social and demographic characteristics were compared in order to determine whether their homicide rates differed. Differences in this criterion variable were presumed to be the result of the primary differentiating feature—that one of the states had the death penalty and the other did not. Such analyses (Bailey, 1974; Sellin, 1958; Sutherland, 1925) consistently demonstrated that there was no difference in homicide rates between "similar" states that varied only with respect to the existence of the death penalty.

The next significant methodological advance came with the advent of correlational studies. The works of Bailey (1977) and Schuessler (1952) are the best-known examples of this trend. These studies sought to show a relationship between executions and the death penalty as well as other exogenous variables. They, too, failed to demonstrate the deterrent effect of executions identified by deterrence theory.

The most recent trend in deterrence studies has been the use of multivariate statistical tools. These analyses have incorporated the use of lag structures as well as a variety of techniques to minimize the effects of autocorrelation. In addition, such techniques lend themselves particularly well to the use of time series designs, a practice that represents an advance in data as well as method. By including a large number of points in time, deterrence studies can more accurately document the effects of executions. Such studies can also be categorized by the type of data used. Most deterrence studies in the 1970s used cross-sectional data (Bailey, 1974; Ehrlich, 1975); aggregates of jurisdictions, typically states, were grouped together for analysis. Recently, there has been a tendency to employ the use of a single jurisdiction in time series analysis. This preserves the advantages of longitudinal design and eliminates some of the potential difficulties inherent in cross-sectional studies, particularly where policy inference is a likely application for the results.

The current study is consistent with these trends in deterrence studies. It proposes a time series design that incorporates a lag structure for the analysis of the deterrence question in five states. A 50-year time series is used to assess the effect of execution on homicides in North Carolina, California, Texas, New York, and Georgia. These five states were chosen for analysis because of their historical use of the death penalty. They are the jurisdictions that have imposed the death penalty most frequently in this country. As such, they are likely candidates for analysis, from a policy standpoint as well as on methodological grounds.

Data Sources

Some of the data for this study were provided by the U.S. Bureau of Prisons. Specifically, the authors have received from that agency an enu-meration of the annual number of executions by state for the time period 1931 to 1980. These data facilitate both the time series nature of the analysis and the approach of using a single jurisdiction (states) as the unit of analysis. The dependent variable, annual rate of murder and nonnegligent manslaughter, was drawn from the Uniform Crime Reports. Other exogenous variables were drawn from the Statistical Abstracts. Selection of these variables was based on an analysis of the death penalty and homicide literature. There was a dual criterion applied for the selection decision: whether the variable was identified in previous research as having both empirical and theoretical relevance to variations in homicide rates. The controls included the proportion of the state population that was male and aged 15 to 29, the proportion of the state population living in urban areas, and the proportion of the state population in nonagricultural employment.

The Current Analysis

Several different analyses were performed. The time series nature of these data made it impossible to address the deterrence issue from several vantage points. Mean homicide rates were compared for three different eras corresponding to the death penalty experience in each of five states. These periods are referred to as (a) "use years," in which the death penalty was in force and executions were carried out, (b) "threat years," in which the death penalty was in force but there were no executions, and (c) "abolition years," in which there was no death penalty in force. This natural division allowed the assessment of three distinctly different eras, each of which can be viewed as representing a particular policy. This permitted a distinction to be drawn between the effect of the actual use of the sanction and the effect of the mere threat of its use, in addition to more typical questions about the effect of its abolition. These comparisons were elaborated in a number of ways, beginning with zero-order correlations and then proceeding to testing for autocorrelation, required only in California.

In Table 1 the mean homicide rate for each state during the three eras identified above is presented. This allows a comparison of the

TABLE 1   A Comparison of Mean Homicide Rates per 100,000
Residents for New York, California, North Carolina, Georgia, and
Texas, 1933–1980, for USE, THREAT, and ABOLITION Periods of
Capital Punishment

STATE	USE	THREAT	ABOLITION
New York			
Mean	3.07	7.76	10.92
Standard Deviation	.74	3.44	.19
N	29	12	5
California			
Mean	4.24	8.00	9.60
Standard Deviation	.96	3.75	.73
N	31	12	5
North Carolina			
Mean	15.96	9.63	12.20
Standard Deviation	5.91	1.32	.79
N	26	17	5
Georgia			
Mean	19.30	13.44	16.40
Standard Deviation	6.83	2.11	2.10
N	32	11	5
Texas			
Mean	12.5	12.09	12.86
Standard Deviation	3.9	2.98	.66
N	32	11	5

behavior of the dependent variable during years in which there were executions (use years), years in which the death penalty was in force but there were no executions (threat years), and years in which the death penalty was not a legally available sanction (abolition years). Because each state has executed different numbers of prisoners, the threat and use estimates are different for each state.

A consistent pattern of findings within each state was not observed; nor can statements be made about the states as a group. It would be expected that a certain commonality of outcomes should emerge for these five states, given their high level of activity in the area of executions. The conclusion to be drawn from the early section of the analysis—where a deterrent effect was observed in some jurisdictions, the opposite effect was observed in others, and in still others

no effect was discernible—is that the penalty has a varying effect, depending on where it is measured. A deterrent effect, however, was observed for executions only in the preliminary examinations of means and correlations and in the regression analysis for New York.

One conclusion seems inescapable from the results presented here: executions have failed to exert a consistent deterrent impact on homicide in the five states most likely to execute.

References

Amsterdam, A. G. (1977). In opposition to the death penalty. In H. Bedau (Ed.), *The death penalty in America* (pp. 346–358). New York, NY: Oxford University Press.

Bailey, W. C. (1974). Murder and the death penalty. *Journal of Criminal Law and Criminology, 65,* 416–423.

Bailey, W. C. (1977). Imprisonment v. the death penalty as a deterrent to murder. *Law and Human Behavior, 1,* 239–260.

Conrad, J. P. (1983). The state as killer. *American Bar Foundation Research Journal, 2,* 451–464.

Ehrlich, I. (1975). The deterrent effect of capital punishment: A question of life and death. *American Economic Review, 65,* 397–416.

Hook, S. (1961). The death sentence. *The New Leader, 44,* 18–20.

Kleck, G. (1981). Racial discrimination in criminal sentencing: A critical evaluation of the evidence with additional evidence on the death penalty. *American Sociological Review, 46*(6), 783–805.

Paternoster, R. (1983). Race of victim and location of crime: The decision to seek the death penalty in South Carolina. *Journal of Criminal Law and Criminology, 3,* 278–363.

Schuessler, A. (1952). The deterrent effect of the death penalty. *Annals, 54,* 284–297.

Sellin, T. (1958). The death penalty. In *Model Penal Code: Reprint, tentative drafts nos. 8, 9, and 10* (tentative draft no. 8). Philadelphia, PA: The American Law Institute.

Sutherland, E. (1925). Murder and the death penalty. *Journal of Criminal Law and Criminology, 15,* 522–536.

Van den Haag, E. (1978). In defense of the death penalty: A legal-practical moral analysis. *Criminal Law Bulletin, 14*(1), 51–68.

Name of Student _____

Student ID # _____

Course Section # _____

Date _____

1. In your college library, locate the *Sourcebook of Criminal Statistics* for the years 1970–1990. Find the homicide rates for states. (Note that the *Sourcebook* sometimes lists this information in a table for "Murder, and nonnegligent manslaughter by state" and sometimes under the label "Murder, and nonnegligent manslaughter rates"). Next, find the annual arrest rate for homicide in Florida, Georgia, New York, North Carolina, and Texas for each year (i.e., 1970–1990). Separate the data into three groups, as follows: 1970–1975; 1976–1983; and 1984–1990. Label each group "Use," "Abolition," and "Post–Supreme Court Decision," respectively. For each of the five states, calculate the mean and standard deviation (SD) for each category (as done in Table 1 of the Decker et al. article).

STATE	USE 1970–1975	ABOLITION 1976–1983	POST–SUPREME COURT DECISION 1984–1990

Florida

Mean   _____   _____   _____

Show your calculations here:

SD   _____   _____   _____

Show your calculations here:

Georgia

Mean   _____   _____   _____

Show your calculations here:

SD   _____   _____   _____

Show your calculations here:

New York

Mean   _____   _____   _____

Show your calculations here:

SD   _____   _____   _____

Show your calculations here:

North Carolina

Mean   _____   _____   _____

Show your calculations here:

SD   _____   _____   _____

Show your calculations here:

Texas

Mean   _____   _____   _____

Show your calculations here:

SD   _____   _____   _____

Show your calculations here:

2. Given your findings, what assessment can be made about the deterrent effect of the death penalty on committing homicide?

_____

_____

CHAPTER 6

Research Ethics

During the past few decades, ethical issues have emerged and become a major concern of many groups, including big business, the military, the government, and academia. So many instances of unethical behavior have surfaced in recent years that all of society now seems concerned with ethical issues. For instance, in the medical profession, we have heard of unnecessary surgeries being performed; in the stock market/investment industry, fraudulent deals and insider trading; in banking, the savings and loan (S&L) scandal; and in the military, $1,000 wrenches and $900 toilet seats. We can all think of countless incidents that have contributed to the general social concern about ethics and ethical behavior.

Universities and colleges have not been exempt from unethical behavior. In the area of research, in particular, competition for grant monies has caused some researchers to engage in unethical practices. When researchers believe in their approaches to solving problems and have invested many years in their work, some will falsify their results so that they can continue to receive funding. They are sure that if they can just continue their research, they will find the breakthrough they are searching for. Also, in some instances, the pressure on academicians to publish causes them to cut corners in their research and publish results before it is appropriate to do so. The accuracy of these results is often questionable, as is the methodology or statistical test employed. These unethical breaches of behavior by researchers underscore the fragility with which the research system operates.

Ethics and ethical behavior are of particular concern to the social sciences, specifically as these issues relate to research and research methods (Braswell, McCarthy, & McCarthy, 1991; Davis, 1989; Longmire, 1991). In the social sci-

ences—including the fields of criminology, criminal justice, sociology, anthropology, and psychology—ethical issues are compounded because research in these areas typically involves human subjects. Thus, the manner in which research is conducted and the findings that are released both have direct consequences for people's lives. Unfortunately, the social sciences are not immune to unethical practices.

ETHICAL ISSUES IN SOCIAL SCIENCE RESEARCH

Numerous ethical questions have been raised about research and research methods of social scientists, but three cases have received considerable attention, not only within their fields but in the news media, as well. A review of each case will illustrate not only the magnitude of the ethical dilemma at hand but the seriousness and nature of the unethical questions and methods employed.

Note that these examples are not representative of all research. Most social scientists conform to the ethical standards that have been established and are accepted today. These three flagrant cases of unethical behavior should be viewed as examples that teach the ethical parameters of research in the social sciences. The development of ethical principles and guidelines is an ongoing process that requires continued refinement as new questions are raised.

The Burt Case

The first case is that of Cyril Burt, a famed psychologist, who, in the late 1970s and early 1980s, was accused of falsifying data related to his study of twins, dating back to 1943 (Broad & Wade, 1982). Burt, who was actively involved in the development of experimental psychology, devoted a considerable amount of his early research to the relationship between heredity and intelligence. Wade (1976) discovered that Burt had reported the same correlations for each set of twins (Davis, 1989), which meant that Burt supposedly had the same findings for each set of twins in terms of the relationship between heredity and intelligence. From a statistical standpoint, these findings were just not possible.

A detailed examination of Burt's notes demonstrated that he had, in fact, invented the correlations. This discovery brought into question the results of his studies, especially those of the last 30 years involving his work on twins. The only reasonable conclusion researchers could draw (and still can) about the results of Burt's work on twins and heredity and intelligence was that the findings had been falsified and thus were not reliable.

One interpretation of this case that suggests a defense for Burt is that he was so sure that his hypotheses were correct that he did not believe he needed to follow the normal research route (Davis, 1989, p. 5). Any defense such as this of falsifying results is unacceptable. This type of unethical behavior is a serious violation of the research method. Many researchers accepted Burt's results and built their own research on it, which makes them victims of Burt's unethical behavior; the same is true of the many students who were taught based, in part, on the results of Burt's work.

The falsification of data and results is certainly not limited to the social sciences. Numerous examples can be found in other fields, especially the medical sciences. The competition for getting research monies and positions is fierce in the field of medical research. What's more, future funding is often based on the results of currently funded research, such that work that shows promise or positive results continues to receive funding. The case of William Summerlin, who was working in the field of cancer research, points out the difficulties of needing to provide results (Davis, 1989).

Summerlin was working on the lack of rejection properties of culture-grown skin, a highly competitive area of research. Because of the pres-

sure he felt to succeed, Summerlin "inked a black patch on two white laboratory mice to convince Good [his boss] that a skin graft between genetically different animals had been successful" (Davis, 1989, p. 7). One of Summerlin's assistants discovered the misrepresentation and brought it to the attention of the proper authorities.

The Humphreys Case

Another type of unethical behavior related to the social sciences is demonstrated by Laud Humphreys' work entitled *Tearoom Trade* (1970) (also discussed in Chapter 4). Humphreys examined the use of public bathrooms and the people who frequented them to engage in deviant sexual behavior. He played the role of the observing participant, facilitating the deviant activities by serving as a lookout.

Had Humphreys's research stopped here, it is likely that only two ethical issues would have been raised:

- That he failed to identify himself as a researcher
- That he observed, facilitated, and failed to report behavior that, in some jurisdictions, violates the law

But Humphreys went beyond making observations in public bathrooms. He copied down the license plates of those individuals who participated in the deviant acts and then retrieved their names and addresses through a connection he had at the motor vehicles department. After obtaining these names and addresses, Humphreys visited the homes of these people, posing as a mental health researcher collecting data for a survey. Humphreys asked the respondents personal questions, which he then correlated with his observations of them in the public bathrooms. At no time did he seek the permission of these people for their involvement in the real purpose of his research.

These surreptitious acts—copying down license plate numbers to track the individuals whom he had observed and then interviewing them under false pretenses—had more serious consequences than Humphreys's original ethical transgressions (as stated earlier).

The Milgram Case

The third case, now famous, is from the work of Stanley Milgram. He was interested in testing under what conditions a person will or will not follow directions that cause him or her to knowingly harm another individual. Milgram's study was motivated, in part, by actions of individuals who were victims of the Holocaust. During their imprisonment, supposedly normal individuals participated in hideous acts against fellow prisoners with the knowledge that they were hurting them.

Milgram (1965) set up an experiment in which lab assistants, dressed in white coats, instructed subjects to send electrical shocks to individuals who answered their questions incorrectly; the subjects sat at the controls of a machine and were told to turn up the current with subsequent incorrect answers, thereby increasing the supposed shock levels. Milgram hired actors to play the individuals receiving the shocks; they could be seen by the real subjects of the study and were instructed to act as if they were being shocked.

In some instances, the subjects refused to administer the shocks, especially when the dials on the machine indicated the electrical dosage to be lethal. The lab assistants assured the subjects that they would accept responsibility for the consequences and urged the subjects to keep increasing the current. Many of the subjects were upset by the situation, since they did not know the recipients of the supposed shocks were actors and not actually being harmed.

This type of experiment would be extremely difficult, if not impossible, to carry out today, given the guidelines in place for informed consent. Briefly, the researcher has obtained *informed consent* when he or she has disclosed to the subject any possible risks or benefits of participation. Furthermore, deceptive tactics, such as those employed by Milgram, might be viewed as being inappropriate.

Assessment of Ethical Issues

People generally agree that the three cases presented are all at the negative extreme of what can be described as a continuum of ethical behavior.

However, not all cases are so black and white. Many times, ethical issues regarding research questions and methods are clouded by considerable amounts of gray; they are not simple issues of right and wrong.

According to Toch (1981), there is no clear distinction between ethical and unethical behavior. "In research, a key difference is that between scientists who are 'doers' and others who are 'talkers.' Ethical prescriptions are most often formulated by the talkers, because what the talkers mostly talk about is doing" (pp. 189–190). Toch suggests that codes of ethics be developed. At the very least, doing so would reduce the number of attacks from individuals outside the profession. In addition, Toch (1981) could not see that with the codes there would be very much damage to the conduct of research.

RESPONSES OF ORGANIZATIONS AND AGENCIES TO ETHICAL ISSUES IN RESEARCH

Professional Academic Organizations

In part because of the problems identified with doing research, a number of professional academic organizations have produced codes of ethics designed to serve as guideposts for researchers. Paul Leedy, in the fifth edition of *Practical Research: Planning and Design* (1993), provides an excellent summary of the Code of Ethics of one such organization, the American Sociological Association (ASA):

1. Researchers must maintain scientific objectivity.
2. Researchers should recognize the limitations of their competence and not attempt to engage in research beyond such competence.
3. Every person is entitled to the right of privacy and dignity of treatment.
4. All research should avoid causing personal harm to subjects used in the research.

5. Confidential information provided by a research subject must be held in strict confidentiality by the researcher.

6. Research findings should be presented honestly, without distortion.

7. The researcher must not use the prerogative of a researcher to obtain information for other than professional purposes.

8. The researcher must acknowledge all assistance, collaboration of others, or sources from which information was borrowed from others.

9. The researcher must acknowledge financial support in the research report or any personal relationship of the researcher with the sponsor that may conceivably affect the research findings.

10. The researcher must not accept any favors, grants, or other means of assistance that would violate any of the ethical principles set forth in the above paragraphs. (pp. 129–130)

Consider item 1: *scientific objectivity*. If the researcher is well versed in the scientific method (discussed in detail in Chapter 1), this will certainly facilitate maintaining objectivity. Closely following the different components of the scientific method will not absolutely guarantee that the researcher will maintain objectivity, but doing so will definitely improve the probability for those who want to be objective.

One component of the scientific method calls for the researcher to identify his or her biases and beliefs as early in the research process as possible. Taking this step gives the researcher the opportunity to control for the influence of his or her biases and beliefs. And when these personal issues are included in the body of the research, the consumers of the results have the opportunity to make informed interpretations of what has been reported. (See also "Value-Neutral Research and the Role of the Researcher," later in this chapter.)

The issue of *honest presentation of results,* item 6 in the ASA code, can best be exemplified by the Cyril Burt case, discussed earlier in this chapter. When researchers present their results in a dishonest manner, as Burt did, they misdirect

others who unknowingly use these tainted results as the basis for further research. Researchers often rely upon the results of previous work to guide their current endeavors and to break new ground, rather than rehash existing findings. When statistically significant but fraudulent findings are reported, they can wrongly influence research that is undertaken to pursue a similar line of thought. This can have costly, long-term, and widespread ramifications for the development and future directions of programs and research. In addition, as stated earlier, the continuous reporting of false results can influence what people in the field believe and thus what textbooks teach, making this a problem for every student who is exposed to material based on falsified research.

Federal Agencies

In addition to academic disciplines developing their own codes of ethics, various federal agencies have promulgated ethical policies that include guidelines for research involving human subjects. The issues of confidentiality, informed consent, and avoidance of harm to subjects are also found in the Code of Federal Regulations (discussed later in this chapter). But looking at studies from the past, a number can be found that were not concerned with protecting subjects from harm. In fact, the purposes of some studies actually brought harm to subjects. Between 1956 and 1961, in a prison in Ohio, doctors from two prestigious institutions used prison volunteers to study whether healthy humans could be inoculated against cancer (Lore, 1990); these individuals were injected with live cancer cells.

While it could be argued that the prisoners volunteered and that their informed consent was obtained, these rationales are somewhat questionable. Can individuals such as prisoners, who are being controlled by the state for extended periods of time, willingly give their consent? Perhaps those who volunteered were motivated to do so because they thought that their participation would bring them some favored status, thereby shortening their sentences or at least making their time in prison easier. Even if this were not the case, the fact that the individuals were injected with a potentially deadly disease would not be appropriate, given ethical guidelines today.

In the 1950s, however, there were no such restrictions or guidelines for involving prisoners in research. In 1955, one year before the cancer research took place, 50 prisoners in the same institution were involved in testing different types of "vaccines as part of the Army's bacteriological warfare program" (Lore, 1990, p. 2B).

A far more problematic issue addresses the current status of the prisoners who participated in these studies. No extended follow-up of medical treatment has been provided for any of the prisoners involved. The truth is that the doctors who performed the medical research have had no contact with the prisoners who participated nor do they even know where these individuals are today. All states now have regulations for the participation of prisoners in medical experiments that would prevent this type of abuse from occurring.

In 1966, in one of the first federal efforts at ethical regulation, Surgeon General William Stewart issued the Public Health Service policy that called for institutional review of research involving human subjects. During this same year, the original policy was revised to include the following:

> There is a large range of social and behavioral research in which no personal risk to the subject is involved. In these circumstances, regardless of whether the investigation is classified as behavioral, social, medical, or other, the issues of concern are the fully voluntary nature of participation of the subject, the maintenance of confidentiality of the information obtained from the subject, and the protection of the subject from misuse of the findings. (Public Health Service, 1966)

Since that time, government policies and regulations have shifted from the level of policy to that of federal statute. Correspondingly, the requirements have become both more rigorous and complex. To make matters even more complicated, "the review requirements, which originally applied only to research funded by the Public Health Service, were extended by the National Research Act of 1974 to all research involving human subjects that is conducted at institutions that receive funds for research under the Public Health Services Act" (Gray, 1979, p. 44).

More recently, the Public Health Services Act, as amended by the Health Research Extension Act of 1985, was updated in 1991. Part 46, "Protection of Human Subjects," was added to the Code of Federal Regulations by the Department of Health and Human Services under Title 45, further delineating the responsibilities of institutions and institutional review boards (IRBs). The updated policy applies to all research involving human subjects that is carried out by federal departments or agencies, their subsidiaries, or institutions subject to their regulation. Research conducted at colleges and universities that receive funds from the federal government is subject to the requirements of this policy.

According to the Department of Health and Human Services (1991, p. 5), research done at colleges and universities that involves (1) normal educational practices, (2) the use of educational tests, or (3) the study of existing data, documents, and records that are publicly available is exempt from standard IRB reviews and is subject only to an *expedited review*. In this type of review, the chair of the IRB reviews the research proposal to determine whether it fits into one of these categories; if it does, the proposal is approved. The chair of the IRB is then responsible for notifying other board members about the action taken.

Institutions engaging in research that comes under the auspices of the federal code are required to establish IRBs, which have the authority to review and approve all research proposals. For an IRB to approve a research proposal, it must satisfy the following requirements:

1. Risks to subjects are minimized (i) by using procedures which are consistent with sound research design and which do not unnecessarily expose subjects to risk, and (ii) whenever appropriate, by using procedures already being performed on the subjects for diagnostic or treatment purposes. . . .

2. Risks to subjects are reasonable in relation to anticipated benefits, if any, to subjects, and the importance of the knowledge that may reasonably be expected to result. . . .

3. Selections of subjects is equitable. . . .
   The IRB . . . should be particularly cognizant of the special problems of research involving vulnerable populations, such as children, prisoners, pregnant women, mentally disabled persons, or economically or educationally disadvantaged persons. . . .
4. Informed consent will be sought from each prospective subject. . . .
5. Informed consent will be appropriately documented. . . .
6. When appropriate, the research plan makes adequate provision for monitoring the data collected to ensure the safety of subjects. . . .
7. When appropriate, there are adequate provisions to protect the privacy of subjects and to maintain the confidentiality of data. When some or all of the subjects are likely to be vulnerable to coercion or undue influence, . . . additional safeguards have been included in the study to protect the rights and welfare of these subjects. (Department of Health and Human Services, 1991, pp. 8–9)

When deemed necessary, IRBs can require that modifications be made in research proposals prior to approval, bringing them in line with these requirements.

VALUE-NEUTRAL RESEARCH AND THE ROLE OF THE RESEARCHER

Questions can be raised about the ethical behavior of researchers to the extent that, as human beings, they have values. Howard Becker (1967), in his presidential speech to the Society for the Study of Social Problems (now a classic article entitled "Whose Side Are We On?"), posits that it is impossible for researchers to engage in *value-neutral* or *value-free research,* which is "uncontaminated by personal and political sympathies" (p. 239).

Given this, Becker suggests that researchers should identify, as much as possible, their own personal and political beliefs so that these issues can be documented when research results are published. In closing his speech, he suggests that researchers should declare whose side they are on. By this, he means that researchers should say, "for instance, that we have studied the prison through the eyes of the inmates and not through the eyes of the guards. . . . We warn people, thus, that our study tells us only how things look from that vantage point" (p. 247).

REFERENCES

Becker, H. S. (1967, Winter). Whose side are we on? *Social Problems, 14,* 239–247.

Braswell, M. C., McCarthy, B., & McCarthy, B. (1991). *Justice, crime and ethics.* Cincinnati, OH: Anderson.

Broad, W., & Wade, N. (1982). *Betrayers of the truth.* New York: Simon & Schuster.

Davis, M. S. (1989). The perceived seriousness and incidence of ethical misconduct in academic science. Unpublished doctoral dissertation, The Ohio State University.

Department of Health and Human Services. (1991). *Protection of human subjects, title 45, code of federal regulations, part 46.* Washington, DC: National Institutes of Health, Office for Protection from Research Risks.

Gray, B. H. (1979). Human subjects review committees and social research. In M. L. Wax and J. Cassell (Eds.), *Federal regulations: Ethical issues and social research.* Boulder, CO: Westview Press.

Humphreys, L. (1970). *Tearoom trade.* Chicago: Aldine.

Leedy, P. D. (1993). *Practical research: Planning and design* (5th ed.). New York: Macmillan.

Longmire, D. R. (1991). Ethical dilemmas in the research setting: A survey of experiences and responses in the criminological community. In M. C. Braswell, B. R. McCarthy, and B. J. McCarthy (Eds.), *Justice, crime and ethics* (pp. 279–296). Cincinnati, OH: Anderson.

Lore, D. (1990, August 26). The convicts who volunteered to be guinea pigs. *The Columbus Dispatch,* p. 2B.

Milgram, S. (1965). Conditions of obedience and disobedience to authority. *Human Relations, 18,* 57–76.

Public Health Service. (1966, July 1). PPO #129. Washington, DC: U.S. Government Printing Office.

Toch, H. (1981, August). Cast the first stone? *Criminology, 19*(2), 185–194.

Wade, W. (1976). *Great hoaxes and famous impostors.* Middle Village, NY: Jonathan David.

Patrons of Porn: Research Notes on the Clientele of Adult Bookstores

Richard Tewksbury
Deviant Behavior
Vol. 11, No. 3, pp. 259–272, 1990

Introduction

The last decade has seen a resurgence of concerns regarding sexual behaviors and values for both individuals and society as a whole. Included in these concerns are issues related to the production, distribution, and use of sexually explicit materials. One aspect of the pornography industry, adult bookstores, has received only occasional research attention (Sundholm, 1973; McKinstry, 1974; Perkins and Skipper, 1981; Potter, 1986, 1989). Similar research focusing on interpersonal interaction—often sexual in nature—has been done in a variety of settings including gay bathrooms, highway rest stops, parking lots, public parks, bars and other "open" public settings (Troiden, 1974; Weinberg and Williams, 1975; Corzine and Kirby, 1977; Delph, 1978). Sexually explicit materials, and the commercial locations selling them, are labeled deviant and frequently provide, or provide referrals to, a variety of deviantly-labeled goods and services (Potter, 1989). However, because of the continued existence of such locales, and their apparent steady flow of business, there appears to be a demand for the products and services they provide.

Little previous research has been conducted about adult bookstores or the patron interaction in such establishments. What is available emphasizes the physical aspects, or the employees of the settings (Perkins and Skipper, 1981; Potter, 1986, 1989). Very little attention has been given to describing patrons and their interactions. McKinstry (1974) focuses on patrons, examining how the interactional patterns and physical setting impact observable patron behaviors. However, he only gathered and utilized data from the retail merchandise area of the establishment, not including the peepshow area in the analysis.

The present paper is a dramaturgical analysis of an adult bookstore video peepshow, focusing on a typology of patrons.

Methodology

Data for the present work is gathered by way of participant observation in one adult bookstore in a major midwestern city over a three month period in 1988. The research employed covert participant observation conducted in an open setting (Lofland and Lofland, 1984). The adult bookstore, and accompanying video peepshow area, is a business establishment accessible to any person over the age of 21 (the posted minimum age for admission) who is willing and able to make the required $3 minimum purchase for admittance. Data comes from participation in surface level interactions (examination of advertisements for individual booths' selections, and viewing of videos/films). The researcher's purpose and role were never misrepresented; it is acceptable behavior to be present and observe others who are present. By structuring the researcher's role as that of a "potential participant" the observer was able to obtain access to interactions and patterns of behavior not otherwise readily observable. A potential participant is one who is present in the setting, and presents an image of a setting native (being knowledgeable of setting activities), but never adverse to nor inclined toward known setting activities.

Source: Hemisphere Publishing, 1990, used with permission.

Typology of Participants

The following typologies present a categorical and analytic perspective on the virtual social identities of patrons of adult bookstore peepshows. The first typology focuses strictly on the behavioral role enactments of such individuals; the second incorporates behaviors, including both given and given off expressions, looking at the overall sexual identity image presented by the individual actors.

Types Based on Roles within the Setting

Categorically speaking, participants may be distinguished by a five category typology: porno watchers, masturbators, sex seekers, sex doers, and the naive.

Porno Watchers

Men categorized as porno watchers were present in the adult bookstore for the express purpose of viewing sexually explicit materials. Porno watchers were the individuals who had the least impact on the interactional processes of the setting. Whereas these men were concerned with viewing sexually explicit materials, they had no sexual interest in other men present; hence they had no desire for interaction. Although not universal, porno watchers tended to be slightly older (over 35). Porno watchers varied widely in their degree of physical attractiveness, and frequently were dressed in either fashionable casual or business attire.

Masturbators

Somewhat similar to porno watchers are men classified as masturbators. As suggested, the primary goal of these men was to seek sexual gratification via masturbation. Masturbators viewed sexually explicit materials, and appeared to use it as a fantasy enhancer. Whereas porno watchers may on occasion masturbate, for masturbators sexually explicit material appeared to be of secondary importance, used as a mode of enhancing sexual stimulation.

Masturbators generally fit into one of two sub-categories, older and unattractive men or business men who remain on premises very short periods of time. Although widely ranging in age, masturbators frequently were better dressed, typically attired in business suits, or in the case of older (50+) men, casual, unfashionable, often ill-fitting clothing.

Sex Seekers

Sex seekers are men seeking others to satisfy their sexual desires. Sex seekers appeared to define the primary function of the adult bookstore as a provider of potential sex partners for the seeker's gratification.

Sex seekers tended to be younger, more attractive, projecting more self-confidence and self-esteem and attired in either business attire or highly fashionable, well-cared-for casual clothing. Sex seekers were highly attentive to their appearance. The usual behavior of the sex seeker was to circulate throughout the establishment and present themselves as available partners for same-sex sexual activity.

Sex Doers

Sex doers are the men whom the sex seekers are seeking. Although this researcher did not personally observe actual sexual encounters, such activities could easily be induced from observations. The observed behaviors which provided strong evidence of sexual activity included physical gesturing between patrons, pairs of men entering and exiting individual booths, propositions (verbal and physical) of the researcher, and verbal and behavioral reactions of other setting participants following attempts by others to proposition them.

Sex doers were the most readily identifiable individuals in the setting. Whereas sex seekers were generally young, sex doers were usually older. Those men observed and classified as sex doers all appeared to be over the age of 35. This group of men also appeared as the most unattractive, with approximately half of them being significantly overweight. Sex doers dress very casually, often appearing disheveled and/or dirty.

The Naive

On occasion men would happen into the adult bookstore video peepshow area who were unaware of setting activities, purposes, and norms. Such men are considered naive about the setting and the activities it houses. Although not necessarily disruptive to the setting, such men may be problematic to the interaction in general (Weatherford, 1986). By being unaware of the sexual component of setting activities, naive men may place themselves, accidentally, in a position to be propositioned by sex doers. Initial observations of naive men are easily misinterpretable; the behaviors are very similar to sex seekers. Naive men appeared, as sex seekers initially appear, to be unaware of the men and activities around them. However, unlike sex seekers, these men truly were unaware of others. When initially tested for their reactions to subtle propositions, naive men either gave no response (because they were unaware or not knowledgeable of propositioning techniques) or attempted to appear polite and courteous, thereby inadvertently yielding signals of willingness. However, when presented with more serious, and therefore more obvious and aggressive propositions, naive men would respond defensively or aggressively.

Conclusions

Patrons of this adult bookstore were not a generic lot. There are some commonly shared statuses, such as race and sex, and some general trends regarding other secondary statuses. However, within this population, some very specific distinctions can be found beyond the merely superficial statuses. Setting participants enact varying roles, and display patterns of role selection according to occupied statuses. The enacted roles and presentational styles of individual actors enable setting co-participants to construct virtual social identities for each other. Each man's virtual social identity then becomes a foundation for the construction of the setting's interactional complex. Considering the array of potential virtual social identities, it is easy to see that interactions may vary widely, as well as each actor's motivations for their respective performed behaviors. The manners in which patrons present publicly perceived behaviors (both those given and given off) differ by categorical, and individual, distinctions. The individual's presentational style and role enactments as elements of this virtual, rather than actual, social identity, structure his setting interactions and degree of integration.

References

Corzine, Jay, and Richard Kirby.
  1977   "Cruising the Truckers: Sexual Encounters in a Highway Rest Area." Urban Life, 6 (2):171–192.
Delph, Edward William.
  1978   The Silent Community: Public Homosexual Encounters. Beverly Hills: Sage.
Lofland, John and Lyn H. Lofland.
  1984   Analyzing Social Settings. Belmont, California: Wadsworth.
McKinstry, William C..
  1974   "The Pulp Voyeur: A Peek at Pornography in Public Places," in Jerry Jacobs (ed.) Deviance: Field Studies and Self-Disclosures. Palo Alto: National Press Books.
Perkins, Kenneth B. and James K. Skipper, Jr..
  1981   "Gay Pornographic and Sex Paraphernalia Shops: An Ethnography of Expressive Work Settings." Deviant Behavior, 2, (2):187–199.
Potter, Gary W.
  1989   "The Retail Pornography Industry and the Organization of Vice." Deviant Behavior, 10 (3):233–252.
Potter, Gary W.
  1986   The Porn Merchants. Dubuque: Kendall/ Hunt.
Sundholm, Charles.
  1973   "The Urban Pornographic Arcade: Ethnographic Notes on Moral Men in Immoral Places." Urban Life and Culture, 2 (1):85–104.
Troiden, Richard.
  1974   "Homosexual Encounters in a Highway Rest-Stop." In Erich Goode and Richard Troiden (eds.). Sexual Deviants and Sexual Deviance. New York: William Morrow and Company.
Weatherford, Jack McIver.
  1986   Porn Row. New York: Arbor House.
Weinberg, Martin S. and Colin J. Williams.
  1975   "Gay Baths and the Social Organization of Impersonal Sex." Social Problems, 23:124–136.

Name of Student _____
Student ID # _____
Course Section # _____
Date _____

1. What ethical problems are connected with conducting covert research?

   _____
   _____
   _____
   _____
   _____
   _____
   _____
   _____
   _____
   _____
   _____

2. What reasons for conducting covert research might justify these ethical transgressions?

   _____
   _____
   _____
   _____
   _____
   _____
   _____
   _____
   _____
   _____
   _____
   _____

3. Make three separate trips to a local shopping mall. While remaining in the common areas of the mall, spend 15 minutes during each visit observing the patrons of one store. Visit the same store each time. Take field notes, and carefully describe the kinds of patrons you observe. Include as much observable information as possible, at minimum, descriptions of gender, apparent age, race, styles of dress, demeanor, interactions, and so on.

Field Notes (attach additional sheets as needed)

Institutional Review Boards: Virtue Machines or Villains?

Bruce L. Berg, W. Timothy Austin, and Glenn A. Zuern
Criminal Justice Policy Review
Vol. 6, No. 2, pp. 87–102, June 1992

Introduction

One hundred years from now the advances in contemporary social science will be history. The most controversial chapters in written accounts of this history, no doubt, will be those that describe ethical, methodological, and political issues surrounding the research enterprise. As controversial as these chapters may continue to be in the future, they hold a singular advantage over writing on these subjects today: they will be in the past not the present, and consequently dispassionate. Issues such as ethical conduct, methodological deceptions, and the politics of research currently invoke extreme passion from social scientists. Interestingly, these passions run equally high among politicians who would see social scientific research regulated as strenuously as the Food and Drug Administration regulates new medicines.

This article examines the history of institutional review boards (IRBs), and the way present day IRBs may be impacting the nature and quality of research in the social sciences.

Research Regulations

The history of regulations, statutes, and research guidelines are largely of recent origin. They have been primarily invoked by biomedical and psycho-experimental research, and only secondarily understood through the natural history of the social sciences (Olesen, 1979; Chambers, 1980). This statement is not by any means suggesting that social sciences are exempt from their share

of exploitive studies. For example, Stanley Milgram's (1963) experiment on authority and following orders, and Laud Humphreys's (1970) study of public sexuality, may also exemplify social scientific indiscretions.

Milgram (1963) was interested in learning about human tendencies to obey authority figures. In order to observe this phenomenon, he told voluntary subjects that they were going to assist in teaching another volunteer a simple word association task. This explanation, however, was a deception, and the "other volunteer" was really one of Milgram's confederates. The subject/teacher was instructed by Milgram to administer an electric shock to the learner (the research confederate) whenever the learner made a mistake. The subject/teacher was told that this electric shock was intended to facilitate learning and should be increased in intensity progressively with each error. Many of the subjects obediently advanced the shock levels to potentially lethal levels.

Actually, the supposed learner felt no electricity at all. Instead, each time the subject/teacher administered a shock, a signal indicated that the learner should react as if shocked. The performance by the learner was sufficient to convince subject/teachers that they were being electrically shocked and aroused considerable emotional anguish and guilt in these subjects.

The other example, Laud Humphreys's (1970) study of casual sexual encounters in public places, has been the focus of considerable ethical debate since its publication. Humphreys was interested in gaining understanding not only about practicing homosexuals, but also about non-homosexuals who briefly engaged in intimate same gender sexual encounters. In addition to observing encounters in public toilets (tearooms), Humphreys developed a way to gain access to detailed information about subjects he had covertly observed.

While serving as a "watchqueen" (a voyeuristic lookout), Humphreys was able both to observe the various encounters and to also catch a glimpse of participants' car licenses. Once Humphreys had license plate numbers, he could locate home addresses of the tearoom participants through the Department of Motor Vehicles. Next, he disguised himself and deceived these men into believing that he was conducting a survey in the neighborhood. The result was that Humphreys was able to collect considerable amounts of information on each of the participants he had observed engaging in public sexual encounters.

Shortly after publication of Humphreys's work in 1970, there was considerable outcry against invasions of privacy, misrepresentation of researcher identities, and deception commonly being practiced during the course of research. Many issues arising out of Humphreys's research continue to serve as fodder for ethical debate. Especially critical among these are the justifications that the subject matter was of significant importance to the scientific community, and that it could not have been investigated in any other manner but through covert strategies.

The blurring of distinctions between biomedical research and that of social scientific inquiry has resulted in official regulations being tilted toward an image of experimental research. In part this results from the origins of official regulations. For example, it is fairly well established that the context in which federal regulations originated was significantly influenced by the Nuremberg Code (Bower and de Gasparis, 1978; Olesen, 1979). This code emerged after the infamous Nuremberg trials where Nazi scientists were held to account for their inhumane behavior during World War II. The Nuremberg Code became the foundation for the "Declaration of Helsinki" adopted by the World Health Organization in 1964, and the "Ethical Guidelines for Clinical Investigation" adopted by the American Medical Association in 1966.

It was also in 1966 that the Surgeon General issued what may have been the first official rules concerning all Public Health Service research. This statement specified that any research financially supported by the Public Health Service was contingent upon an institutional review committee. The committee was charged with the responsibility of assuring that any research procedures would not harm human subjects and that subjects were informed of any potential risks (and benefits) from their participation. In essence, the institutional review board for research was born.

Several revisions of this general policy occurred throughout the late 1960s, and finally, in 1971 the Department of Health, Education, and Welfare (DHEW) published a booklet entitled, "The Institutional Guide to DHEW Policy on Protection of Human Subjects." This booklet extended the review requirements to all DHEW grant and contract activities involving human subjects—including "non-medical" and "non-experimental" studies. The booklet also spelled-out the requirement of obtaining "informed consent" from subjects before including them in research projects.

In 1974, the National Research Act was passed by Congress, and the National Commission on Protection of Human Subjects of Biomedical and Behavioral Research was created by Title II of this law. The National Research Act directed all institutions that sponsored research to establish institutional review committees. Today these committees are more commonly called Institutional Review Boards, or simply IRBs.

IRBs and Their Duties

Among the most important factors effected by the DHEW regulations are those regarding the establishment of locally appointed Institutional Review Boards and the requirements for obtaining written informed consent from research subjects. Both of these requirements have drawn heavy critical fire from social scientists (Meyer, 1977; Gray, 1977; Fields, 1978). Qualitative researchers, especially those involved in ethnographic research, have been particularly vocal. Their concerns often pertain to the way formal requirements for institutional review and written informed consent damages their special fieldworker/informant relationships (Wax, 1977; Cassell, 1978).

The National Commission for the Protection of Human Subjects, created by the National Research Act of 1974, has reviewed their own guidelines (DHEW, 1978) and offered revisions (*Federal Register*, 1978). These revisions are more specific about the role that the IRB should play. For example, the *Federal Register* points out that board members may be liable for legal action if they exceed their authority and interfere with the investigator's *right* to conduct research. These revised guidelines also recommend that the requirement for written informed consent could be waived for certain types of *low risk styles of research*. Unfortunately, the guidelines remained nonspecific in identifying the characteristics endemic to ethnographic research which might qualify for exceptions.

Because their research procedures are more formalized and require contacts with subjects, the more limited and predictable characteristics of quantitative methodologies are generally simpler to define. As a result, the specific exemptions or styles of research that can be expedited through IRBs largely are quantitative survey types, observation in public places, research involving educational tests (diagnostic, aptitude or achievement), and archival research (*The Belmont Report*, 1978).

Clarifying the Role of IRBs

Initially, IRBs were charged with the responsibility of reviewing the adequacy of consent procedures for the protection of human subjects in research funded by the U.S. Department of Health, Education, and Welfare (DHEW). This mandate was soon broadened to include a review of all research conducted in an institution receiving any funds from DHEW—even when the study itself did not (Burstein, 1987; Code of Federal Regulations, 45 CFR 46, 1989).

As part of the IRB's review duties, they were to assure that subjects in research studies were advised both of their potential risks from participation, and possible benefits. This task seems to have evolved among some IRBs to become an assessment of risk to benefit ratios of proposed studies. In some cases, this is based upon the IRB's impression of the *worth* of the study. In other cases, this may be based upon the IRB's presumed greater knowledge of the subject and methodological strategies than potential subjects are likely to possess (Burstein, 1987). Thus, in many cases, IRBs, and not subjects, predetermine whether the subject will even have the option of participating or declining participation in a study.

Today, many IRBs have further extended their purview to include evaluation of methodological strategies, not, as one might expect, as these methods pertain to human subject risks but in terms of the project's methodological adequacy. The justification for this, apparently being, that even where minimum risks exist, if a study is designed too poorly it will not yield any scientific benefit.

Several problems immediately surface when one considers the original intent of IRBs and their current practices. These include the question of informed consent; the calculation of risk/benefit; and what and who decides when a research design is *good* (Burstein, 1987). Further complicating issues is the fact that these actually are three overlapping questions, often weaved together as one.

Informed Consent

What proper informed consent involves according to Federal regulations, and how an IRB interprets this requirement, may differ. According to the Code of Federal Regulations (45 CFR 46, 1989), "General Requirements for Informed Consent" include:

> Except as provided elsewhere in this or other sub-parts, no investigator may involve a human being as a subject in research covered by these regulations unless the investigator has obtained the legally effective informed consent of the subject or the subject's legally authorized representative.

This general requirement specifies a number of recommended inclusions, such as a statement about what the study involves; a description of any reasonable and foreseeable risks or discomforts to the subject; a description of any benefits afforded to the subject; and disclosure of any possible alternative treatments, if any apply, that might be advantageous to the subject. Other suggested criteria include a statement addressing confidentiality of records identifying the subjects; explanations about any medical treatments that may be available if injury occurs in the course of the research; information about who the subject can contact in the event he or she is so injured; and a statement that the individual understands his or her participation is voluntary.

The general requirements, however, also provide for exceptions and alterations to some of these inclusions. Section C (Code of Federal Regulations, 45 CFR 46, 1989:10) reads:

> 6(c) An IRB may approve a consent procedure which does not include, or which alters, some or all of the elements of informed consent set forth above, or waive the requirement to obtain informed consent set forth above, or waive the requirement to obtain informed consent. . . .

The policy outlines situations acceptable for waivers or alterations to usual requirements for informed consent (Code of Federal Regulations, 45 CFR 46, 1989:10):

(1) The research involves no more than minimal risk to the subjects;
(2) The waiver or alteration will not adversely affect the rights and welfare of the subjects;
(3) The research could not practicably be carried out without the waiver or alteration; and
(4) Whenever appropriate, the subjects will be provided with additional pertinent information after participation.

Thus, in many cases, researchers may entirely avoid the necessity for a signed written consent form. The decision rests largely in the hands of the IRB members, and the ability of the researcher to convince these members that a waiver is warranted.

Risk/Benefit Concerns

The question of level of risk to participants is likewise vague and ambiguous. While the language of the federal regulations remains largely directed toward medical and biomedical risks to subjects, its auspice blankets the social sciences as well. In this regard, psychological risks often seem to loom large. Again, there are instances where this may be fairly clear cut, but there are likely greater instances where this potential risk is simply unpredictable. Consider, for example Philip Zimbardo's study of a mock prison (Zimbardo, 1972; Haney, Banks, and Zimbardo, 1973). Zimbardo hypothesized that the conditions of prison as a social setting—and not the personalities of the people involved—are the major cause of prison violence.

Zimbardo placed twenty-four male college student volunteers in a mock prison. The men had agreed to take part in this two week long experiment for a daily payment of $15.00. All twenty-four men had been screened to assure they were exceptionally physically and psychologically healthy. Half of these men were randomly assigned as guards, and half as prisoners.

Designated "prisoners" were arrested in their homes—without warning—by the Palo Alto police. After being fingerprinted and photographed at the police station prisoners were taken in hand-cuffs to the Stanford County Prison on campus. Conversely, guards were given an orientation, where they were warned about the dangers of prison work. Guards were also admonished to keep the prison secure at all times. Zimbardo and his team of researchers now waited to see what would happen.

What happened next was entirely unforeseen by anyone. Within hours, the two groups had begun taking their *roles* very seriously. Both groups began to act much like stereotypical guards and inmates—both groups rapidly put aside all they had ever learned about appropriate behavior and human decency. Guards showed increasing hostility and even brutality toward prisoners, including forcing prisoners to engage in humiliating tasks such as cleaning toilet bowls with their bare hands.

Prisoners similarly began to act-out as inmates. Within the first five days of the experiment five prisoners had to be removed from the study because they began showing signs of "extreme emotional depression, crying, rage and acute anxiety" (Haney, Banks, and Zimbardo, 1973:81). Before the end of the first week, and with the threat of a possible jail break, the experiment had to be canceled.

The Zimbardo study is often discussed regarding the ethical conduct of research. Yet, even had the regulations for informed consent been in place (the study predated the 1974 appearance of the National Research Act), and followed meticulously, problems still would have surfaced. No one ever suspected the magnitude of the effect this experience would have on subjects. It would have been impossible for an IRB to accurately predict the psychological risk and subsequent psychological and emotional harm to subjects.

Although speculative at this point, it is likely that most universities simply appoint a group of faculty to their IRBs for some unspecified timeframe. The underlying assumption here is that as university faculty they should be automatically qualified to serve in such a capacity. Unfortunately, the assumption that because a faculty member has managed to secure work in a university setting he or she is the best choice for an IRB is unacceptable if not naive. IRB members are expected to serve as gate-keepers of virtuous research. At minimum, then, each member should have experience that includes serving as the principal investigator on a study involving human subjects. Ideally, universities should strive to have IRB membership reflect a diversity of researchers. Experience from physical and social science disciplines, and we would hope, given the relationships between subjects and investigators, ethnographers also would be represented. Furthermore, membership should require ratification by other members of the university community, and not merely reflect an administrative appointment. Finally, membership should be for a specified time period, to allow attitudes and prevailing viewpoints on the board to change over time.

References

The Belmont Report
   1979   Department Of Health Education And Welfare. Pub. no. (05) 78-0012.
Bower, R.T. and P. de Gasparis
   1978   Ethics in Social Research. New York: Praeger.
Burstein, A.G.
   1987   The virtue machine. American Psychologist (Feb.):199–202.
Cassell, J.
   1978   Risk and benefit to subjects of fieldwork. American Sociologist. 13(August):134–143.
Chambers, E.
   1980   Fieldwork and the law: New contexts for ethical decision making. Social Problems. 27(3):330–341.
Code of Federal Regulations (45 CFR 46)
   1989   Protection Of Human Subjects. Washington, D.C.: Department of Health and Human Services, National Institute of Health, Office for Protection from Research Risks.
DHEW
   1978a   Report And Recommendations On Institutional Review Boards. Washington, D.C.: Department of Health Education and Welfare, Pub. no. (05) 78- 0008.
Federal Register
   1991   Federal policy for the protection of human subjects: Notices and rules (Part II). June 18 (FR Doc. 91-14257)
   1978   Protection of human subjects: Institutional review boards. November 30 (43 FR56174).
Fields, C.M.
   1978   Universities fear impact of rules to protect research subjects. The Chronicle Of Higher Education (March 12):5–6.
Gray, B.G.
   1977   The functions of human subjects review committees. American Journal Of Psychiatry. 134:907–909.
Haney, C., C. Banks, and P. Zimbardo
   1973   Interpersonal dynamics in a simulated prison. International Journal Of Criminology And Penology. 1:69–97.
Humphreys, L.
   1970   Tearoom Trade: Impersonal Sex In Public Places. Chicago: Aldine.
Meyer, R.E.
   1977   Subjects' rights, freedom of inquiry, and the future of research in the addictions.

American Journal Of Psychiatry. 134(8):899–903.

Milgram, S.
1963 Behavioral study of obedience. Journal Of Abnormal And Social Psychology. 67:371–378.

Olesen, V.
1979 Federal regulations, institutional review boards and qualitative social science research. In Murray L. Wax and Joan Cassell, Federal Regulations: Ethical Issues and Social Research. Boulder Colorado: Westview Press:103–118.

Wax, M.L.
1977 On fieldworkers and those exposed to fieldwork: Federal regulations and moral issues. Human Organizations. 36(3):321–327.

Zimbardo, P.
1972 Pathology of imprisonment. Society. 9(April):4–8.

Name of Student _____

Student ID # _____

Course Section # _____

Date _____

1. You have been hired by a leading university to create guidelines for membership on their institutional review board (IRB). The university is particularly interested in directing your attention toward several areas.

   a. What background should IRB members be required to have?

   _____

   _____

   _____

   _____

   _____

   _____

   _____

   _____

   _____

   _____

   _____

   b. Should IRB members be appointed by the university administration or elected by the faculty? Justify your answer.

   _____

   _____

   _____

   _____

   _____

   _____

   _____

   _____

   _____

   _____

c. Should IRB membership be set as a specific term or duration? Should members be eligible for re-election or re-appointment?

_____

_____

_____

_____

_____

_____

_____

_____

_____

_____

d. What sorts of research, if any, should be exempt from review? Again, justify your answer.

_____

_____

_____

_____

_____

_____

_____

_____

_____

_____

_____

2. You are a member of an IRB at a leading university. The following study has been presented for review:

The research will involve a study of third-grade students in a reading class. The class will be divided into two approximately equal-sized groups. One group will be instructed using a special modular reading program that has been previously validated and designed to increase students' reading skills and comprehension. The other group will not receive any special training. The researcher expects that students who received special instruction will, on average, show a minimum increase in reading level of two units by the end of the semester. The students who did not receive special instruction are not expected to show any improvement.

a.   What are some of the ethical problems presented by this research plan?

_____

_____

_____

_____

_____

_____

_____

_____

_____

_____

b.   How might each of these ethical problems be avoided or eliminated?

_____

_____

_____

_____

_____

_____

_____

_____

_____

_____

_____

3. You are a researcher who has recently studied marijuana growers. As part of your study, you interviewed 50 large-scale marijuana farmers. Although you conducted these interviews in neutral locations, some of them contain various pieces of identifying information, such as the names of seed suppliers, other marijuana farmers, and various midlevel dealers. Somehow, the local police department has learned about your research and asked you to turn over your tapes of the interviews.

a.   Will you refuse to release this information and risk going to jail? Explain your answer.

_____

_____

_____

_____

_____

_____

_____

_____

_____

_____

b.   What could you have done to better ensure the confidentiality of your findings?

_____

_____

_____

_____

_____

_____

_____

_____

_____

_____

_____

CHAPTER 7

Policy Implications

ETHICS VERSUS POLITICS

Ethical and political issues are sometimes thought of as being closely related. However, they are not the same issue. One way to differentiate between the two is to link *ethical* concerns with methodological design and *political* concerns with the use of research findings. For example: Does the design include activities that in any way injure subjects or place them at serious risk of injury? Is participation voluntary or coercive? Are there undue invasions of privacy? Will the research further deteriorate conditions for subjects or the environment?

These questions about research design clearly fall in the purview of ethical issues. How findings are used, how they were intended to be used, and what impact they may have on people, such as those used as subjects (e.g., drug users who were not actual subjects in the study), are all political issues. For instance, suppose a researcher makes arrangements with police officers to take urine samples from suspected violent felons immediately upon arrest. This activity would raise "red flags," for both ethical and political reasons. Depending on the purpose of the research, however, the issues would vary.

Assume the researcher wants to find out whether these violent felons used drugs and/or alcohol when committing their crimes in order to better identify precursors of violent behavior. The researcher would naturally need to get informed consent from each suspected felon prior to obtaining the urine sample. The researcher would also need to offer the usual types of confidentiality assurances and provide security for all records

and urine analysis data. These are all important ethical concerns.

What if, however, the researcher's purpose is to establish a data set in order to argue that some violent criminals are polydrug users and should be sentenced more severely than single-drug users who become violent? Now, the researcher enters the world of politics.

In the truest sense, ethical considerations are not entirely separate from political ones, but they are distinguishable. How researchers plan to use findings from their own research seems to be reasonably within their control. How others who pay for or read about research in scientific journals use those findings is not so easily controlled, however. These issues can be difficult for researchers, especially inexperienced ones, to reconcile. As Punch (1986, pp. 13–14) suggests, too often, academics, textbooks, and journal articles espouse an image of conducting social research for students that is "neat, tidy, and unproblematic." Yet experienced researchers immediately recognize that such an image is idealistic, not realistic.

The argument here is *not* that every researcher must search his or her soul constantly throughout the design and implementation of a project. Such silly and naive sentimentality is itself a false image of research. There are enormous differences between revealing the innermost thoughts and trepidations contained in one's research diary (a journal routinely kept by many social scientists during research) and addressing certain political and ethical concerns.

The following sections will review a number of the general and largely pragmatic issues involved in the politics of research. The soul searching will be left to each individual researcher's conscience.

GATEKEEPERS AND THE POWERFUL

Why a researcher chooses a particular topic and slant, how he or she gains access to subjects and settings, and even which data-gathering techniques he or she selects may all have political overtones. Many studies describe in detail the enormous significance of their findings and argue that the topic was chosen for some lofty humanitarian reasons. Students of research often develop images of people such as Margaret Mead, Franz Boas, and Bronislaw Malinowski, intrepidly going off into the wild to study primitives and literally getting dirty with data. The fact is, though, that much of today's research (when it is not the secondary analysis of nearly sterile data sets) is research *by convenience and accessibility.*

Convenience can be a legitimate reason to undertake research, particularly when linked to accessibility and a topic that is research worthy. Yet some researchers fear that their findings will not be taken seriously if it is discovered how conveniently the data were collected. In truth, on occasion, social scientists simply find themselves in the right place, at the right time.

Adler (1985) describes how she learned that her next-door neighbor was a drug smuggler and how through him, she gained access to the world of middle-level drug smugglers. Certainly, the study of drug smuggling is important and respectable research that needs to be undertaken. Because of the circumstances, Adler found herself in a convenient position to undertake that study. Had she intentionally sought to locate a drug smuggler to use as a guide to the world of drug smuggling, she may not have been successful.

Many researchers gain access to research settings because of personal relationships with *gatekeepers,* who are usually people with special information, connections, or control over some setting (Berg, 1995; Bogdan & Taylor, 1975). Given these assets, gatekeepers often have the ability to facilitate research or to disrupt, slow, or even prevent it from occurring. When Berg (1990a, 1990b) was interested in studying train-

ing in a police academy, he sought the advice of one of his students, who was a state police officer. While discussing the project with the student, Berg learned that not only was the student an officer but president of the State Police Association. Because of the student's relationship with the police commissioner, Berg was given considerable access to seven police academy programs (including several that, coincidentally, were located five minutes from his home, further increasing the convenience quotient of the research) (Berg, 1990a, 1990b).

Financial considerations also affect research. The kind of research done (quantitative or qualitative), the nature of the data collected (large- or small-scale), and even the research topic selected may be controlled by "purse strings." In 1968, two important pieces of federal legislation were passed: the Juvenile Delinquency Prevention and Control Act and the Omnibus Crime Control and Safe Streets Act. As part of the provisions of these acts, two agencies were created: the Office of Juvenile Delinquency and Youth Development and the Law Enforcement Assistance Administration (LEAA). Under the auspices of these agencies, considerable federal funding became available for law enforcement training, education, equipment, and research. In addition, delinquency prevention became a primary research funding target. Model programs sprang up across the United States, evaluation studies were initiated on existing programs, and federal funds were made readily available for law enforcement and delinquency research of almost any type.

In the mid-1980s, when public concern over acquired immune deficiency syndrome (AIDS) was significantly heightened, federal funds for attitudinal studies on AIDS became readily available. Studies were undertaken in public settings as well as inside correctional facilities. Drug researchers suddenly began to include AIDS components to their research in order to qualify for federal and state monies. The funds for attitudinal research on AIDS began to dwindle by 1991, as better information filtered down from epidemiological research studies. However, this example clearly illustrates that the availability of funding from federal and state sources significantly influences the amount and type of research undertaken in the social sciences.

Access can also be affected when researchers enter the realm of the *powerful* or *elite*. Researchers have, in fact, seldom penetrated these largely uncharted territories (Punch, 1986). Instead, most researchers have focused on what may be labeled *holding categories,* or low-level and marginal social groups. There are, for example, few empirical studies on powerful and elite individuals, such as corporate executives, crime bosses, drug king pins, congresspeople, high-ranking police and military personnel, and so forth. On the other hand, there are countless studies on people from the lower social strata or who have marginal qualities or interests: drug addicts, the poor, the mentally impaired, patrons of topless bars and porno shops, and so on.

Some researchers believe that it is not adequate simply to conduct research on categories of people who are easy to access. But gaining access to study the powerful and elite poses many potential pitfalls. Persons of power would likely be able to control what areas of their lives a researcher could access.

These problems with accessing the elite are somewhat analogous to the problems a researcher faces when entering a correctional setting with the permission of the warden. Although the warden may give the appearance of cooperation, the researcher can never be certain that he or she will have *full access* to every location in the prison that he or she desires to explore. In the name of security, the warden may limit where the researcher can go, with or without a correctional officer escorting him or her. Even when given access, the researcher may find inmates and prison workers to be inhibited, resistant, or uncooperative, due to their knowledge of the warden's cooperation with the researcher.

INSTITUTIONAL REVIEW BOARDS (IRBS)

Another political factor in research is the institutional review board (IRB), an internal agency or institutional mechanism designed to assess research proposals and assure protection of human subjects. Usually, members of the institution or agency are placed on a panel that reads research plans and considers whether they can be undertaken legally, safely, and ethically (see also Chapter 6).

Ideally, when an IRB determines that there may be problems with a research design, it notifies the researcher and discuss its concerns. If the researcher can assuage the board's concerns, perhaps by modifying the design, permission to undertake the study will probably be given. If, on the other hand, no agreement can be obtained between the researcher and the IRB, the institution or agency will not allow the researcher to carry out the study under its name or using its resources.

In a utopian sense, the IRB is there to protect those people (subjects) who might not otherwise be able to protect themselves. From this view, the IRB is a benevolent protector. Of course, this view suggests that the subjects of most research studies are unprotected or powerless.

One of the complaints many researchers utter when submitting proposals to IRBs is that the people sitting in judgment over their designs may never themselves have conducted research. Some IRB members may be clinicians whose methods are somewhat different from those of social scientists. Other members may, at one time, have been skilled researchers, but the passage of years and lack of research involvement may have eroded their ability to make legitimate assessments and offer quality advice. It is interesting to note that members of IRBs are often selected on the basis of convenience or because they volunteer, not because of their experience, skills, or knowledge.

Thus, the politics of IRBs sometimes take on a gamelike appearance: The researcher tries to hammer out a proposal that will meet the demands of the IRB, even when the design may not make good methodological sense to him or her. In this situation, the researcher might tell the IRB whatever it takes to get the design approved but then do what he or she wants or believes is correct in carrying out the project.

Under such devious circumstances, we might be tempted to question the integrity of the researcher. We must be cautious, however, and consider the actions of the IRB that may have motivated the researcher to compromise his or her integrity. We might also question the appropriateness of some actions of IRBs when members clearly have little or no empirical experience or their skills have become dull from lack of use.

Regrettably, no uniform standards can be established that would ensure an appropriate and equitable review of all research proposals. Since every research project has different benefits and problems, no single criterion of ethical appropriateness or safety can be applied. What can be done, however, is to staff IRBs with members who have, at minimum, some recent experience in conducting empirical research and who have themselves operated ethically. Perhaps seats on IRBs should also be elected positions, rather than appointed ones. Then individuals who were qualified and maybe even dissatisfied with previous board actions could run for positions.

THE USE OF RESEARCH FINDINGS

When we read research studies, we assume that the information and findings they present are accurate. Researchers operate on the assumption that as long as they tell the truth, they will be believed. In fact, all researchers are charged with the responsibility of providing accurate information, all the time. To do otherwise would mean undermining the amount of confidence people place on study results. But just how applicable or generalizable those findings may be is a separate question.

Just because a given research finding is accurate and truthfully presented does mean that it is useful. The terms *accurate* and *useful* are not synonyms. Although used similarly in lay parlance, scientifically, we know that *usefulness* speaks to practical application, whereas *accuracy* suggests correctness.

We have all heard reports about caffeine, nicotine, saccharin, NutraSweet, and cholesterol, specifically, that high concentrations of these products have caused blindness, cancer, and heart attacks in lab animals (chiefly rats). These studies were undertaken carefully and in controlled laboratory conditions and seem to yield highly accurate results—about rats. But do these results translate accurately for humans?

On the surface, examples such as these may seem somewhat extreme. Nonetheless, they do illustrate the validity of these questions: Do research findings apply in real-world settings? Is there genuine reason to believe that these studies have practical implications that can be generalized to humans?

For instance, when a study has been conducted on delinquent youths in Syracuse, what implications will the results have for youths in California? If fear of crime is studied among blind people living in Pennsylvania, will the findings be relevant to sighted persons living in the same state? What about to blind people living in Michigan?

In effect, the issue becomes: To what extent will results generalize to different locations and situations? How exact must situations be before findings from a study in one situation can be used to explain phenomena that occurred in another situation? Concerns such as these are often discussed in research books, as they regard dimensions of the sample and various demographics of people in the sample. But there are other "nonpeople" dimensions, or what Katzer, Cook, and Crouch (1991, p. 176) call *ecological representativeness:* elements of a study beyond the level of people.

Ecological representativeness includes, for example, instrumentation: Would the same results have been obtained if an in-depth interviewing strategy had been used instead of a questionnaire? What if a telephone interview had been used instead of a face-to-face one? Would the results have differed if the methodological design had been triangulated and included both multiple data-gathering strategies and multiple researchers? What would have happened if the wording or order of the questions in the interview schedule had been altered? Might different kinds of subjects had been obtained if the study had been conducted in the winter instead of the summer? Would a researcher of the opposite gender have come to the same conclusions?

These kinds of questions should be considered along with more traditional questions about the researcher's sampling strategy. In some studies, in which the researcher has meticulously identified a representative sample, generalizability at the people level may be accounted for. However, people who *use* research findings and who consider their possible implications must also consider other dimensions: ecological representativeness.

Since it would be impossible outside the confines of theory to design a study that generalized across all dimensions, researchers usually work with what they view as the most important dimension: people. In fact, many times, the other "nonpeople" elements may not matter much. Environments may be essentially alike, other data-gathering strategies may offer more or less information but not necessarily different findings, and so forth. People, however, will assuredly have differences. When a researcher develops a careful sampling procedure, readers of the results can be relatively confident about generalizing those findings along the people dimension. Even when a study uses a sample other than a representative one (e.g., an accidental, purposive, or weighted sample), the people dimension is usually covered. In an effective report, the researcher will describe the extent of limitations on generalizing results at the people level.

At times, however, the other dimensions *do* matter. In these instances, using other elements would create differences in the results. Although the researcher may not adequately consider the differences that will prevent consumers of research from generalizing findings to their situations, consumers should do so. Thus, the next obvious question is: What should we look for when determining the degree of generalizability of research findings?

The crux of generalizability is the removal or suppression of obvious differences between the phenomenon and situation described in the research and those in which the results are to be applied. If we can demonstrate that the differences between the study situation and the application situation are relatively minor, then the results can safely be applied.

Sometimes, it is easier to consider how situations are *similar* than it is to determine how they are *different*. For example, since researchers are usually concerned with the people dimension, they may report demographic comparisons between their sample and some larger population. When comparisons show similarities among proportions of males to females, educational levels, age cohorts, economic levels, religious affiliations, and related characteristics, generalizability may be relatively easy to establish. In other cases, however, there may be differences that matter but that are not as obvious. In these situations, we must assess the adequacy of methods used by the investigator, the theoretical arguments offered, and the kinds of evidence presented.

In an absolute vacuum, any minor change in the research environment could alter the results of a study. In the real world of research, however, things are not quite that sensitive. The reader must consider the likelihood that the results would have differed had alternative theories been applied, different data-gathering strategies been employed, or various other measures of strength and association been used.

It is important for inexperienced researchers to keep in mind that there is no single best way to evaluate the usefulness of a study's findings. The evaluation process is based largely on the concerns of the research consumer. A study that is determined unsuitable for one consumer may be just right for another. In some cases, then, the differences between a study and a particular application situation do not invalidate the results overall. Of course, in other situations, identifying a faulty method or theory or an incorrect measure may indicate that a research report is unacceptable in any situation. There is, however, no foolproof way to undertake the enterprise of research, and readers should be cautious when evaluating application plausibility and generalizability.

GENDER AND RESEARCH POLITICS

Only during recent years have women scientists entered the top ranks of the social and behavioral sciences. This is because the predominant form of social structure in modern history has been patriarchal: male-dominated families, governments, and lineages. The major mechanism used to maintain this structure has been to keep women in positions subordinate to men, including subordinate intellectual roles.

The processes, theories, and products of the social sciences have been deeply influenced by this ideological mechanism. In fact, we find relatively few great women social scientists in the forefront of social science history. Agnew and Pyke (1987, p. 242) echo White's (1975) suggestion that "variables such as the decreased likelihood of sponsorship, lack of role models, atypical (interrupted) career paths, and exclusion from the 'old boys' network' all operated to dissuade women from careers in science."

Social scientists are trained to consider certain relevant issues regarding gender, including researcher reactivity, gender performance, attitudes, educational levels, earning capacity, and other demographic characteristics. These issues become second nature in conducting research. However, certain personal views held by the researcher may affect or even bias the study results, either intentionally or unconsciously.

Without question, a vast amount of contemporary research and theory has been built upon a patriarchal (and chiefly White, western European) ideological foundation that suggests:

1. Females are different from males along most variable divisions.
2. These differences have a basic biological origin.
3. Men's position on variables is superior (Agnew & Pyke, 1987; Pyke, 1982).

This Euro-patriarchal bias has had a significant impact on the production of social scientific research. Among today's researchers, in addition to this traditional Euro-ideology, there is a feminist orientation (complete with its own set of biases) and, more promisingly, an egalitarian perspective.

When we read a research report and assess its relative merits, gender bias is an important factor to consider. Bias may arise from the way in which the researcher's personal orientations affect the construction of a question or focus. For example, consider the following series of statements:

1. Girls are less aggressive than boys.
2. Girls are arrested for shoplifting less frequently than boys.
3. Girls are physically weaker than boys.

In addition to the Euro-patriarchal cultural bias obvious in all these statements, there is an inherent inaccuracy: They suggest that *all* females are more whatever than *all* males. Such forms of language bias may be culturally ingrained and operate unconsciously. Nonetheless, they create

an inferential bias that should be considered when evaluating research findings.

In addition, bias may be reflected in the topic selected for investigation or the way in which results are presented. Until about the last 30 years, serious research on gender roles, women deviants, and even occupational motivations among women has been all but nonexistent. In the past, when studies examined these issues, they involved comparisons with men, often showing preferences for male subjects (Agnew & Pyke, 1987; Carlson, 1971; Pyke, Ricks, Stewart, & Neeley, 1975). More serious is the fact that studies that use exclusively male samples are more likely to generalize to the opposite sex than studies using only female subjects (Agnew & Pyke, 1987; Greenglass & Stewart, 1973). In short, contemporary social science literature not only lacks adequate research and theory about women but may foster imprecise or fallacious information based on the overgeneralizations from research involving exclusively male subjects.

Ideally, we could study research in which phenomena had been studied from a variety of ideological orientations (e.g., Euro-patriarchal, feminist, egalitarian, etc.). If a finding was consistent from these different perspectives, readers' confidence in it could be much greater. At present, however, increasing the sensitivity of the social sciences to address gender bias should promote more objective research.

REFERENCES

Adler, P. (1985). *Wheeling and dealing*. New York: Columbia University Press.

Agnew, N. M., & Pyke, S. W. (1987). *The science game* (4th ed.). Englewood Cliffs, NJ: Prentice-Hall.

Berg, B. L. (1995). *Qualitative research methods for the social sciences* (2nd ed.). Boston: Allyn and Bacon.

Berg, B. L. (1990a). First day at the police academy: Stress reaction training as a screening-out technique. *Journal of Contemporary Criminal Justice, 6*(2), 89–105.

Berg, B. L. (1990b). Who should teach police? A typology and assessment of police academy instructors. *American Journal of Police, 9*(2), 79–100.

Bogdan, R., & Taylor, S. J. (1975). *Introduction to qualitative research methods*. New York: Wiley.

Carlson, R. (1971). Where is the person in personality research? *Psychological Bulletin, 75,* 203–219.

Greenglass, E., & Stewart, M. (1973). The underrepresentation of women in social psychological research. *Ontario Psychologist, 5,* 21–29.

Juvenile Delinquency Prevention and Control Act of 1968 (Public Law 90-445), Title I.

Katzer, J., Cook, K. H., & Crouch, W. W. (1991). *Evaluating information.* New York: McGraw-Hill.

Omnibus Crime Control and Safe Streets Act of 1968 (Public Law 90-351), Title I.

Punch, M. (1986). *The politics and ethics of field work.* Beverly Hills, CA: Sage.

Pyke, S. W. (1982). Confessions of a reluctant ideologist. *Canadian Psychology, 23,* 125–134.

Pyke, S. W., Ricks, F. A., Stewart, J. C., & Neeley, C. A. (1975). The sex variable in Canadian psychological journals. In M. Wright (Chair), *The status of women psychologists.* Symposium presented at the meeting of the Ontario Psychological Association, Toronto, Canada.

White, M. S. (1975). Women in the professions: Psychological and social barriers to women in science. In J. Freeman (Ed.), *Women: A feminist perspective* (pp. 227–237). Palo Alto, CA: Mayfield.

Estimation of Individual Crime Rates from Arrest Records

Alfred Blumstein and Jacqueline Cohen
The Journal of Criminal Law and Criminology
Vol. 70, No. 4, pp. 561–585, 1979

Introduction

This paper addresses patterns of individual criminality, a matter of fundamental concern for
understanding and controlling crime. Despite an
enormous volume of research into the causes
and prevention of crime, very little is known
about the progress of the individual criminal
career. In particular, neither the number of crimes
an individual commits each year, the crime rate,
nor the changes in that rate as a person ages
and/or accumulates a criminal record is known.
Such knowledge about individual careers is basic
to our understanding of individual criminality, and
in particular, to our understanding of how various
factors operate on the individual either to encour-
age or to inhibit criminal activity.

Basic knowledge about individual criminality
also has immediate practical import for developing effective crime control policies. For example,
incapacitation—physically preventing the crimes
of an offender (e.g., through incarceration)—has
emerged as a popular crime control strategy. But
the benefits derived from incapacitation in terms
of the number of crimes prevented will vary
greatly, depending on the magnitude of the individual's crime rate; the higher an individual's
crime rate, the more crimes that can be averted
through his incapacitation.

One incapacitation strategy calls for more
certain and longer imprisonment for offenders
with prior criminal records. But if individual crime
rates decrease as a criminal career progresses,
there are fewer crime-reduction benefits gained
from incapacitating criminals already well into

their criminal careers than from incapacitating
those with no prior criminal record. Clearly then,
evaluating the crime control effectiveness of various incapacitation strategies requires information
about the patterns of individual career criminality.

Prior Research on Criminal Careers

Prior research on criminal careers is largely limited to case studies and biographical or autobio-
graphical sketches which cannot be considered
characterization of the typical offender. The major
exceptions are the Gluecks' [1937; 1940] longitudinal studies of criminal careers in the 1920's and
the Wolfgang [1972] study of delinquency in a
birth cohort. Another major source of data on
adult careers is the FBI Careers in Crime File.
Some analysis of this data is published in the
staff report of the President's Commission on the
Causes and Prevention of Violence [Mulvihill,
Tumin, and Curtis, 1969].

The Glueck studies found a steady decrease
in the proportion of criminals who were still active
offenders during successive follow-up periods.
This was taken as evidence of an increasing
dropout from criminal activities with the passage
of time.

These results have served as the basis for the
hypothesis that individual criminality declines with
age, perhaps because of the aging process and
its associated increased maturity and/or declining
vigor. The Gluecks' "age of onset" theory represents further refinement of this hypothesis, where
time until criminal activity ceases is determined

by intervals after the start of a career, rather than as an explicit function of chronological age.

The available findings concerning the effects of aging, however, are based on measures of the incidence of arrests in the total population. They may result from changes either in the individual arrest rates of offenders with age or in the number of persons actively engaged in crime at any age. To the extent that the arrest patterns that have been observed are due to variations in the size of the criminal population at each age, these patterns do not reflect variations with age in the rate of criminal activity of active individual criminals.

Data

The data to be used here are from the FBI computerized criminal history file. They include the adult criminal records through early 1975 of all those individuals arrested for homicide, rape, robbery, aggravated assault, burglary, or auto

theft in Washington, D.C., during 1973. The data include the adult arrest histories of those 5,338 offenders and include records for 32,868 arrests. Despite the large size and richness of the data set, there are some features of the data that limit the generality of the results to the United States as a whole.

Table 1 compares the characteristics of the Washington, D.C., arrestees with those of persons included in the reported arrests in the *Uniform Crime Reports* (UCR) for 1973 [Federal Bureau of Investigation, 1974]. The two populations are not directly comparable because persons with more than one arrest are counted more than once in the UCR arrest data. This multiple counting alone, however, would not account for the observed differences. The Washington, D.C., arrestees are clearly not representative of arrestees in United States cities in general. Nonwhites are heavily over represented as they are in the general D.C. population. (In the 1970 census, the population of Washington, D.C., was 71 percent nonwhite com-

TABLE 1   Comparison of Washington, D.C., Arrestees with Arrests in United States Cities in 1973

	1973 WASHINGTON, D.C.	1973 UCR ARRESTS FOR CITIES	
	Arrestees	Total	Persons ≥ 18
RACE:			
White	8.1%	69.0%	
Nonwhite	91.8%	31.0%	
SEX:			
Male	89.7%	84.4%	
Female	10.3%	15.6%	
AGE:			
< 18	0.1%	26.5%	—
18–20	18.6%	13.9%	18.9%
21–24	24.4%	14.1%	19.2%
25–29	19.9%	10.5%	14.3%
30–34	12.3%	7.5%	10.2%
35–39	8.4%	6.1%	8.3%
40–44	5.0%	5.8%	7.9%
45–49	4.6%	5.3%	7.2%
≥ 50	6.7	10.0%	13.6%

Federal Bureau of Investigation, *Uniform Crime Reports: 1973* (1974).

pared to 12.3 percent nonwhite for the total population of the United States.)

It should also be noted that the arrestees used here are not drawn from the population of offenders, since there is no reasonable way of generating such a random sample. Only those offenders who come to the attention of the criminal justice system (CJS) through the arrest process can be identified. As a result, as long as criminals differ in their crime committing activity and in their vulnerability to arrest, the arrestees in any year cannot be representative of all offenders in general. Offenders who are more criminally active and/or more vulnerable to arrest are more likely to be arrested at least once in a year, and thus, they will be over represented among the arrestees in a year.

The arrestees, however, are representative of those offenders who are detected by the CJS. From the perspective of direct crime control through incapacitation or rehabilitation, the criminal behavior of those offenders who are available for sanctioning should be the focus of study, for it is their crimes that can be reduced directly.

Methods

Several factors are considered as potentially influencing individual arrest rates during a criminal career. The first is age. It is well established that most criminals eventually stop committing crimes. What is not known is whether this dropout occurs suddenly or after a gradual decline in criminal activity. The second factor to be considered is the length of the criminal record. While it is not empirically substantiated, the traditional view has been that the presence of a criminal record indicates a higher than average criminal intensity, and thereby justifies harsher sentences. This idea has been given statutory form in a few jurisdictions. Individuals specializing in different crime types also might have characteristically different arrest rates.

The last factor considered is possible trends over time in arrest rates. These trends might reflect general increases or decreases in criminality over time that are independent of age, or they might arise from a cohort effect where different cohorts, i.e., groups of offenders all beginning their criminal careers at the same time, have characteristically different arrest rates. Such a cohort effect might, for example, reflect the effect of being socialized at different times.

To explore the import of each of these factors, individual arrest rates are estimated by:

- age of the offender,
- number of prior arrests in a record,
- crime type "specialties," and
- year of observation

Results

Analysis of variance was performed on the individual arrest-rate estimates. These results report that arrest rates vary with age, crime type, number of prior arrests, and time, with crime type interacting with age and with prior arrests. The marginal means reported indicate that arrest rates increase with the number of prior arrests, decrease with age, and have been increasing generally over time. The particular approach used to characterize individuals by crime type makes very little difference in any of these results.

Conclusions

Using the arrest histories of cohorts of active offenders, this investigation isolated variation in the individual arrest rates during the careers of active offenders from variations in the size of the offender population. Contrary to previous findings of a decrease of arrest rate with age when rates per total population are used, it was found that individual arrest rates actually increase with age for burglary, narcotics, and the residual category "all other" offenses, and that rates are trendless for robbery, aggravated assault, larceny, auto theft, and weapons offenses. At the same time, individual arrest rates are generally trendless with respect to the number of prior arrests in an individual's record, and tend to increase in later cohorts for all crime types except aggravated assault, auto theft, and narcotics.

Controlling for time served after sentence does not result in any meaningful differences in these results. The estimated time served of less than two months per arrest is not sufficiently long to significantly alter the variations in individual arrest rates observed during a career.

These results were obtained by using samples of active criminals (persons with at least one arrest before and after the observation period) and by controlling for variations in time served in institutions. Admittedly, the results must be regarded as only preliminary because of the limited number of years the cohorts were observed (from four to seven years). Further replications with other cohorts of active criminals are needed.

The findings of increases in individual arrest rates with age and increases for later cohorts can be reconciled with the prior findings of decline in criminality with age from cross-sectional analyses. First, the peak in arrests per capita previously observed at younger ages can be partially attributed to a large number of offenders actively engaging in crime at those ages. It is not due to significant variation in individual arrest rates over age for those persons who remain active as offenders. Also, the younger people at any time tend to be from later cohorts whose individual arrest rates were found to be higher. Thus, the cohort effect, where people beginning their careers in more recent years have higher arrest rates, would also contribute to the peak in arrests at younger ages. For the same reason, the decrease in per capita arrest rates as people get older is due to the combination of the greater dropout from criminal activity as people age (resulting in smaller numbers of active older criminals) and the lower arrest rates of older people who come from earlier cohorts.

References

Federal Bureau of Investigation
  1974 *Uniform Crime Reports: 1973.* Washington, D.C.: U.S. Government Printing Office.
Glueck, S., and E. Glueck
  1937 *Later Criminal Careers.* New York: Knopf.
  1940 *Juvenile Delinquents Grown Up.* Cambridge, MA: Harvard University Press.
Mulvihill, D., M. Tumin, with L. Curtis
  1969 *Crimes of Violence.* Washington, D.C.: U.S. Government Printing Office.
Wolfgang, Marvin, R. Figlio, and T. Sellin
  1972 *Delinquency in a Birth Cohort.* Chicago: University of Chicago Press.

Name of Student _____

Student ID # _____

Course Section # _____

Date _____

1. Locate in your school library either the *Uniform Crime Reports,* by the Federal Bureau of Investigation, or the *Sourcebook of Criminal Statistics,* by the Bureau of Justice Statistics. Using the volumes for 1989–1993, create a comparative table of annual arrest rates for race, gender, and age in rural and urban settings. (See Table 1 in the Blumstein and Cohen article for a model.) Include arrest rates for the following crime categories: homicide, rape, robbery, aggravated assault, burglary, and auto theft. (If you want to create more than one table per year to represent the data, go ahead, but be sure that the variables in each table will allow you to answer the questions that follow.)

   COMPARATIVE TABLE   Arrest Rates for Race, Gender, Age, and Rural/Urban Settings by Homicide, Rape, Robbery, Aggravated Assault, Burglary, and Auto Theft: 1989–1993

2. What is the general pattern of arrest rates for each category of crime?

    a.   Homicide

    b.   Rape

    c.   Robbery

    d.   Aggravated assault

    e.   Burglary

f.   Auto theft

3.   What are the general patterns of crime for rural compared to urban settings?

4.   How do arrest rates compare for males versus females? What might explain this finding?

_____

_____

_____

_____

_____

_____

_____

_____

_____

_____

_____

5. How do arrest rates compare for Whites versus non-Whites in urban versus rural settings? What might explain this pattern?

_____

_____

_____

_____

_____

_____

_____

_____

_____

_____

_____

_____

_____

_____

_____

_____

_____

_____

Death Penalty Opinions: A Classroom Experience and Public Commitment

Robert M. Bohm
Sociological Inquiry
Vol. 60, No. 3, pp. 285–295, August 1990

Introduction

Although the issue of the death penalty probably was not crucial to the outcome of the 1988 Presidential election, the message about the death penalty was not lost on the American public. In a post-election poll conducted by the Gallup organization, fifty-seven percent of Bush voters and thirty-eight percent of Dukakis voters responded that the death penalty was a very important issue in deciding for whom to vote. In another 1988 Gallup poll released in December, ninety percent of Republicans, eighty-one percent of Independents, sixty-nine percent of Democrats, and seventy-nine percent of all Americans polled expressed support for the death penalty. Not only did a majority of Americans support the death penalty, but the seventy-nine percent figure represents a nine percent increase from a Gallup poll conducted in January, 1986, and the largest percentage of Americans to support the death penalty since the polling of opinions about the death penalty began in 1936 (Gallup and Gallup, 1988).

For those who seek abolition of capital punishment, one feature of the public support noted is that most Americans know very little about the death penalty and its effects (Sarat and Vidmar, 1976; Ellsworth and Ross, 1983; Bohm and Aveni, 1985; Finckenauer, 1988). The same appears to be true of Canadians, too (Vidmar and Dittenhoffer, 1981). Although Americans express opinions about many social issues of which they are ignorant, many abolitionists would like to believe that support for the death penalty is a function of a lack of knowledge about it and that opinions are responsive to reasoned persuasion.

In a series of studies, the influence of knowledge about the death penalty was examined, i.e., the influence of classroom instruction and discussion on death penalty opinions and the reasons for those opinions (Bohm and Aveni, 1985; Bohm, 1989; Bohm, Clark, and Aveni, forthcoming). In the studies that focused exclusively on the effect of knowledge on death penalty opinions, the experimental stimulus, knowledge, was found to change the opinions of a substantial number of subjects. In 1985, support decreased thirteen percent (sixty-eight percent vs. fifty-five percent) and opposition increased by the same amount (twenty-one percent vs. thirty-four percent) (N = 44); in 1986, support decreased thirty-two percent (seventy-one percent vs. thirty-nine percent) and opposition increased thirty-nine percent (seventeen percent vs. fifty-six percent) (N = 41); and in 1987, support decreased twenty-six percent (eighty-two percent vs. fifty-six percent) and opposition increased twenty-four percent (eighteen percent vs. forty-two percent (N = 50). However, only in the case of blacks were a majority of subjects persuaded to oppose the death penalty (see Bohm and Aveni, 1985; Bohm, 1989).

Procedure

Subjects for the study were 109 undergraduates of a medium-sized southern university: fifty-nine subjects in an experimental group and fifty-four in a control group. The experimental group was enrolled in a special class on the death penalty in America, while the control group consisted of students enrolled in two other courses offered during the same semester. Subjects were not randomly assigned to either group. Forty-two subjects in the experimental group were criminal justice majors or minors, and many of them had been exposed to some material on the death penalty in previous classes. The reason student subjects were used was to employ a prolonged stimulus experimentally. Brevity of exposure to the experimental stimulus is a weakness of previous research (cf. Sarat and Vidmar, 1976; Lord, Ross, and Lepper, 1979; Vidmar and Dittenhoffer, 1981).

The death penalty class met two hours a day, five days a week for four weeks (a total of forty hours) during the May, 1988 term. The assigned text for the course was Bedau's *The Death Penalty in America*, Third Edition (1982). Additional course work included lectures, guest speakers, films, and discussion.

The instructor was forthright about his opposition to the death penalty but emphasized that his opinion should not influence the opinion of anyone else. Both sides of all issues were presented, and no intentional preference was shown for either side, except when the instructor played devil's advocate to whichever position was taken by a student. An adversarial role was assumed to provoke thoughtful considerations of the issues. Students were fully aware from the outset that their grades in the class were independent of their views. Results from the class and unpub-lished results of a six-month follow-up study of the instructor's 1985 class suggest that demand characteristics had negligible effect.

Measures

Death penalty opinions were ascertained publicly at the beginning of each class period. Students were asked: "Which of the following statements best describes your position toward the death penalty for some people convicted of first-degree murder?" Response categories available to the students ranged from "very strongly opposed" (1) to "very strongly in favor" (7) on a seven-point Likert-type scale.

Results

In Table 1, the percentage distribution of pretest and posttest death penalty opinions by total subjects in both experimental and control groups is shown. Percentages are reported for both the seven response categories and three collapsed categories (favor, oppose, undecided).

In sum the data suggest that the experimental stimulus had little effect changing death penalty opinions. Only seven of the fifty-nine experimental subjects (twelve percent) changed

TABLE 1
Percentage Distribution of Death Penalty Opinions on the Pretest and Posttest by Total Subjects in Both Experimental and Control Groups

	EXPERIMENTAL		CONTROL	
	Pre	**Post**	**Pre**	**Post**
Favor	62	57	67	55
Uncertain	7	7	11	9
Oppose	31	36	22	36
Very strongly in favor (7)	22	22	22	20
Strongly in favor (6)	20	20	28	13
Somewhat in favor (5)	20	15	17	22
Uncertain (4)	7	7	11	9
Somewhat opposed (3)	7	8	11	13
Strongly opposed (2)	10	14	2	6
Very strongly opposed (1)	14	14	9	17
N	(59)		(54)	

their opinions toward the death penalty during the semester. Two subjects increased the intensity of their support.

Discussion and Conclusion

Most reasons given for not changing a death penalty opinion during the class are familiar to those who have studied the subject. Those who oppose the death penalty cite religious reasons, that the death penalty is morally wrong, that no one has the right to take another's life, including the state, there is arbitrariness and discrimination in administration of the death penalty, and there is the chance of executing innocent people.

Proponents of the death penalty argue that capital punishment is a proper or just punishment for murder, especially aggravated murder, that the death penalty serves as a deterrent, that murderers do not deserve to live, that we need the ultimate weapon for the ultimate crime, that the death penalty makes the family of the victim feel better, that nobody can guarantee that a murderer will not get out of prison and kill again, and that capital punishment shows the value of human life. Despite their support, many proponents acknowledge that the death penalty is not administered fairly.

One reason that can be suggested for why the majority of subjects did not change their opinions is public commitment. An implication of these findings for abolitionists is that people should not be asked to publicly commit to a death penalty opinion. However, this strategy poses a dilemma. Allowing people to form opinions about the death penalty privately may be more effective in generating opposition, but such a task is certain to prevent any bandwagon effect, that is, the desire of people to align with a popular movement for death penalty opposition.

References

Bedau, Hugo A. 1982. *The Death Penalty in America.* Third Edition, edited by Hugo A. Bedau. New York: Oxford University Press.

Bohm, Robert M. 1989. "The Effects of Classroom Instruction and Discussion on Death Penalty Opinions: A Teaching Note." *Journal of Criminal Justice* 17:123–131.

Bohm, Robert M., and Adrian F. Aveni. 1985. "Knowledge and Attitude about the Death Penalty: A Test of the Marshall Hypotheses." Paper presented at the annual meeting of the American Society of Criminology, San Diego, CA, November.

Bohm, Robert M., Louise J. Clark, and Adrian F. Aveni. Forthcoming. "The Influence of Knowledge on Reasons for Death Penalty Opinions." *Justice Quarterly* 6.

Ellsworth, Phoebe C., and Lee Ross. 1983. "Public Opinion and Capital Punishment: A Close Examination of the Views of Abolitionists and Retentionists." *Crime and Delinquency* 29:116–169.

Finckenauer, J. O. 1988. "Public Support for the Death Penalty: Retribution as Justice Deserts or Retribution as Revenge?" *Justice Quarterly* 5:81–100.

Gallup, George, Jr., and Alec Gallup. 1988. "Public Support for Death Penalty is Highest in Gallup Annals." Early release by the *Los Angeles Times* Syndicate.

Lord, Charles G., Lee Ross, and Mark R. Lepper. 1979. "Biased Assimilation and Attitude Polarization: The Effects of Prior Theories on Subsequently Considered Evidence." *Journal of Personality and Social Psychology* 37:2098-2109.

Sarat, Austin, and Neil Vidmar. 1976. "Public Opinion, the Death Penalty, and the Eighth Amendment: Testing the Marshall Hypothesis." *Wisconsin Law Review* 17:171–206.

Vidmar, Neil, and Tony Dittenhoffer. 1981. "Informed Public Opinion and Death Penalty Attitudes." *Canadian Journal of Criminology* 23:43–56.

Name of Student _____
Student ID # _____
Course Section # _____
Date _____

1. Ask five people you know who are not in your class (family, friends, roommates, etc.) to answer the following questions:

   Subject #1

   a. On the scale below, indicate your response to this question: Should people convicted of first-degree murder be given the death penalty?

Very Strongly in Favor	Strongly in Favor	Somewhat in Favor	Uncertain	Somewhat Opposed	Strongly Opposed	Very Strongly Opposed

   b. Briefly indicate why you feel this way about the death penalty.

   _____

   _____

   _____

   _____

   _____

   Subject Information

   Gender _____
   Race _____
   Age _____

Subject #2

a. On the scale below, indicate your response to this question: Should people convicted of first-degree murder be given the death penalty?

Very Strongly in Favor	Strongly in Favor	Somewhat in Favor	Uncertain	Somewhat Opposed	Strongly Opposed	Very Strongly Opposed

b. Briefly indicate why you feel this way about the death penalty.

_____

_____

_____

_____

_____

Subject Information

Gender _____

Race _____

Age _____

Subject #3

a. On the scale below, indicate your response to this question: Should people convicted of first-degree murder be given the death penalty?

Very Strongly in Favor	Strongly in Favor	Somewhat in Favor	Uncertain	Somewhat Opposed	Strongly Opposed	Very Strongly Opposed

b. Briefly indicate why you feel this way about the death penalty.

_____

_____

_____

_____

_____

Subject Information

Gender _____

Race _____

Age _____

Subject #4

a. On the scale below, indicate your response to this question: Should people convicted of first-degree murder be given the death penalty?

Very Strongly in Favor	Strongly in Favor	Somewhat in Favor	Uncertain	Somewhat Opposed	Strongly Opposed	Very Strongly Opposed

b. Briefly indicate why you feel this way about the death penalty.

_____

_____

_____

_____

_____

Subject Information

Gender _____

Race _____

Age _____

Subject #5

a. On the scale below, indicate your response to this question: Should people convicted of first-degree murder be given the death penalty?

Very Strongly in Favor	Strongly in Favor	Somewhat in Favor	Uncertain	Somewhat Opposed	Strongly Opposed	Very Strongly Opposed

b. Briefly indicate why you feel this way about the death penalty.

_____

_____

_____

_____

_____

Subject Information

Gender _____

Race _____

Age _____

2. Form small groups of five or six people in class, and pool your data. Working as a research team, develop a table to show the frequency distribution for each of the seven points on the Likert scale. (See Table 1 in the Bohm article for a model). Provide the results of your collaborative effort here.

3. Conduct a content analysis using the subjects' brief explanations of why they feel as they do about the death penalty. Develop a narrative description of the reasons given by subjects for their positions.

_____

_____

_____

_____

_____

_____

_____

_____

_____

_____

_____

_____

_____

_____

_____

_____

_____

_____

_____

_____

_____

_____

_____

_____

4. Are the subjects' reasons distinguishable along demographic lines (e.g., age, race, or gender)? Why do you think this is so?

_____

_____

_____

_____

_____

_____

_____

_____

_____

_____

_____

_____

_____

_____

_____

_____

_____

_____

_____

_____

_____

_____

_____

_____

_____

Drugs, Alcohol, and Social Styles of Life QUESTIONNAIRE

Dear Student:

The following questionnaire is designed to gather data about various aspects of social life among college students in the United States, which will contribute to our understanding of many important questions. We hope, therefore, that you will fill out the questionnaire with thought and care.

Most of the questions that follow can be answered by circling a number; others ask that a brief answer be written in. You may skip certain questions, if you want to. We would prefer, however, that you answer all of them.

The information in this questionnaire will be used strictly for research purposes. The only information that will be made public are group responses, such as averages and percentages. *Do not* sign your name or in any other way identify yourself on the questionnaire or the answer sheet.

The success of this study depends on your completing this questionnaire to the best of your ability. We appreciate your help with what we believe is very important research.

Sincerely,

Robert J. Mutchnick
Bruce L. Berg

Date: Month _____ Day _____ Year _____

Directions: For each of the following questions, either *circle* or *write in* the appropriate response. Please provide only 1 answer per question.

I. BACKGROUND INFORMATION

1. What is your gender?
    1. Male
    2. Female

2. My age on my last birthday was: _____

3. I would identify my race as:
    1. White (non-Latin)
    2. Black
    3. Latin
    4. Asian
    5. Other: _____

4. My present class standing in school is:
    1. Freshman, first semester
    2. Freshman, second semester
    3. Sophomore
    4. Junior
    5. Senior
    6. Other: _____

5. Using the four-point scale shown below, indicate your approximate overall high school grade point average:
    1. A = 4.0
    2. B = 3.0
    3. C = 2.0
    4. D = 1.0

II. ABOUT MY FAMILY

6. At the time I finished high school, my parents were:
    1. Both living together
    2. Divorced
    3. Separated
    4. Father was dead
    5. Mother was dead
    6. Both parents were dead
    7. Temporarily living apart for reasons other than marital problems

7. Please circle the *highest level* of education completed by your *father:*
    1. Some grade school
    2. Completed grade school
    3. Some high school
    4. Completed high school
    5. Completed high school and had other noncollege training (e.g., technical)
    6. Some college
    7. Completed college
    8. Some graduate work
    9. Graduate degree (e.g., M.D., M.A., J.D., Ph.D.)

8. Please circle the *highest level* of education completed by your mother:
    1. Some grade school
    2. Completed grade school
    3. Some high school
    4. Completed high school
    5. Completed high school and had other noncollege training (e.g., technical)
    6. Some college
    7. Completed college
    8. Some graduate work
    9. Graduate degree (e.g., M.D., M.A., J.D., Ph.D.)

9. My father's main occupation is (or was): _____
    (Indicate the name or title of his job (e.g., "doctor," "supermarket manager," etc.)

10. My mother's main occupation is (or was):_____
    (Indicate the name or title of her job (e.g., "doctor," "supermarket manager," etc.)

11. About how many hours a week does (or did) your father work outside the home?
    _____ hours each week

12. About how many hours a week does (or did) your mother work outside the home?
    _____ hours each week

13. How much would you say your father likes (or liked) the kind of work he does (or did)?
    1. Dislikes his work extremely
    2. Dislikes his work considerably
    3. Dislikes his work somewhat
    4. Neither dislikes nor likes his work
    5. Likes his work somewhat
    6. Likes his work considerably
    7. Likes his work extremely well

14. How much would you say your mother likes (or liked) the kind of work she does (or did)?
    1. Dislikes her work extremely
    2. Dislikes her work considerably
    3. Dislikes her work somewhat
    4. Neither dislikes nor likes her work
    5. Likes her work somewhat
    6. Likes her work considerably
    7. Likes her work extremely well

15. Using one of the six names shown below for social class, please select the one you think best describes your family:
     1. The lower class
     2. The working class
     3. The lower-middle class
     4. The middle class
     5. The upper-middle class
     6. The upper class

16. I usually get money for things I want to buy:
     1. From my job
     2. From my parents
     3. From my friends
     4. By stealing
     5. By selling drugs

III. Personal Habits

17. In the last 30 days, how many cigarettes have you smoked?
     1. I have never smoked cigarettes
     2. I have not smoked cigarettes in the last 30 days
     3. Less than one cigarette per day
     4. Approximately one full cigarette each day
     5. More than one, but fewer than five cigarettes per day
     6. About one-half pack per day
     7. About one pack per day
     8. More than one, but less than two packs per day
     9. Two or more packs per day

The next several questions are about alcohol. In each, the term *a drink* means one can or bottle of beer, one 4 ounce glass of wine, or one shot of straight liquor (e.g., gin, vodka, scotch), including mixed drinks.

18. Have you ever had a drink of beer, wine, or liquor—not just a sip or a taste?
     1. Yes
     2. No

19. How often do you usually have beer?
     1. I never drink this beverage
     2. I have at least one drink of this beverage every day
     3. I have at least one drink three or four days a week
     4. I drink once or twice a week
     5. I drink about three or four times a month
     6. I drink about once a month
     7. I drink irregularly but at least several times a year
     8. I drink at least once a year

20. How often do you usually have wine?
     1. I never drink this beverage
     2. I have at least one drink of this beverage every day
     3. I have at least one drink three or four days a week
     4. I drink once or twice a week

5. I drink about three or four times a month
6. I drink about once a month
7. I drink irregularly but at least several times a year
8. I drink at least once a year

21. How often do you usually drink liquor (or mixed drinks)?
    1. I never drink this beverage
    2. I have at least one drink of this beverage every day
    3. I have at least one drink three or four days a week
    4. I drink once or twice a week
    5. I drink about three or four times a month
    6. I drink about once a month
    7. I drink irregularly but at least several times a year
    8. I drink at least once a year

22. When you *do* drink alcoholic beverages, how many drinks do you usually have during a single drinking occasion (e.g, at a single party, restaurant, friend's house, etc.)?

    A. *Cans/bottles of beer:*
       1. I never drink this beverage
       2. Twelve or more drinks
       3. About eight drinks
       4. Six drinks
       5. Five drinks
       6. Four drinks
       7. Three drinks
       8. Two drinks
       9. One drink
       10. Less than one full drink

    B. *Glasses of wine:*
       1. I never drink this beverage
       2. Twelve or more drinks
       3. About eight drinks
       4. Six drinks
       5. Five drinks
       6. Four drinks
       7. Three drinks
       8. Two drinks
       9. One drink
       10. Less than one full drink

    C. *Drinks of liquor:*
       1. I never drink this beverage
       2. Twelve or more drinks
       3. About eight drinks
       4. Six drinks
       5. Five drinks
       6. Four drinks
       7. Three drinks
       8. Two drinks
       9. One drink
       10. Less than one full drink

23. Do you usually drink with other people?
    1. Yes
    2. No

24. Do you ever drink alone?
    1. Yes
    2. No

25. Regarding drinking with others, which of the following statements most accurately describes you?
    1. I never like drinking alone
    2. I sometimes like drinking alone
    3. I do not care if I drink alone or with others
    4. I sometimes like drinking alone
    5. I always like drinking alone

The next several of questions are about drugs. (Please remember that your answers are strictly confidential: They will never be connected with your name, your class, or any other identifying information.)

26. In your lifetime, how many times (if any) have you used *marijuana* (also called "grass," "pot," "dope," "smoke," "joints," "reefer," etc.)?
    1. I have never heard of this substance
    2. I have never used this substance
    3. Once
    4. Two or three times
    5. Four to nine times
    6. At least ten times
    7. I use it regularly (at least once daily)
    8. I use it often (at least three times a week)

27. During the past 30 days, how many times (if any) have you used *marijuana?*
    1. I have never heard of this substance
    2. I have never used this substance
    3. Once
    4. Two or three times
    5. Four to nine times
    6. At least ten times
    7. I use it regularly (at least once daily)
    8. I use it often (at least three times a week)

28. In your lifetime, how many times (if any) have you used *angel dust* (also called "PCP")?
    1. I have never heard of this substance
    2. I have never used this substance
    3. Once
    4. Two or three times
    5. Four to nine times
    6. At least ten times
    7. I use it regularly (at least once daily)
    8. I use it often (at least three times a week)

29. During the past 30 days, how many times (if any) have you used *angel dust?*
    1. I have never heard of this substance
    2. I have never used this substance
    3. Once
    4. Two or three times
    5. Four to nine times
    6. At least ten times
    7. I use it regularly (at least once daily)
    8. I use it often (at least three times a week)

30. In your lifetime, how many times (if any) have you used *LSD* (also called "acid") or other *hallu-cinogens* (such as "magic mushrooms," "mescaline," etc.)?
    1. I have never heard of this substance
    2. I have never used this substance
    3. Once
    4. Two or three times
    5. Four to nine times
    6. At least ten times
    7. I use it regularly (at least once daily)
    8. I use it often (at least three times a week)

31. During the past 30 days, how many times (if any) have you used *LSD?*
    1. I have never heard of this substance
    2. I have never used this substance
    3. Once
    4. Two or three times
    5. Four to nine times
    6. At least ten times
    7. I use it regularly (at least once daily)
    8. I use it often (at least three times a week)

32. In your lifetime, how many times (if any) have you used *cocaine* (also called "coke", "blow," "snow") other than *crack?*
    1. I have never heard of this substance
    2. I have never used this substance
    3. Once
    4. Two or three times
    5. Four to nine times
    6. At least ten times
    7. I use it regularly (at least once daily)
    8. I use it often (at least three times a week)

33. During the past 30 days, how many times (if any) have you used *cocaine?*
    1. I have never heard of this substance
    2. I have never used this substance
    3. Once
    4. Two or three times
    5. Four to nine times
    6. At least ten time
    7. I use it regularly (at least once daily)
    8. I use it often (at least three times a week)

34. In your lifetime, how many times (if any) have you used *crack* (small pellets, or "rocks," of processed cocaine)?
    1. I have never heard of this substance
    2. I have never used this substance
    3. Once
    4. Two or three times
    5. Four to nine times
    6. At least ten times
    7. I use it regularly (at least once daily)
    8. I use it often (at least three times a week)

35. During the past 30 days, how many times (if any) have you used *crack?*
    1. I have never heard of this substance
    2. I have never used this substance
    3. Once
    4. Two or three times
    5. Four to nine times
    6. At least ten times
    7. I use it regularly (at least once daily)
    8. I use it often (at least three times a week)

36. In your lifetime, how many times (if any) have you used *heroin* (also called "smack," "junk," etc.)?
    1. I have never heard of this substance
    2. I have never used this substance
    3. Once
    4. Two or three times
    5. Four to nine times
    6. At least ten times
    7. I use it regularly (at least once daily)
    8. I use it often (at least three times a week)

37. During the past 30 days, how many times (if any) have you used *heroin?*
    1. I have never heard of this substance
    2. I have never used this substance
    3. Once
    4. Two or three times
    5. Four to nine times
    6. At least ten times
    7. I use it regularly (at least once daily)
    8. I use it often (at least three times a week)

38. In your lifetime, how many times (if any) have you used prescription drugs for recreational purposes (that is, used them when you were not sick)?
    1. I have never heard of this substance
    2. I have never used this substance
    3. Once
    4. Two or three times
    5. Four to nine times
    6. At least ten times
    7. I use it regularly (at least once daily)
    8. I use it often (at least three times a week)

39. During the 30 days, how many times (if any) have you used prescription drugs recreationally?
    1. I have never heard of this substance
    2. I have never used this substance
    3. Once
    4. Two or three times
    5. Four to nine times
    6. At least ten times
    7. I use it regularly (at least once daily)
    8. I use it often (at least three times a week)

For each of the questions in the next item (# 40), please fill in the appropriate age. If you have never tried one (or more) of these substances, please write the word "never" in the blank.

40. About how old were you the first time you (if ever):
    1. Had a drink of alcohol (beer, wine, or liquor)? _____
    2. Used marijuana? _____
    3. Used angel dust? _____
    4. Used LSD or some other hallucinogen? _____
    5. Used cocaine (other than crack)? _____
    6. Used prescription drugs recreationally _____

41. As far as you know, about how many of your close friends get drunk on alcoholic beverages once a week or more?
    1. None
    2. A few
    3. Some
    4. Most
    5. All

42. As far as you know, about how many of your close friends get "stoned" or "high" on marijuana at least once a week?
    1. None
    2. A few
    3. Some
    4. Most
    5. All

43. As far as you know, about how many of your close friends get "stoned" or "high" on some other drug at least once a week?
    1. None
    2. A few
    3. Some
    4. Most
    5. All

IV. Leisure Activities

44. What would you say is your hobby (or hobbies)?_____
_____

45. What do you usually do when you have leisure or spare time?_____
_____

46. What sports activities do you enjoy watching (either in person or on television)?_____
_____

47. Do you enjoy reading for pleasure?
     1. Yes
     2. No

48. Do you enjoy outdoor activities, such as fishing, boating, hiking, or swimming?
     1. Yes
     2. No

49. How often are alcoholic beverages used as part of your leisure-time activities?
     1. Never
     2. Sometimes
     3. Occasionally
     4. Often
     5. Always

50. How often are drugs used as part of your leisure-time activities?
     1. Never
     2. Sometimes
     3. Occasionally
     4. Often
     5. Always

51. During my lifetime, I have had sexual relations (referring to intercourse) outside of marriage:
     1. Never
     2. Once
     3. Two or three times
     4. Five times or more

52. The first time I had intercourse, I was:
     1. I have never had intercourse
     2. Under the age of 16
     3. 17 years old
     4. 18 years old
     5. 19 years old
     6. 20 years old
     7. 21 years old
     8. Over 21 years old

53. When I have intercourse, I practice "safe sex" (use condoms or other latex barriers)
     1. I never have intercourse
     2. I never practice safe sex
     3. I sometimes practice safe sex
     4. Sometimes I do, and sometimes I don't

    5. I usually practice safe sex
    6. I always practice safe sex

54. About how many hours a week do you spend on school work (e.g., studying, doing projects, homework) outside the classroom?
    1. I spend no time on school work
    2. At least one hour per day
    3. Two to three hours a week
    4. Four to six hours a week
    5. Ten or more hours each week

The next several questions are about various activities that may be called illegal. (Again, please remember that everything you tell us will be held in the strictest confidence and that you will not in any way be connected to your answers.)

V. Illegal Behaviors

55. When I run into the store for just a minute and park by a meter, I put money in the meter:
    1. I always put money in
    2. I sometimes put money in
    3. I'm not sure whether I do or I don't
    4. I usually do not put money in
    5. I never put money in

56. In my lifetime, I have shoplifted:
    1. Never
    2. Once
    3. Two to four times
    4. Five to ten times
    5. More than ten times

57. During the past 30 days, I have shoplifted:
    1. Never
    2. Once
    3. Two to four times
    4. Five to ten times
    5. More than ten times

58. When I shoplift, I usually take items valued at:
    1. I never shoplift
    2. Under $5
    3. Over $5 but under $10
    4. Over $25 but under $50
    5. Over $50 but under $100
    6. Over $100

59. In my lifetime, I have had fights in which someone was physically injured:
    1. Never
    2. Once
    3. Two to four times
    4. Five or more times

60. During the past 30 days, I have had fights in which someone was physically injured:
    1. Never
    2. Once
    3. Two to four times
    4. Five or more times

61. When out on a date, I have forced someone to do something sexually that they did not want to do (they said "no"):
    1. Never
    2. Once
    3. Twice
    4. Three times
    5. Four or more times

62. When out on a date, I have been forced to do something sexually that I did not want to do (I said "no"):
    1. Never
    2. Once
    3. Twice
    4. Three times
    5. Four or more times

63. I have been the victim of a crime:
    1. Never
    2. Once
    3. Twice
    4. Three times
    5. Four or more times

64. In my lifetime, I have taken items that did not belong to me:
    1. Never
    2. Once
    3. Twice
    4. Three times
    5. Four or more times

65. During the past 30 days, I have taken items that did not belong to me:
    1. Never
    2. Once
    3. Twice
    4. Three times
    5. Four or more times

66. In my lifetime, I have been arrested for a crime (breaking any law):
    1. Never
    2. Once
    3. Twice
    4. Three times
    5. Four or more times

67. During the past 30 days I have been arrested for a crime:
    1. Never
    2. Once
    3. Twice
    4. Three times
    5. Four or more times

VI. Fear of Crime

Directions: Use the following scale in answering the next 10 questions.
(Circle the number adjacent to each question.)

1. Strongly Agree
2. Agree
3. No Feelings About It
4. Disagree
5. Strongly Disagree

		Strongly Agree	Agree	No Feelings About It	Disagree	Strongly Disagree
68.	I feel comfortable walking around my neighborhood alone at night.	1	2	3	4	5
69.	There are some places in my neighbor hood where I would avoid walking alone at night.	1	2	3	4	5
70.	I feel comfortable walking around my neighborhood alone during the day.	1	2	3	4	5
71.	There are some places in my neighbor-hood where I would avoid walking alone during the day.	1	2	3	4	5
72.	I keep a weapon in my car, such as a club or heavy tool, just in case I need to protect myself.	1	2	3	4	5
73.	I sometimes carry some sort of weapon, such as a knife, gun, or mace, just in case I need to protect myself.	1	2	3	4	5
74.	I always check to see who is at the door before opening it.	1	2	3	4	5
75.	I usually feel comfortable being alone in my home during the day.	1	2	3	4	5
76.	I usually feel comfortable being alone in my home at night.	1	2	3	4	5
77.	I own a dog because it makes me feel safer.	1	2	3	4	5

Random Numbers Table

	(1)	(2)	(3)	(4)	(5)	(6)
1	19700	61566	16588	57781	50250	50122
2	12035	25910	76505	38090	87768	78400
3	85734	83376	95758	89069	30105	28856
4	74652	26832	59302	17800	35511	23092
5	93920	15554	38120	96290	47942	37472
6	17679	97040	75386	83093	82386	37040
7	82645	76572	81091	91017	64990	13358
8	41832	48410	92159	13126	60768	89909
9	34732	78953	81672	10465	46734	62756
10	31673	77137	45190	36959	13246	46758
11	18730	72434	52457	28407	13900	22675
12	34560	95725	42083	14229	92160	54620
13	32590	43376	18526	22283	24627	79057
14	59235	49826	82672	72057	67743	68005
15	23270	70432	74743	76563	50553	41189
16	47213	44879	72030	98216	86658	68020
17	99954	36464	83605	29050	89340	72369
18	28341	67579	49807	90544	77907	54574
19	19756	96697	79342	73408	88672	76819
20	49173	71690	81778	62606	91560	32209
21	18490	31480	78272	17958	75370	42848
22	20967	32970	98327	56120	51642	57230
23	88568	85271	95399	71300	88131	42267
24	50350	28182	39168	65760	34273	90246
25	92479	86891	67269	60669	40132	86055
26	43460	79914	43260	22735	39830	49600
27	82510	59354	81066	65344	48754	36271
28	61375	25480	11359	12212	92327	53201
29	26728	10946	99670	94568	69485	74217
30	62212	54931	58838	20926	88342	86222

The authors gratefully acknowledge the work of Dr. Robert Sechrist, Geography and Regional Planning Department of Indiana University of Pennsylvania, who used Turbo Pascal to generate this random numbers table.

31	41202	12557	54744	80519	29057	24855
32	46902	69848	96074	25763	17640	32236
33	28482	59594	91614	40160	32675	37468
34	26056	98382	99092	33982	27763	30201
35	22327	90150	26342	47051	77496	22576
36	36990	66542	52858	38887	79786	19864
37	38679	59409	54589	15900	72350	45102
38	63720	25732	39756	31734	46167	88049
39	32889	70316	28520	34600	63721	73779
40	18481	36542	34316	69902	14846	71196
41	63198	60494	29649	93450	67972	86823
42	23905	87880	41880	13000	99602	14148
43	60457	45398	47945	62924	98220	33843
44	53841	97798	17372	45036	56652	85190
45	41100	17740	67180	40058	67071	53999
46	40909	56957	55690	28331	75010	47344
47	44160	31460	56535	83130	21581	50430
48	79501	46488	34518	79679	68043	85901
49	90927	72072	68447	78477	16494	20904
50	92387	98495	28755	78265	83918	92213
51	72170	79710	42714	58923	19720	44741
52	35630	38256	50600	59628	72108	37330
53	11853	31702	16844	62574	93652	25972
54	17350	61753	60317	77574	68792	30000
55	85627	82196	42658	47854	71153	92758
56	37550	69472	66371	22343	83444	56684
57	45031	53374	91440	64793	37775	53050
58	90060	56433	21000	95017	59188	51372
59	61982	87304	71549	82571	20237	65030
60	58685	58481	51420	38192	39399	31606
61	89799	23622	86746	73301	81156	12643
62	51284	54830	46372	22886	49551	34672
63	95431	51880	54823	52072	20019	15279
64	79093	26847	88628	91704	31325	65443
65	97934	40009	66935	73237	80409	23167
66	39542	73092	68190	58257	17955	30163
67	13194	19399	59416	82951	63487	46925
68	39095	80607	95902	62819	35830	26490
69	49060	92389	74118	27963	47712	92197
70	22360	52460	45655	84246	47351	89781
71	41801	96399	25023	20651	14822	90680
72	74360	91523	49104	81370	46025	95636
73	61124	44147	71084	60314	82058	97721
74	27516	40525	96656	51250	66821	18685
75	38355	66821	18685	38355	66813	95338

76	10712	40644	70365	78740	78328	44688
77	42166	27730	47624	63190	13455	90249
78	33848	50900	69385	74293	72476	29028
79	58202	27826	21770	66730	49314	80019
80	41267	41764	47610	87978	84676	18577
81	85148	54520	64911	34095	69441	69745
82	47270	52349	71791	33822	26455	58601
83	40290	18672	32405	18061	81944	57744
84	25630	76900	79080	11449	45658	55811
85	97340	38834	60495	49807	35800	75517
86	14859	34277	64150	17862	34675	77294
87	21432	13413	87818	58167	24122	57570
88	119090	92247	21285	96522	33544	61979
89	59620	36424	58040	54209	58343	58828
90	85981	37420	98051	42362	31583	43136
91	65844	90660	87767	58771	56687	66543
92	41837	53142	31031	32448	33982	13419
93	28678	97102	24271	86251	38899	68465
94	15895	58821	26802	12896	34657	46149
95	15948	20588	64717	84648	27219	77250
96	40584	31931	73932	42035	95353	72858
97	13214	31718	65207	31852	53609	11126
98	50149	91442	18955	89821	30999	17078
99	68491	25028	42638	88176	73235	30810